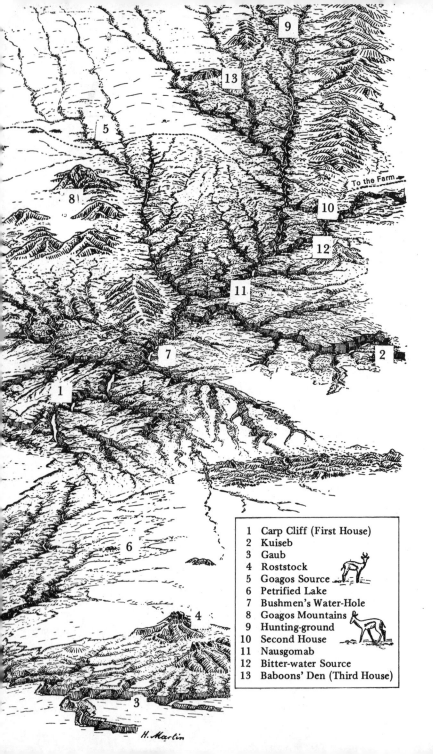

To the Farm

1 Carp Cliff (First House)
2 Kuiseb
3 Gaub
4 Roststock
5 Goagos Source
6 Petrified Lake
7 Bushmen's Water-Hole
8 Goagos Mountains
9 Hunting-ground
10 Second House
11 Nausgomab
12 Bitter-water Source
13 Baboons' Den (Third House)

H. Marlin

Henno Martin

The Sheltering Desert

Robinson Crusoes in the Namib

AD. DONKER / PUBLISHER

AD. DONKER (PTY) LTD
AN IMPRINT OF JONATHAN BALL PUBLISHERS (PTY) LTD
P O Box 33977
Jeppestown
2043

First English edition by William Kimber, London, 1957
Second English edition by SWA Scientific Society, 1974
This edition first published 1983
Reprinted in paperbooks 1988, 1991, 1994, 1996, 1998. 1999, 2001

ISBN 0 86852 150 7

Typeset by Triangle Typesetters (Pty) Ltd, Johannesburg
Printed and bound by NBD, Drukkery Street,
Goodwood, Western Cape

Foreword

Forty years have passed since I, my friend Hermann and the dog Otto sought the shelter of the desert in order to escape the madness of the Second World War. We found the shelter we were looking for and we found adventures of survival which confronted us forcibly with the primitive traits of our own nature. Even after half a lifetime, the scenes of our desert existence are sharply etched into my memory, and every visit to the Namib feels like a return home.

When I wrote this book twenty-seven years ago, the game which had provided us with food and joy was being wiped out by unscrupulous hunters. Now the 'Carp Cliff' and its surroundings and the red dunes to the south of the Kuiseb canyon have been incorporated into the Namib Game Park, and it is a pleasure to record that springbok, gemsbok and zebra have recovered to some extent, and that at the Desert Research Station Gobabeb, on the lower Kuiseb River, scientists are studying the conditions under which life exists in this unique desert.

Forty years ago, as Hermann and I lived like carnivores, whilst day by day the cruelties of the great war were brought by the radio into the serenity of our desert evenings, our thoughts and talks were much occupied with the riddles of the evolution of life and of man, of his astonishing cultures and his fateful failings. In the meantime, the dangers which we recognised then have grown and continue to grow at an increasing rate. Our deductions about the link between the complexity of human nature, with its capability for both sublimely altruistic and devastatingly destructive behaviour, and mankind's evolution from primitive hunting families to competing warlike societies, seem to be as relevant today as they were during the great war.

Readers interested in this aspect are referred to the late Robert Ardrey's book *The Social Contract* in which the peculiarities and the innate dangers of human nature are traced to their animal roots. Many of our present troubles are aggravated by the prevalent socio-political theories which do not acknowledge the discrepancy that exists between the demands of modern societies and some parts of our hereditary make-up. By blaming all the evils of this world on its social structures these theories mobilise our inherited aggressiveness against other individuals, groups, races and nations, encouraging ever more costly combats with ever more disappointing results. It is essential to realise that a part of the struggle for physical and spiritual survival has to be waged within ourselves against innate tendencies which, though once a condition of man's evolution, have now become serious obstacles to our further existence and development.

For me the most important gain of our life in the Namib was the experience that the human mind can rise above even the most savage conditions. Whether this faculty will enable us to master the avalanching dangers with which an unbalanced blind progress coupled with a grave misunderstanding of man's nature are now confronting us, only the future can show.

Windhoek, July 1980.

Henno Martin

The End of the Road

The heavy iron gates of Windhoek Prison fell to behind us with a clang. I turned round for a moment. Above the inner arch of the gates was an inscription, a little faded but still legible: *Alles zur Besserung!* Those reassuring words had obviously been left over from the days of German rule. So we were to be improved, reformed, rehabilitated as its inmates! In the ordinary way I should have laughed, but we didn't feel much like laughing.

The formalities were soon settled. Our names: Hermann Korn and Henno Martin. Profession: geologists. Then our belts and bootlaces were taken away. After that the cell doors closed behind us. We were separated now and my sick comrade lay in the next cell.

I didn't feel too good myself; we had been on the move all day in order to reach our destination before nightfall. The feeble light of a lamp in the prison yard fell through the bars of my cell window. I could not sleep.

I lay on my back and stared into the semi-darkness. How narrow and confined this small space was after the wide horizons and the high heavens of the desert in which we had lived for so long!

And the experiences that lay behind us! We had tried to escape from a world convulsed by war, and up to a point we had succeeded. For two and a half years we had made ourselves independent of human society, disappearing into the desert, living the life of primitive hunters, governed only by the harsh laws of the wilderness and our own limitations.

Lying there I lived it all over again. Many pictures rose in my mind: the beauty of nature, the animals of the wilds, the pangs of hunger and thirst, the occasional physical exhaustion, the silent nights and the glistening stars. That part of our lives was all over now: what came next?

Well, for one thing we shouldn't have to stalk our breakfast in the morning; it would be brought to us in our cells, ample proof that human society had got hold of us again.

I closed my eyes and thought of the past.

Flight

It was the first year of the Second World War. The German armies had occupied Holland and were already breaking through the first defences of the Maginot Line. Windhoek was in a swirl of war propaganda, and enthusiasm, fear and anxiety coloured every discussion. Even a scientist could hardly hope to keep his head in that hysterical atmosphere. But my friend Hermann Korn and I had already decided that this was not our war. We had seen it coming for a long time, and in fact that was the reason why we had left Europe in the first place. We wanted no hand or part in the mass suicide of civilised peoples.

But now it looked as though the war was about to catch up with us; more and more Germans were disappearing behind the barbed wire of internment camps. Any day the same fate could overtake us. It was a dread thought for two men used, in their scientific work, to the desert expanses and the freedom of the endless rolling plains, and we were determined to maintain our personal neutrality and to defend our independence to the best of our ability. One evening, sitting on the stone steps of our house, we reviewed the situation and wondered if there was anything we could do about it. And then suddenly we remembered what we had once said half in joke: 'If war comes we'll spend it in the desert!'

The idea fascinated us. With suppressed excitement we began to discuss the practical possibilities, weighing up the pros and cons. By the time the light of the zodiac stood over the western hills the idea had become a decision: we would go into the desert and live there in complete isolation until the war was over. One living thing we did propose to take with us, and that was our dog. There was no need to ask him what he thought about it; he was always ready to come, and whenever he saw signs of packing he would wag his tail joyfully. His name was Otto. We had called him that because it's a name that looks the same fore and aft, and so did Otto when he was a puppy — the same shape too! This was no longer the case, but he was still Otto.

Our preparations took four days, and then we started on our journey with our heavily loaded lorry. Our objective was the dry canyon of the Kuiseb river, a place not easily accessible, though by South West African standards it wasn't far: about 200 kilometres from Windhoek. The easiest way to get there would have been to take the *pad* (as they call any sort of passable track) running from the uplands down along the Kuiseb valley into the 'Namib', which is a Khoi-Khoin (Hottentot) word for desert and is the name used for the area between the uplands and the Atlantic. But for us that was just the way to avoid. The inhabitants of the isolated farms we passed would certainly spot our lorry and then the police would find out which way we had gone the moment they cared to inquire. We therefore decided to make a wide detour over Okahandja and Karibib. Incidentally, in notifying the authorites we were leaving town we had given Karibib as our destination.

As soon as we had left Karibib our adventure began; henceforth we were subject only to the laws of the wilds. From Karibib we turned into the hills and rested there until darkness fell; we wanted to make quite sure that no one from even the remotest farms should see us passing. During the night we drove along the skirt of the Chuos mountains across the wide Sphinx plains. Once in the glare of our head-lights we spotted a number of gemsbok or oryx gazelles. For a few hours we slept in a sandy pit, and when the stars began to pale our lorry drove into a grey and barren ravine which led down into the still deeper canyon of the Swakop river. This dried-out river-bed was notorious because of its deep, loose sand, but we already knew it and we let some of the air out of our tyres until they were soft and broad enough to give us a better grip. Then we went through the sand with our engine screaming. This hussar tactic was successful, and once on firmer ground we pumped up our tyres again. On the south side a similar ravine led us up again to the surface of the Namib and we reached a little-used track which ran along the wildly fissured Swakop canyon right down to the coast.

Even in full sunshine this part of the desert is rather colourless, and the general grey is broken only occasionally by a dyke of black basalt. In the pale twilight of the dawn the sky and the desert merged imperceptibly and it was absolutely impossible to estimate distances in that uncertain light. On one occasion we thought we could see a dilapidated hut ahead of us, but it turned out to be a rusty petrol tin. But then a large, dark shape loomed up and didn't budge. It turned out to be a cow. She was standing in the middle of the *pad,* and beside her lay a new-born calf, already dead and torn and bleed-ing. Slinking around were three wild dogs, *Lycaon pictus,* which hunt in packs like wolves and wreak havoc amongst herds of game or cattle and flocks of sheep. They stared at us balefully with their ugly hyena-like heads.

The cow probably belonged to a half-caste family which lived in a small clay hut below in the Swakop

11

canyon. The lean and half-starved beast was doing its best to defend the dead calf, lunging with its horns against the hungry steppe dogs. When we came up she turned her head to us as though seeking help, but we could do nothing; we couldn't afford to waste even one of our precious cartridges.

The wild dogs followed our movements closely and no doubt they were greatly heartened when we drove on, and they knew they could be certain of their feed. For us that pathetic little scene on the first morning of our journey was symbolic of our entry into a cruel and ruthless struggle for existence.

Before long we left the track to cross south-eastwards through the desert to reach Kuiseb canyon. Tyre marks remain visible for a long time in desert landscape and so we turned the lorry onto a stretch of basalt, scoured and polished by the wind, whilst with the help of an old sack we obliterated our tyre marks for quite a stretch.

It was broad daylight now and the sun shone down over the endless plains though in the hollows and fissures the shadows still gathered like dark water. Our immediate objective was a sandy pass across a dark slaty ridge, but we knew that we must not go on for much longer, because we were on the direct air line Windhoek-Swakopmund, and in the open desert a lorry with windows to catch the sun and a long trail of dust behind it can easily be seen from the air. We reached a shallow dried-out valley where the ground was encrusted with salt and there we drove our lorry under a low rock face and stopped for a snack. We looked round carefully. Beyond a few thin grey-green tamarisks there was no cover and to the eyes of fugitives our lorry seemed unusually large and very shiny. We wiped it over with oily rags and threw dust over it. After that it was far less conspicuous.

12

'I think we'll make it,' said Hermann. 'It'll be at least ten days before they start looking for us.'

'At least,' I agreed, 'and then they'll almost certainly start the search around the Brandberg.'

'Why?' demanded Hermann, raising his eyebrows.

'Well, that's where we were last working, wasn't it? And then, before we left I made arrangements that they should.'

'Such as?'

'I jotted down a little calculation to discover how far x-number of litres would take us, and I very cautiously put down only the first letters of the destinations in question, and blotted it. When the police examine the blotting pad, as they will do when they realise we're missing and search the place, they'll assume we've gone to the Brandberg area.'

Hermann grinned. 'Not bad,' he said. The Brandberg was 320 kilometres farther north. A good deal later we learned that in fact this was the first area the police had searched for us.

We now sat under the burning sun in a drying east wind and waited for evening. We had stretched a tarpaulin at an angle over the lorry and this gave us a bit of shade. We put our antenna over a couple of bushes and taking our power from the lorry battery we switched on the radio, and there, in the desert, we listened to the latest war communiqués. They were about the German tank drive into France. The voice that came to us out of the ether seemed unreal and fantastic, and yet alive as though in a dream. Through the hot, sharp gusts of the east wind we could almost hear the roar and rattle of the heavy tanks.

Otto lay under the lorry and panted. The heat affected us too, and we felt thirsty, but we had to go easy with the small quantity of water we had with us.

After our night drive we were too tired to discuss the war situation at any length. At last the sun went down and we allowed ourselves a little water. After that we started up and drove through a small dried-up water-course and over wide stony plains scoured smooth by the winds. Hermann was at the wheel. We had not been under way long when the lorry came to a stop in the loose sand of a dried-out gully and we had to let air out of our tyres before the wheels could get a sufficient hold. Once on firmer ground we stopped again to pump up the tyres — not a very pleasant occupation, and it made us irritable. We were tired too, and reacting to a rather disagreeable remark of mine Hermann told me to get on with it myself, and silently I took the wheel.

When the evening shadows lengthened the many grooves, ridges and patches of debris showed up against the grey of the desert in deep black stripes. The twilight seemed to rise out of the hollows and the horizon was beginning to darken, but we were anxious to put a few more kilometres behind us before we stopped for the night. Suddenly as I swung the wheel over to avoid a rock my elbow hit the hooter and for some reason the contact jammed and there was a sudden loud, uninterrupted howl in the silence. It was quite impossible that any human being was remotely within earshot but the sudden noise brought my heart into my throat. I pulled up, sprang down and with trembling hands I searched in the tool-box for a screwdriver. Hermann cursed, and Otto, who didn't know what the noise was all about, leapt down from the lorry and added to it by barking furiously. Hermann shouted at him and he stopped barking, but the hooter went on howling. It seemed a small eternity before I managed to break the contact, and then suddenly the silence all around us was

14

immense and we realised how foolish we had been to let such an unimportant incident upset us. We looked at each other and then we both laughed — at which Otto began to jump around again and bark with joy.

But we decided not to go any further, and a few hundred metres away we dug ourselves sleeping hollows in the sand protected by a wind-bitten rock face. We had hardly slept at all the night before and we suddenly felt dog-tired. We were very soon in our sleeping-bags and fast asleep with Otto rolled up between us.

The First Hunt

The next day we were already on our way before sunrise. We were driving over a flat stretch of steppe chalk, the nose of our lorry turned towards the blue pyramidal shapes of the Tumas and Amichab mountains, which rose over the bare straight plains ahead like islands in the sea. They served as landmarks. The clear air was still cool and it was a pleasure to drive. Otto was tremendously excited, because to the left of us there were springbok leaping around and the east wind brought their scent direct to his nose.

Two hours later we were picking our way with difficulty over broken ground at the foot of a mountain. Then we drove over a stretch of red sandy ground completely barren except for five lonely stunted camel-thorn trees. After a while several gemsbok showed their grotesque black and white faces. We didn't seem to interest them much, and they just trotted off indifferently. With growing anxiety we noticed that there wasn't a blade of fresh grass anywhere, only the greyish weather-beaten stubble of last year's growth still jutted through the red sand here and there.

A long, gentle slope strewn with brown boulders slowed us down until we had almost to feel our way forward and the needle on the temperature gauge climbed to boiling point. Before long we had, willy-nilly, to replenish the water in our radiator from our water-bag, a canvas sack holding a few litres, in which, thanks to evaporation through canvas, the water remains cool even on the hottest day. Ahead of us was a great ochreous depression over which a shifting heat haze trembled looking almost like blue smoke. Two small mountains with serrated ridges were our immediate objective. We climbed up the eastern ridge to get a better view and with half-closed and smarting eyes we tried to penetrate the haze. At the far, southern end of the vast chalk plain we discovered a shining white rocky bastion. Somewhere there must be the Kuiseb canyon, and we could see a pattern of clearly defined gullies branching out like filigree work into the lighter plains around.

In that flickering heat it was not easy to distinguish the main watershed. With our glasses we did our best to make out the few and infrequent landmarks in the bare stretches, because we wanted to get as near as possible to the main canyon without losing our way between the many side ravines. We knew that we could be certain of finding water only in the main Kuiseb valley.

Our lorry now crept forward at a snail's pace over sharp chalky rubble which chewed up our tyres. The first landmark we passed was a dried-up camel-thorn bush, and it was some time before we came across the second — the white bastion seemed hardly nearer than before. A springbok scampered over the glistening plain before us, seeming airborne in the distorting heat waves. Our eyes were inflamed and it was difficult to keep them open against the dazzling light. Then we spotted a speck of green! It drew us like a magnet. It was a small *vlei,* a round depression in which perhaps every few years a little water collects, a poor, waterless oasis surrounded by a few trees struggling to stay alive.

It certainly wasn't anything marvellous, and yet what a joy it was to stop in the sparse shade of those aru trees and recover our breath! We decided to spend the night here and then look around for a suitable permanent camping place.

By the time we had unloaded and had a meal the afternoon was far advanced and the heat had been dissipated by a breeze from the west. In the slanting rays of the sun we could now see isolated blades of grass amidst the chalky debris. Obviously a little rain had fallen here at some time, and this probably meant that there was game in the neighbourhood. We were soon proved right, when we saw two white points on a dark rocky ridge moving as we watched; no doubt — two springbok grazing. Would we be able to get within range? The plain between afforded practically no cover. Our trouble was that we had no rifle; we had been compelled to surrender it at the beginning of the war, and all we had now was a Luger-parabellum pistol and a shotgun. And our stock of ammunition consisted of only forty-four cartridges for the gun and about three hundred rounds for the pistol.

When we discussed the matter, Hermann was optimistic as usual, whilst Otto, who stood there with wagging tail and seemed to know what we were talking about, had no doubt at all. In the end we decided to try, and I took up my position at some considerable distance from the two animals, taking cover between two chalk boulders. With the shot-gun by my side and a pair of field-glasses glued to my eyes I watched Hermann and Otto gradually working their way towards the ridge. Then it was plain that Otto had got wind of the springbok and wanted to race on ahead; I saw Hermann threaten him with his hand. The dog obeyed, remaining a little distance behind as Hermann advanced still further, partly bent double, partly crawling.

Finally Hermann came to the ridge. He could

hardly expect to get any nearer undetected, but the springbok were still over a hundred metres away. Then I saw him slowly raise the pistol and aim. I almost stopped breathing in my excitement; not for a moment did I let the antelopes out of my sight. Then came the shot. The springbok on the right jumped into the air twice, and both of them stared in obvious surprise towards the rocky ridge. Hermann was aiming again, but before he could fire a second time Otto's patience was exhauted, and he tore ahead after the antelope, which now raced off easily in long, springing bounds — unfortunately not in my direction.

We met again at the *vlei* and we didn't waste many words on the inquest; we both realised that we had quite a lot to learn. Otto returned much later, crawled under the lorry, and lay there panting.

The Canyon

The first morning hour was always wonderful. The sharp, jagged edges of the rocks threw long blue shadows over the desert like windslab over the snow. To the east the uplands rose above the plains like a steel-blue wall and the glistening white bastion seemed only a stone's throw away. But when we finally stopped at its foot our speedometer had registered another eight kilometres.

How were we to get to the top? A rather steep slope strewn with shingle struck me as passable and I raced up in low gear with small pebbles flying in all directions. We made it and I breathed a sigh of relief. But the smile faded from my face even before it had properly formed, because the world seemed to end suddenly under our front wheels. I swung the wheel round, in my haste jabbing Otto in the nose with my elbow, and the lorry slewed round just in time. We were not on a plateau at all but on a narrow ridge, and we stared down uneasily into a confusion of wild grey crags, rocky summits, black shadows and a labyrinth of gorges. Then we saw the deeper cleft formed by the main canyon, and at its bottom the white sandy bed glistening between innumerable dark ravines and ridges. Beyond them dazzling stretches of chalk spread out again, and still further away was the blue shimmer of jagged mountains, whilst on the horizon we could see the red sand of the dunes.

We stared down in fascination. It was an impressive and intimidating sight, a landscape inconceivable under a more temperate sky and in milder latitudes. Barren cliffs fell away steeply into deep ravines all around the main canyon like a wild and gigantic maze. They had a name, the 'gramadoelas', and as someone had aptly said, they looked as though the Devil had created them in an idle hour.

The thought that this wild, barren landscape was to be our home for perhaps quite a long time filled me with misgiving and yet at the same time with a feeling of elation. Hermann observed soberly: 'They won't find us so easily here.' That was very obviously true. To the east the barren landscape gradually merged into grass steppes, but in the dry years even the steppes were reconquered by the desert.

Through a narrow pass we now reached the main plateau of our rock bastion, which covered an area of rather less than three kilometres in length by rather more than five hundred metres in breadth. Apart from a small camel-thorn tree and a few gnarled noni bushes in a small, deep *vlei* it was quite barren. We hid our lorry in the *vlei* and tried to find a way down into the canyon. We had to know whether there was water before taking any further decisions.

A zebra track led us past white walls hollowed out by the wind and house-high rugged boulders which had plunged down from overhanging cornices above. Down below began a maze of steep gullies and micaceous schist ridges. There were obviously not many places in which the lower, partly overhanging slopes of the main canyon were negotiable, and from above it wasn't easy to see just where those few places were. We decided to follow the zebra track. After all, zebra had lived in these parts from time immemorial and we could safely rely on their instinct and experience.

The track ran along the ridges, and we could see why: the sides fell away in steep, smooth and polished steps, and naked rock was everywhere: an impassable chaos of sharp ribs and shiny schist slabs. The small grey vaal bushes and the isolated balsam shrubs hardly looked like living plants. We were astonished that anything at all could grow in this hot, dry wilderness of rock and stone.

Suddenly we heard one or two sharp whistles and we looked up. Above us stood a pair of klipspringer, small mountain antelope. They were perched on a high rock looking down at us curiously. Then another whistle sounded, and the two bounded from crag to crag like rubber balls and finally disappeared into a nearby gully.

With difficulty we continued our way along the zebra track which led us down to the broad sandy bed of the canyon. A few hundred metres further on we discovered a water-hole, and we all drank to our heart's content. When we had time to look around, we were amazed to spot a big imprint of a cloven hoof. The track of zebra and antelope were clearly visible in the damp ground, but this was the spoor of a far bigger animal. Hermann, always imaginative, said something about giraffes, but I laughed at him. Then we realised that it was a cattle spoor, and we remembered that many years ago cattle had gone wild on an isolated farm further upstream and that they were now roaming in the mountains and valleys like game, but we certainly wouldn't have expected to find them so far out in the desert. Water was obviously available, but what about food? As far as we could see there wasn't a blade of grass anywhere.

Following the spoor we found the track of a smaller animal, and then an even smaller one. No doubt remained in our minds: cattle had passed this way: a bull, a cow and a calf. At every bend of the twisting and turning canyon we reconnoitred carefully before going on; not wishing to upset the valuable beasts. We didn't set eyes on them, though we did, to our delight, find a good deal more water. Beyond almost every bend in the canyon we came across another water hole. And then we made the second important discovery of the day.

In a small pool in which the water was very low we saw a dead fish floating. Closer examination showed it to be a carp — right in the desert! Obviously there must be others, living carp close at hand! We waded into the pool knee deep and felt around in the mud. Suddenly Hermann gave a shout: 'Here's one!' He didn't manage to grab it but he did succeed in driving it up to the shallow end of the pool, where the surface of the water was agitated violently. Otto barked madly, and finally Hermann managed to grab and hold the carp. It was about twenty-five centimetres long and Hermann was very proud of his catch. As it was midday and we were hungry we decided to cook it straight away.

But how were we to cook it without a pot or a pan? We decided to fry it on a flat stone. There was plenty of dry driftwood around for a fire. Then we realised that we had no salt. So far we had seen no incrustations around any of the water-holes, but a little distance away were a few tamarisk bushes. They sweat out salt and they are therefore able to live in salty ground water, unlike any other bush or tree. We made a small fire between the rocks, sprinkled some broken tamarisk twigs over our first catch in the desert, and then waited patiently until it was done. It took quite a time. Later on we learned a much better way of cooking fish.

Where did that carp come from originally? Probably they had been swept down through broken dams from upland farms during the great rainy period of 1934; which meant that these holes had carried water

23

all that time — an encouraging thought. On the other hand, the dried-out bed of the Kuiseb showed that it had not flowed for more that a year, and that was disturbing. Still — fish in the desert; it was a wonderful discovery! Gratefully we named our rock bastion 'Carp Cliff'.

Whilst the light held we wandered around, looking into the side valleys in the hope of finding a suitable place to set up our new home. We found nothing that pleased us so we went back to the *vlei* for the night. Because the plateau was exposed and widely visible we decided not to make a fire.

Our First House

The eastern corner of Carp Cliff was separated from the main part of the plateau by a pass with steep chalk steps. We had to build a path before we could get the lorry through, shifting great chalk boulders and filling out the drops with stone slabs. It was hard work but it proved worthwhile because round the very next bend we found an overhanging cliff, hollowed out into a half circle round a patch of flat ground. Such places had been favoured as homes by men of the Stone Age. It was well situated too, facing south, so the great overhang would protect us from the direct rays of the sun. In addition, a long-established zebra track led down into the canyon. Even more important: the nearest farm was over fifty kilometres away and there was only one difficult and very inaccessible entrance to our gramadoela hideout. We could hardly hope to find a better place.

The western end of the rock shelter was broadest and we decided to make our 'living-room' there. We set up our two folding chairs, an old metal trunk to serve as a table, and two empty petrol-tin cases placed one on top of the other as a cupboard. The radio went into the top one.

Next to the 'living-room' was the 'kitchen'. There wasn't a great deal of kindling wood around so it was essential that our oven should not have too much draught. We dug out a long right-angled pit and faced it with stone slabs which we carried up from the foot of the chalk cliff. Our kitchen cupboard was also made up of empty cases. Along the rock face we made a low ledge on which we piled the contents of our potato and orange sacks. Our tinned goods, jam, sauerkraut and tomato purée, also found a place on this ledge. Supplies like flour, sugar, rice and dried fruit we proposed to leave in the driving cabin of the lorry. So far, unfortunately, we didn't know where we were going to park the lorry itself.

Behind the kitchen, and in the least-sheltered spot, we made our 'bedroom', a very simple matter. It consisted of two dug out 'made-to-measure' sleeping hollows in the hard ground with scooped-out special places for hips and shoulders. We then spread canvas over the hollows and put our sleeping-bags on top, together with blankets, sheets and pillows. During the day the whole was covered up with a tarpaulin.

In the afternoon we paused to survey our handiwork. So far our new home didn't look too homely, but at least we had a roof over our heads. As our water reserve was nearly exhausted we packed watersacks and field water-bottles into our rucksacks and climbed down into the underworld again. The evening shadows were already gathering in the gullies and we could see that there were fresh spoor on the zebra track. When we reached the last rock corner we reconnoitred before going down into the canyon, thinking of the cattle traces we had seen. But apart from a few tamarisk bushes and one or two young acacia trees of a type which grow in dried-out riverbeds with shallow ground water, there was nothing to be seen.

From the entrance of the zebra track into the canyon it was only about a hundred metres to a water-hole with a stretch of dark moist soil protected at one end by low shrubs. I scooped up the cool, rich earth with my hands and the idea of a garden occurred at once. Those few square metres of fruitful soil lay under the hot grey rock face in an area of dust-dry white sand like a promise, and whilst we drew our water we talked about fresh vegetables and juicy tomatoes. Then a sudden whistle made us look up. Right above us stood a klipspringer on a ledge of rock. Hermann just had time to grab Otto by the tail and at the same moment I raised my shot-gun. The report echoed from rock to rock round the canyon and the little antelope pitched down near the water-hole.

Our return, loaded with water and the dead antelope, was laborious, though the animal was only small. It meant a climb of over two hundred metres. At least we had the consolation of knowing that we weren't likely to go stale for lack of exercise.

That evening whilst a small golden sickle of moon stood in the western sky we sat in our new home and ate the cooked liver and brain of the klipspringer whilst Otto enjoyed its neck. We also finished off the last crust of the bread we had brought with us from Windhoek. After our meal we sat talking for a long time, discussing the war situation and our chance of being able to keep our end up in this desert. The Southern Cross hung sparkling under our cliff ceiling and the outlines of our chalk bastion were clearly defined between the bright stars and the amorphous depths below us. There was absolute silence as though the arid stillness of planetary space were dropping slowly from the stars.

We were well aware that we should have to live a life in the raw so to speak, and would be tried to the limits of our physical endurance. That was the law of the wilderness. And spiritually our lot would not be much different. Our lives would be primitive and almost savage and ruthless — and we would have to accept it, or be unable to survive at all. But if we were to remain sane we should have to preserve our finer susceptibilities and the faculties of the spirit. These seemed contradictory requirements but they would have to be reconciled. Men who had failed to find the proper combination in such conditions sometimes lost their reason altogether. And very often discordance had led to violence and killing.

In the starry immensity of that still night we both realised that the future would demand a great deal of us; that in addition to the adventure of living from the chase there would be adventures of the mind too. No doubt we could learn to live as bushmen lived, but we should never be able to go back to their level of thought and feeling.

The following days were taken up with a dozen and one jobs. The wind generator to replenish our battery had to be assembled and erected outside our quarters. And for a whole day we searched around for a suitably concealed spot to park the lorry. Finally I found a place under an overhanging cliff about five kilometres away. After that it took us another half-day to negotiate the boulder-strewn gully and tuck the lorry away under the rock face. Then we jacked her up and took off the wheels, covering them up to protect the tyres as far as possible. The heavy lorry battery had to be carried back to our cave dwelling, and we doubted that our old rucksack could stand the weight. It might tear and the battery smash to pieces on the hard rock. We decided not to risk such a calamity — it would have cut us off from the outside world entirely!

With the aid of an old puttee we made a loop to take the weight of the battery in addition to the rucksack straps and in this way we succeeded in transporting the valuable burden safely over the rock-strewn way to our cave. For the first time in days we were able to listen to the radio again, but we were

28

really over-tired and didn't enjoy it. To add to it all a cold south-west wind was blowing right into out 'house' and we sat shivering in the darkness listening to the contradictory British and German war communiqués. And what we heard was not calculated to raise our spirits either. In the end we began to snap at each other for no particular reason, and finally we squabbled and turned in without even saying good-night.

When we woke up the next morning our squabble was forgotten. We looked out over the intricate, clearly defined pattern of light and shade on ridge and gully below, over the steep chalk steps now turning golden in the morning sun, away to the blue shimmering mountains behind them and on to the red dunes on the horizon. It was as refreshing as a morning dip. Hermann stayed in bed and smoked his pipe happily whilst I made the coffee.

Hunger

But the lovely morning made no difference to the fact that we were ravenously hungry. The klipspringer I had shot had long ago been eaten, and the supplies we had brought with us had to be strictly rationed; for example, for breakfast we allowed ourselves half a cupful of flour, which we mixed into a sort of pap to make it go further. In addition we allowed ourselves a teaspoonful of sugar each and the same amount of jam. And unless we managed to bag something during the day, that would have to do us until evening. Small wonder that we found we couldn't stick to the labour plan we had worked out! After about an hour of heaving stones to build a protective wall between 'kitchen' and 'living-room' against the bitter south wind, we gave way to the more and more indignant rumblings of our empty bellies, went up on the rocky ledge above and looked around for something to eat.

With our field-glasses we studied the tracks which led down into the canyon, scanning the white chalk faces and ledges, and even the more distant prospects. For some time we concentrated on a couple of small black spots, but they didn't move, and when after five minutes they still hadn't moved we realised they were bushes.

To the north and the north-east lay a desolate maze of gullies and ravines. To the south we could overlook part of the canyon. Far beyond it we saw a yellowish patch to which we now turned our attention. There must be grass growing there, and where grass grew there would be game. But even so, how could we transport our bag through the steep gorges and gullies of the main canyon? It looked almost impossible. Once again we went over the whole area with our glasses, and once again we saw nothing. Even Hermann with his never-failing optimism admitted that it would be senseless to set out on the off-chance. Suddenly the desert around us felt strange and hostile. And yet we had often stayed in the Namib for long periods at a time and we had thought ourselves well acquainted with conditions there. But a scientific expedition with ample supplies was one thing; life in the wilderness for good was quite another.

Yet such sage distinctions didn't relieve the pangs of hunger. Hermann decided on more carp, and he spent the rest of the forenoon making fish-hooks out of steel wire. In the meantime I turned an old petrol tin into a water container to hold about ten litres, a very necessary item, for we had to go down into the canyon to fetch water at least every other day.

When we had both finished our jobs we set off armed with hook and line to try our luck in the water-hole. As bait we had saved up a few bits of meat, some cooked macaroni and one or two blow-flies. We had no idea what bait you used for carp but we hoped that in the desert they wouldn't be too particular.

We settled down to fish and it wasn't long before Hermann's line began to jerk. Our eyes sparkled hopefully: a bite! But it was a frog. I had never cared a great deal for rod-and-line fishing since a keeper caught me when I was a little boy, confiscated my tackle and gave me a terrible wigging. However, beggars can't be choosers so I did my best and after a while I had a bite too — another frog. And yet there were carp in the pool! Indeed, now and again we could see their dorsal fins above the surface of the

31

dark-green water.

Now we changed our bait to bits of the frogs we had caught, but we still caught nothing but frogs. Finally our patience and our store of curses gave out, so we gave up and made our way down the canyon in the hope of finding a klipspringer or two. We didn't even see one, or any fresh cattle traces. When we got back to the water-hole we discovered that the frogs had eaten the rest of our bait, so all we took home in the end was enough water for about a day and a half — and an even keener hunger than before.

That evening we cooked just over a hundred grams of macaroni with a few tiny bits of bacon to flavour it — and of this modest supper Otto had to have his share.

In the night we heard zebra pounding past beneath our rock shelter.

The next day we climbed up onto the ridge again and had another good look round. Then we separated, one going west and the other east along the game tracks leading down into the canyon. Two tracks following the long eastern ridge showed relatively fresh gemsbok spoor, and we hoped to catch a beast returning from a water-hole. We learned only later that gemsbok don't go down to the water-holes at night or even in the early morning, but only during the day.

The Bullfight

The morning twilight hung over the rocky chaos below like grey mist as we clambered over the chalk debris of the east ridge. Hermann, armed with our pistol, followed the more frequented game tracks, whilst with the shot-gun and Otto on the lead, I went along the other. Deep below us to the right, between steep walls, lay the winding canyon. At every bend I could see a small patch of the white sandy river-bed glistening amidst the darker rocks.

Suddenly I saw an unusual black spot in the still shadowless grey early-morning light. I looked at it through my field-glasses and my heart gave a bound: there in the river-bed below stood a great steer. It was undoubtedly the bull whose spoor had so astonished us on the very first day. He was grazing near a small water-hole. I slapped Otto across the haunches in joy and together we ran back to where Hermann was crouching in a rocky niche, watching his game path. Long before we got near I began to shout and wave my arms, and Otto barked furiously. Hermann got up and came to meet us.

'Do you want to frighten everything away?' he demanded.

'The bull!' I exclaimed breathlessly.

He stared at me perplexed for a fraction of a second, then he grasped what I meant and together we ran back to where I had first spotted the beast. We could hardly hope to get within range without being noticed; a few scattered tamarisks were all the cover available. Should we try to approach from two sides? If the bull took fright and ran off it would be almost impossible to get in a favourable shot. And he would soon get wind of anyone approaching down canyon. But supposing one of us made use of the slight breeze to drive him slowly towards the other? Presumably as soon as he sensed anyone approaching he would retreat, but owing to the steep sides he certainly wouldn't be able to escape either to left or right. This seemed the best idea so we decided that Hermann, armed with the pistol, should take cover ahead whilst Otto and I drove the bull towards him.

By this time Otto had realised that something unusual was in the air, and he was wagging his whole rear eagerly. He was clearly quite satisfied with the honour of accompanying me — perhaps because I had the shot-gun. Beyond the next bend we found a fairly reasonable way down. I waited for about a quarter of an hour to give Hermann time to take up his position. In the meantime the sun had risen. The canyon itself was still completely in shadow, but black shadows could already be seen below the schist slabs on the mass of ridges. The whole scene looked like an intricate woodcut.

Finally Otto and I made our way down, wading slowly through the white sand. In the canyon ahead of us great grey rock walls rising one behind the other seemed to bar the way, but as we approached, each one in turn revealed a new stretch of canyon. I kept a careful look-out and sighed with relief as I spotted the massive body of the bull through the sparse branches of a line of tamarisks which stood between me and the bull, and afforded some cover.

Slowly and cautiously I made my way closer. Above all I mustn't startle the beast and send it galloping away in blind fright. But after a while I realised that the bull wasn't reacting in the least though he must have got wind of me. Through my field-glasses I could see that he was cropping young rushes that were growing in the mire near the water-hole. Only two tamarisks were between me and him now and still he gave no sign. My heart was pounding as I stepped out from behind the last tamarisk. At that moment the bull raised his massive head, looked at me balefully and then charged. I released Otto, raised my shot-gun and let the bull have a charge straight in the face at twenty paces.

The sound of the shot was still reverberating through the canyon when he appeared behind me. I dodged, but he was just as good at side-stepping as I was. He almost had me, but with a tremendous effort I leapt up the side of the canyon and like a monkey pulled myself onto a ledge.

The bull stood below and glowered up at me. Otto was hanging onto his tail. Now Hermann ran up, stood with straddled legs, took good aim and shot the bull behind the ear. He collapsed as though struck by lightning, a huge black mass in the white sand. What a mountain of flesh! But was the bull actually dead? I picked up a lump of rock and hurled it at his head, whereupon he sprang to his feet and I hurriedly sought safety on my ledge again.

Otto had seized the bull's nose and the bull tried to crush him into the sand. Hermann went quite close now and shot the bull in the forehead. The only effect was a sudden imperious jerk of that great head which tossed the dog away like a ball. When Otto had picked himself up he confined his attentions to the bull's rear.

Hermann tried again with another shot behind the ear. This seemed to be the most effective spot and the bull dropped again and lay motionless in the sand for a while, but then he got up once more and stood there defiantly. We retreated a little. Hermann's ammunition was exhausted; we hadn't reckoned with so much shooting. I still had a shot cartridge, but what was the good of that?

The bull was obviously in a bad way. He stood there rather uncertainly and waggled his great head. One eye, which had been wounded by the shot, was closed and swollen. We felt sorry for the poor beast but at the same time we were full of wild delight, for we were now sure that he wouldn't escape us. First, however, we had to go back to get more ammunition and also an axe, a big knife, a rope and our sleeping-bags because if we abandoned the carcass for the night the hyenas wouldn't leave us much.

As we clambered up the steep slope we realised what hard work it would be to get the meat up to our shelter.

'It isn't worth it,' I said. 'It would be much more sensible if we camped down with the bull until we've eaten him.'

We returned loaded with sleeping-bags, coiled rope, a frying-pan, two empty petrol-tins cut open at the top, a water container, empty cans, salt, flour, an axe, herbs and the many odds and ends we had decided we would need.

The bull was lying in the sand with his head up and he watched us defiantly as we came closer. We left our packs on the rock and approached cautiously. When we were near he scrambled to his feet and came for us with lowered horns. Those wild cattle were the product of a merciless weeding out of the unfit and those that had survived were unbelievably strong and tough. How on earth could we end the poor beast's sufferings and get the meat we wanted? A shot in the heart perhaps? But where exactly was the heart in that enormous body? Neither Hermann nor I had ever slaughtered an ox and we had no idea.

But we had to try. Hermann took aim and fired. The bull advanced a few steps, but then lay down near a small acacia tree. He wasn't dead yet, and an hour later he was still prepared to fight. Another shot — in the head this time — seemed to have no effect at all.

By this time Hermann and I were both quite shaken. It was a shocking business and our inability to end it made us feel ashamed. Suddenly the solution struck me. I made a lasso, threw it over the bull's horns and tied the end to the tree, greatly limiting the bull's freedom of movement. Hermann then went up and shot him behind the ear. The great head fell again and whilst the bull was unconscious I sprang forward and slit his throat with the sharp kitchen knife we had brought with us. We sighed in relief — at last we had finished the wretched butchery.

By the time we had drawn the bull's entrails the sun was already sinking behind the white bastion of Carp Cliff and it was time for us to find somewhere to spend the night. About a couple of hundred metres beyond lay a rib of rock jutting out from the canyon side and beneath it the almost level ground was made up chiefly of old, dried-out droppings from rock dassies, animals remotely related to — of all creatures — the rhinoceros. By this time it was like turf and we shifted our things up there and scooped out a couple of sleeping hollows.

Otto, who had already had his fill, now curled up on Hermann's sleeping-bag and went to sleep — we had to gather kindling first, but this chore over we sat together at a blazing fire and fried ourselves a piece of the bull's liver in its own kidney fat. How indescribably satisfying it was to be able to eat meat to our hearts' content! Finally we clambered to our feet heavily: there was still work to be done; our bag had to be secured for the night against the hyenas. Quite near at hand was the dried-out trunk of an acacia tree which had been carried there at some time by the river in spate. We set light to it, and when we were satisfied it would glow and smoulder throughout the night to the confusion of all hyenas we went back to our hollows and crawled dead tired into our sleeping-bags.

The Big Feast

It was a cold night and there was no need to fear that the meat would go off, and long before sun-up we were at work skinning the carcass and cutting it up. The skinning was a very much more difficult job than we had imagined. During the night the meat had grown so cold that our fingers were soon numbed and we had to light a fire to thaw our hands from time to time. The sinews of the bull were enormously tough and quickly blunted our knives, so we had to look for a couple of flints to sharpen them with; after that it was easier.

As we cut away the great pieces of meat we carried them to a shady place under the projecting rock rib. Even the smallest pieces were not wasted, but packed into a petrol can. We were neither of us skilled butchers of course and we found we had taken on a difficult and laborious job. Hours passed, the sun beat down on our aching backs, sweat made our eyelids sticky, and our hands were slimy with blood and grease. Otto lay replete under a tamarisk and whined contentedly in his sleep whilst we toiled.

At last we were able to withdraw the backbone from the hide, which, despite all our care, had got a bit sandy. We washed it, dug a hole near our sleeping quarters, lined this with the hide, and now packed the meat into it and then drew the hide together. It was high time: the flies were beginning to buzz and we had already had to cut away several patches of fly-blow.

And then we sat down to a good midday meal as a reward for our labours: liver dumplings with a little rice. It was our first midday meal for many days. The food gave us such pleasure that we decided to allow ourselves a little celebration at least every Sunday — if it were only in the form of an extra spoonful of sugar or a dozen currants.

During the afternoon I cut up the fat on a piece of driftwood whilst Hermann reduced it in the frying pan. It was astonishing how much fat that bull had managed to accumulate in such a dry year. We poured the precious liquid into two aluminium bowls we had immersed to the brim in a shallow part of the pool and in this way we obtained two blocks of wonderful dripping.

The powerful head of the slaughtered bull lay beside the bare backbone on the sand and I hacked it open to get at the brain, which was to be our supper. This operation revealed that none of our bullets had gone right through the beast's skull. In the hard struggle for existence in the desert the bones and the cranium of these wild cattle seemed to have become much tougher than those of ordinary cattle; or perhaps our ammunition, some of which was quite old, was not particularly good.

After sundown we laid the meat out on the rock around our sleeping place to let it get cold again during the night. The temperature was again very low, but though this was uncomfortable for us, the meat was the important thing. We were having the first cold nights of the approaching winter, which was fortunate because neither of us knew much about preserving meat, and if the weather had been warm we should certainly have lost a good deal of it. We now possessed enormous quantities, well over a hundred kilograms, and if we could succeed in preserving it all we should have ample food for quite a long time to come.

We decided to turn some of it into dried meat, what they call biltong in this part of the world; the rest we hoped to be able to smoke, though we had tried before without much success. The most important thing was to keep the meat cold and free from flies until a dry crust formed over it. In the uncertain light of the early morning we were busy cutting up thin strips to make biltong, which were then hung up to dry. Biltong has a long history in South Africa; when the Boers set out on their great inland trek over a hundred years ago they took biltong with them in their saddle-bags; and much later, in their gallant but ultimately hopeless struggle against the British, biltong allowed them to carry out many an apparently impossible patrol and raid.

Finally we had cut up practically the whole carcass: into strips for biltong, and into larger pieces for smoking. We put them into the skin, sprinkling salt between the layers and covering up the whole with tamarisk branches as a protection from the sun. The biltong was to pickle for twelve hours, and the meat to be smoked for forty-eight hours. For breakfast we had heart and kidneys, an excellent dish.

After we had used all the best pieces we still had a large amount of lesser quality meat: sinewy pieces, gristly bits, the flesh on the enormous neck, and so on. It seemed a pity to waste it, so we decided to try our hand at making beef extract. Our two petrol tins had a capacity of about eighteen litres each, and they seemed quite suitable for the purpose, though it wasn't long before we realised that with making beef extract, as with so many other things, an ounce of practice was worth a pound of theory.

Although the tin was full of water, bits of meat settled at the bottom and caught there. By the time we discovered it the precious liquid was already burnt and it hurt us to pour it away.

We then scoured out the empty tin with sand and started again, but more carefully this time. The liquid was becoming richer and richer, and every two hours we poured it into the other canister and then scraped all the bits and pieces off the bottom for fear they might catch. Every four hours the boiled-out meat was replaced by fresh meat.

We hadn't forgotten the pangs of hunger we had endured previously and from time to time we would fish out particularly tasty bits of meat from the liquid, sprinkle them with salt and eat them with gusto. Otto was getting fatter and fatter and beginning to look more and more like the shape which had earned him his name in the first place. Most of the time — when he wasn't eating — he was just lying down and sleeping.

By evening both of our canisters were full to the brim with a golden-brown liquid which gave off a wonderful aroma. It tasted no less wonderful than it smelt, and Hermann grinned: 'I've always fancied a cup of bouillon made from a whole ox,' he said.

The next morning we removed the layers of fat which had formed like sheets of ice in the night, and the extract manufacture continued. Before long the liquid was so thick that the fire had to be kept low allowing the brew to simmer gently. Whilst Hermann supervised the process he made hooks to hang up the smoked meat. In the meantime I broke open the marrow bones on a suitable slab of rock to get at the marrow inside them, which gave us enough soft marrow-fat dripping to fill two empty jam tins. We were to be thankful again and again for our supply of this, for without it we should have been reduced to the tallow-like fat of the antelope, with which, at a pinch, you could fry, but certainly not cook.

There was a good deal of other work to be done too. To dry the biltong we stretched a rope above our sleeping place — we couldn't risk fixing it between the tamarisks in the river-bed, because only the night before the hyenas had dragged away the last of the bull's head, and they would certainly have left nothing at all of our biltong. But there are no convenient hooks let into the natural rock face, so we had to make wooden wedges and hammer them into fissures to give us something to fix our rope to.

And of course we needed a smoke chamber. A little above our sleeping quarters we found a roof-like rock with a horizontal ledge running back into a deep niche. Parallel to the ledge we built a wall of the same height from rock slabs and across the two we laid tamarisk branches to form a rack on which the meat could lie. Before we had finished the job it was evening, but we worked on for a while hanging up the biltong.

By this time we thought we had deserved a good supper, so with a forked branch of green wood as a spit we grilled ourselves a couple of juicy ribs over the glowing fire. As the fat dripped onto the glow, flames would leap up, licking the meat and throwing dancing shadows on the rock ceiling. Otto lay stretched out next to Hermann with his muzzle on his paws, staring into the fire and sniffing the wonderful smell of grilling meat. Somewhere far away a jackal howled and the stars sparkled over the dark velvet battlements of the canyon.

It was a warm evening and we were happy and contented. How often we had longed to play at Robinson Crusoe as children, and here we were experiencing the real thing as grown men! But now our feelings were even more deeply rooted I think; the

43

atavistic instinct seemed to manifest itself. After all, countless generations before us had found the height of happiness and contentment in a rock roof like ours, a heap of glowing embers, and fresh meat from the chase sizzling over it as a reward for dangers braved and hunger endured.

Our contentment was not quite so complete when we turned in and tried to sleep. In the warmth the dung we were lying on gave off an acrid penetrating odour we hadn't noticed before. Hermann groused and grumbled and I tried to console him with the thought that a little thing like smelly dung would hardly have upset our Stone Age forebears; to which he replied that he wasn't a forebear.

The hyenas were noisy that night. I suppose they smelt our biltong. Several of them gathered for a concert and before long the din was so horrible that we even forgot the stink. They would start off with deep, gurgling chesty tones, rise rapidly into a crescendo of hee-hawing like love-sick donkeys, and end in peals of hysterical cackling laughter which echoed and re-echoed round the canyon walls. This concert went on for hours.

Bees Make Honey

As soon as we awoke in the grey light of the morning we looked at our biltong. It was still too moist for the warmth of the day and the attentions of the flies so we packed it away in the hide again and hung the meat we wanted to smoke on the rack we had prepared the day before. It looked agreeably pink and pickled. The *pièce de résistance* was undoubtedly the great tongue, and this we hung up in the farthest corner of the niche where it would get most smoke. Neither of us had any idea how long you had to smoke meat. I knew that on the peasant farms in the Black Forest, hams and sides of bacon hang up in the chimney all the winter, but Hermann seemed to remember that when you took a ham to the pork butcher to be smoked it was ready within two or three days. We decided to try two days.

Our conversation in this period revolved almost exclusively around food and the various problems connected with it. Gnawing hunger was a thing of the past, at least for the time being, but we didn't find it altogether easy to live on meat alone. Every night great steaks were hung up to cool off and the following day we grilled them for our midday meal. During the day they were wrapped in sacking and blankets to keep them cool. For breakfast we still had our porridge of flour with a teaspoonful of sugar and another of jam, together with a cup of coffee. In the evenings we cooked some macaroni perhaps, or allowed ourselves a little rice to go with our meat. Nutritionally this was ample, but we felt a great desire for fruit and sweet things.

'We'll have to find a bees' nest, that's all,' said Hermann one evening.

There were plenty of bees around; we could see them drinking at the water-holes and zealously visiting the little clumps of wild saxifrage that managed to exist between the stony debris at the bottom of the canyon. But where in the innumerable fissures and cracks of the canyon was their nest? We knew that bushmen located bees' nests by studying the flight direction, finding the nest where the lines converged. This method obviously required a good deal of time and patience. Well, at least we had plenty of time.

So whilst Hermann looked after the meat-smoking I sat down near a clump of saxifrage in the hot sand and studied the flight of the bees. There were a good many of them, and as soon as I had been able to detect a general direction in their flight I marked it in the sand. Then I went on to another clump of saxifrage some distance away and continued my watch there. It soon became obvious that most of the bees flew off up canyon, so I went a hundred metres or so in that direction and repeated my observations at a water-hole. Slowly I worked my way forward and I began to feel quite hopeful. In the afternoon we changed over and Hermann carried on. He tried to interest Otto in the business, declaring that a dog ought to be able to scent the bee line to the nest. Once or twice as a puppy he had tried to play with them, and he could still remember what had happened. But, even without Otto's assistance, by evening Hermann had traced the general bee line to the next canyon bend. Unfortunately at that point it turned steeply upward and the bees disappeared from sight in the upper reaches of the canyon.

The next day I tried again higher up and I discovered that from there most of the bees flew down the canyon, but near the bend I lost sight of them again. Their nest was obviously somewhere in the upper part of the canyon face and it was impossible to look for it there so we had to give up the search — which was a pity because we had already worked out some wonderful recipes for using the honey ... We came to the conclusion that Samson must have enjoyed the special favour of Jehovah when he found his honey so easily ...

To console us, our smoked meat was taking on a beautiful golden-brown appearance, and we celebrated our success with a small piece of chocolate per man and dog. We had done most of the work now and we were able to spare a day for visiting our permanent quarters again. How refreshing it was to climb up out of the narrow, hot and barren canyon to the light, airy plateau. To see the wide horizon and the pattern of the landscape spreading out beneath us again was sheer delight, and we waved happily to the light-blue table mountain of the Gamsberg and to the jagged outline of the marble mountain Tinkaneib. Standing under the high white roof of our desert home we realised for the first time just how light and agreeable it was and how perfectly it fitted into the vast expanse of the Namib.

Everything was just as we had left it. Those golden oranges were still on our kitchen ledge; if they had been real gold the sight of them could hardly have given us greater pleasure. And when we ate one the luscious flesh tasted heavenly. We felt happy and contented again, and our spirits soared as we looked out over the bright landscape and the wild maze of gullies and canyons beneath us.

We switched on the radio, and light music from Cape Town sounded gaily under our roof. Hermann whistled the melody as he prepared a large piece of meat for pickling; then he measured our breakfast rations for the coming week. In the meantime I was cutting two lids out of a couple of empty tins to fit our one-kilo tins of meat extract, which we had brought up with us. But suddenly the music broke off and an announcer began to read the latest war communiqúe. The unheralded switch was shattering and it brought home to us that in the great civilised world outside, the margin between safety and desperation was no wider than it was here in the primeval world of the wilderness. Of course we had already known that in theory, but it came on us at that moment with a real shock.

The announcer reported that German troops were advancing on Paris and that the German High Command had threatened to bomb the city if the French defended it. My thoughts raced to and fro like frightened horses tearing along a fence. For me that fence was the recognition that in thousands of years of history nothing fundamental had changed in the condition of human existence — and it seemed to be much the same in man's spiritual life too. Only meantime many more men inhabited the world and by co-operation, science and technical developments they had magnified the destructive capacities of the Stone Age a myriad times.

Of course there was nothing new in this either; it was just that it was suddenly made horribly clear to us. And that fence, which extended from the grey mists of the past right into the uncertain gloom of the future — I thought I could see it running through the endless heat haze of the desert before me — was a barbed-wire barrier for my own soul which had just experienced such happiness in seeing the wide horizons after days of bloody toil in the underworld below.

All the afternoon I was sullen and hardly said a word. That night when we were once again lying on our bed of dung I could not help thinking of that imaginary fence. My first reaction was bitter cynicism and a rejection of all the material and spiritual values which mankind had developed in the course of thousands of generations. But at the same time I felt that I should have to overcome that cynicism if I were to survive here in the desert. Cynicism is a sharp enough weapon in the hurly-burly of an overcrowded town; it gives you elbow-room and it also gives you a satisfactory feeling of superiority. But what's the use of elbow-room in a desert? And what's the use of cynicism when the enemies you have to contend with are the broiling sun and the parching winds — when your only aim is to survive amidst the swift, sure-footed, cruel and lovely animals of the desert?

My feelings that night were vague and intangible. After all, our life in the desert had only just begun, and we were still strangers here. We were still tied by a score of strings to the busy life of the urban civilisation we had only just left. We still had not grasped that dogged persistence and absolute patience, essential for the primitive life we were to live, could be acquired only by a complete spiritual revaluation and abandonment of all our involved relations with human civilisation; and that before we could truly call the desert our home we would have to be conditioned by sun and wind, hunger and thirst.

Carp Pond and Garden

Biltong and smoked meat grew drier every day, but we decided to wait until the process of dehydration had reduced the weight very considerably and made it easier to transport from our temporary quarters to our permanent home. But this meant that we had to stay below in the canyon to protect it from the depredations of the hyenas. The daylight hours we used for a closer exploration of the canyon and its side ravines. We also found ourselves longing more and more keenly for some change in our monotonous diet of meat.

The presence of the carp in the water-hole was a constant challenge to our ingenuity, but further attempts at catching them merely produced further frogs. After repeated failures we gave up fishing and consoled ourselves with the thought of smoked ox tongue. Hopefully we boiled it for a few hours, but when we took it out we turned our heads away in disgust; it had gone rotten inside. There was nothing for it but steaks again. They were still juicy and tender, but somehow they no longer gave us the same pleasure; we were tired of them.

'I'm going to shoot a carp to-morrow,' Hermann announced firmly — so firmly in fact that I didn't raise the obvious objection that a carp really wasn't worth one of our precious bullets. And the next day when he took his pistol to the water-hole I still made no objection. I understood his feelings only too well. Several times he aimed and lowered his pistol again. Finally he fired. When the surface of the dark water was smooth again there was a carp floating belly upwards. Hermann had shot the two-kilogram fish neatly through the neck. Crisply fried it tasted like the food of the gods, and we ate every bit of it, sucking each separate bone. When we had finished we both agreed that the expenditure of ammunition had been worthwhile; still, it obviously couldn't continue so we eagerly discussed every feasible method of catching fish we had ever heard of.

As far as we were concerned there was no great choice. We hadn't a net, and not enough string to make one. There were no flexible reeds for weaving the lobster-pot type of basket, and the crippled thorn bushes and the brittle tamarisk twigs were of no use. And the water was too muddy for spearing fish or shooting them with a bow and arrow. We even discussed the possibility of discovering some form of fish poison such as was obtained from lady's-smock or cuckoo flower in Germany; there might be something of the sort amongst the Euphorbiaceae of the desert. But messing around with unknown poisons could be a dangerous business, and the idea of eating fish caught that way was not attractive.

In the end we came back to the idea of a net. I had a pair of old cellular underpants, but that didn't seem too hopeful. We wondered whether we could make a net by tearing a sheet into strips, but finally we decided to sew two sheets end to end and my underpants as well and to bone the whole with tamarisk branches. With this fence net we hoped to drive the carp into a corner and catch them there. Satisfied that we had solved the knotty problem we awarded ourselves a piece of chocolate each, and this raised our spirits so high that we also decided to start a garden at our drinking-water hole.

The next morning we carried two rucksacks full of smoked meat up to our cave and when we went down to fetch water we took packets of seed with us. We pulled out the few tufts of grass which were growing in the patch of good earth, dug it over with two pieces of wood, made a tilth and levelled it.

How encouraging the pictures on the packets looked! Purple radishes, green and gold mangel-wurzel, reddish-gold carrots, and shining scarlet tomatoes! We now sowed two beds of radishes and one each of mangelwurzel, tomatoes, carrots and parsley. In our minds' eye we could see a harvest of wonderful vegetables. When we had well watered the soil we took thin thorny branches from a young acacia tree and laid them over the beds to protect them from the birds. Throughout all this Otto lay quietly under a bush; he wasn't interested in gardening. In fact he couldn't understand what we were wasting our time on; hadn't he drawn our attention to a fresh gemsbok spoor on the way down?

By the time we had negotiated all the winding bends of the canyon it was evening. We had brought two potatoes with us from our cave and we now baked them in the hot ashes of our fire and roasted half-dried biltong to go with them. The roasting made the meat tender again and it went down well with the baked potatoes — with a knob of butter it would have been a real delicacy.

The next morning there was a strong east wind and sand was being swept along in clouds and hurled against the sides of the canyon like pelting rain. It was not surprising that all the walls and rock faces just above the dried-out bed were smooth and polished. A gust of wind got stuck in the corner of our shelter whirling up dust and mica flakes which rained on us and our possessions. When we woke up our hair, ears, eyelids were full of sand and there were little dunes on our already rather grubby pillows.

Our frying-pan, with fat in it, was now half-full of sand and mica dust, and because the top of our jar of apricot jam hadn't been closed properly a layer of dust had formed on the jam too.

When we went out into the river-bed the full force of the wind lashed us with sand and schist. Through half-closed eyes we watched curtains of it being hurled up the rock walls. Looking up canyon as though expecting something different there, our eyes met the glistening white bastion where our cave was. The sky itself seemed dusty. This east wind of the Namib was no stranger to us and we knew that it would probably last for three days.

With hardly a word we packed our things together, taking as much of the smoked meat as we could carry, and we then clambered laboriously up the steep zebra track to our cave. Twice more, heavily loaded, we made the same hard climb and then we had all our meat up above. We now suspended a rope along our bedroom wall, fastening it to jutting pieces of rock or to wooden pegs we rammed into fissures. When we had finished, dark pieces of meat and long strips of biltong dangled along the light-coloured wall making a pleasing and highly nutritious picture.

Labour and Contemplation

To celebrate the gathering in of our meat harvest we had decided to treat ourselves to something extra-special: smoked meat with sauerkraut. We had been looking forward to it for several days. Actually it would have been better if we hadn't. The meat certainly smelt all right in the pot, and Otto obviously thought so too, but when the great moment came and we tasted it we looked at each other in dismay: it was horribly salty.

We had no time to go into the matter — not that it would have been much use anyway — for at that moment the light music on the radio was suddenly cut off and a loud fanfare of trumpets told us that some special announcement was about to be made. A roll of drums sounded, followed by a military march, and then the fanfare again. After which came the voice of the announcer: 'Stand by to receive a special message from the headquarters of the Führer.'

It was some time before this special announcement actually came through, and we sat silently, listening to a lively brass band, which for us was accompanied by the booming of the east wind through the canyon. I was haunted by sad and disturbing thoughts. The radio, the newspapers, the films — everything was now harnessed to totalitarian propaganda. Thoughts, feelings and opinions were being manufactured and mechanically churned out. How much room was there, or would there ever be again, for reason and mutual understanding? Of all the technical developments of recent years it seemed to me that the technique of mass communication was the most dangerous. Wouldn't mass hysteria and mass slaughter be the obvious consequences once technology had violated the protean creativeness of man?

Finally the announcement came: France had surrendered. We discussed the situation at length.

The east wind was still howling and the stars flickered uncertainly in the warm whirl of air. What would happen now? Would Hitler try to invade England? And how long would it be before the United States came to England's aid? Or would Hitler now try to make peace? There were a dozen and one reasons to support any supposition you liked. The future proved them wrong — all of them.

After we had turned in we lay awake for hours. This may not have been altogether due to the disturbing news; we had drunk vast quantities of tea after our salty meal. But when we finally got to sleep we slept well on into the next day. The east wind was still rushing through the canyon and we felt glad that there was no need for us to be there now. But we had to go down again right after breakfast because we had no more water.

The first thing we did was to visit our garden. It looked a sad sight. Some love-lorn zebra stallion had danced all over it. Our turnip bed was ruined. We realised now that we should have to enclose it if we wanted anything to grow. We didn't much care for the idea because an enclosed space is visible a long distance off. Few would fail to recognise the hand of man, and there was always the danger that Khoi-Khoin tribesmen might come our way. So far we had seen no fresh human traces. We had found the remains of a fire which had probably been laid by Hottentots but it might easily have been years old. How important was this garden to us? How long would we be able to remain in good health living on meat alone without vegetables? We weren't sure. And supposing that blacks did discover our presence, did that necessarily mean that they would tell the police? We were afraid it did.

In the end our own desires tipped the balance — as they so often do. We decided to tend our garden and fence it in. That afternoon we went down into the canyon again and felled a number of young acacia trees which formed a thorny group beyond the waterhole. It wasn't very hard work; the axe just bit into the soft wood of these swift-growing trees. But their thorns were sharp and they stuck into our flesh, so it was to the accompaniment of a good deal of grumbling that the trunks were finally hewn and got into place to form a barrier against marauding animals.

After that we put the garden in order and watered the beds with a field water-bottle. The wind would soon enough dry out the ground so we gave it a good soaking. Then we carried water up to our cave and finished the day digging thorns out of our flesh with a needle.

We had enough water for four days now so there was no need to go down to the canyon for a while, but there was enough other work to do. For one thing, our cave dwelling wasn't yet comfortable enough, particularly when the south wind blew, so we built a breast-high wall against the south wind. The next job was to make the net for the carp, so we sewed two sheets and a couple of underpants together to make one length, and along it we sewed a cord with loops at regular intervals. Tamarisk branches were to be stuck through these loops from side to side in order to give this primitive net the rigidity to enable us to push it forward through the water without its giving way. When we had finished our handiwork didn't look anything like a net — despite the cellular pants we had sacrificed — but we hoped it would come up to expectations.

Food was still the centre of all our thoughts and discussions. Our smoked meat was salty and we could consume it only in small quantities at a time. If only we had bread! Perhaps we could save a little flour from our breakfast ration to make bread with, but where were we to get the wood we would need for baking it? We wondered whether there was some sort of bread which could be baked quickly and we thought of Swedish crisp bread.

We measured out two rations of flour and mixed it with water to a thinnish paste without salt — the meat was salty enough! We then spread the paste on to a flat piece of carefully greased tin and put it over bits of glowing charcoal. And lo and behold, the result was a golden-brown crisp biscuit-like bread. We were very proud of ourselves. With the remainder of our butter — a bit rancid by this time — and a scrap of cheese it tasted excellent.

We also decided to ration our jam differently: from now on each of us was to have his own tin of jam — to last three weeks. In this way if either of us fancied two or three spoonfuls at once he could have it without upsetting the other — he would have to make up for the extravagance by going without later.

This was the day on which we listened to the report of the signing of the Franco-German armistice in the Compiègne forest, and we wondered how Hitler thought he was ever going to come to an understanding with France after this deliberate humiliation.

Then came a windless and relatively warm day. It was the weather we had been waiting for to tackle our carp — the water in the pool had been very cold.

We got up early and went down into the canyon. First of all we visited the garden. The first seedling leaves of the radishes and mangelwurzel were just visible and the sight of their delicate green quite moved us. The soil was still moist but we carefully watered the beds again. From there we went to the other pool higher up the canyon where the carp were. The tamarisk was the only tree which offered us straight enough branches for our 'net', so on the way we cut pieces of a suitable length.

The water was still cold and we shivered when we waded into it; evaporation in the dry air was more than enough to counteract the slight warmth provided by the rays of the winter sun. But once we were thoroughly wet it wasn't so bad. Extending the 'net' over the breadth of the pool we slowly and carefully pushed it ahead of us. Where it wasn't big enough to reach right to the bottom we stirred up the mud with our feet to prevent the fish from escaping underneath it. Finally we had drawn the whole pond and had cut off one corner with our primitive gear. We forced the tamarisk branches into the mud at the bottom and to our great delight we could feel the fish nosing and flapping against the material in their attempts to escape. Now that we had our hands free it was not difficult to catch the carp in this small area. Our first 'beat' produced the respectable bag of fourteen big carp. Then we caught six more. The smaller fish we put back into the water — they'd come in when they were bigger!

It was an unexpectedly large haul and we were now faced with the problem of what to do with twenty fat carp. We certainly couldn't eat them all before they went bad.

'Simple,' said Hermann, 'we'll just dam up one end of our drinking water hole and make a carp pond.'

The solution was brilliant, so we packed the fish into the wet 'net', and ran back with them as fast as we could, taking it in turns to carry the heavy rucksack. It took us an hour to get back, and by the time we had reached our water-hole ten of the carp were dead. The remaining ten we put into our carp pond, which we improvised by sealing off a corner of the pool with a stone wall. We hid our fish-net in a fissure in the rock face, then we cleaned and scaled the dead fish and took them with us up to our cave where we fried the three biggest. We ate a good deal — grinning at each other with satisfaction, saying again and again how wonderful they tasted — but there was a good deal of fish left over and we didn't want to waste it. This time it was my turn to have a good idea: you could souse fried herrings, so why not carp. Why not indeed? So we soused the rest of the fried carp.

There were now seven fish over and we decided to smoke them. But how to smoke fish? Warm or cold? And for how long? Neither of us knew. We discussed the matter during supper and decided to try with cold smoke, since fish goes off far more quickly than meat. We built ourselves a smoke chamber next to our sleeping quarters between two rocks which could be closed with a sack. What we needed now was a smoke lead, so we scooped out a trench in the ground and a pit for the fire, covering both of them with slabs of rock. We rubbed the fish with salt, hung them up in the smoke chamber on wire hooks, and sat up until midnight keeping the slow fire smouldering so that it would give off as much smoke as possible. A light wind was blowing and now and again it blew the fire into flames and we had to damp it down again. The words fell slowly with long pauses in between, whilst the Southern Cross, like a great illuminated clock hand, moved round under our rock roof.

When we got up the next morning I immediately inspected the smoke chamber. The fish were golden brown but they struck me as still rather raw so we continued to smoke them until midday. Then we fried one; it tasted excellent, and the flesh was firmer than is usually the case with smoked fish.

Good Times

The days passed quietly and without incident. Thanks to our ample supply of carp we were never hungry now. The very next day after our first successful attempt we tried again in another pool, catching nineteen more, which we hurried back to our carp pond. Before long we had over forty fine fat carp swimming around in it awaiting our pleasure. When we went down to fetch water it was now the easiest thing in the world to catch a couple of fish to fry for our supper. At the same time our skill in smoking increased. We used more charred wood and we smoked the fish for five or six hours only.

And in our garden we pulled the first radishes and mangelwurzel tops.

One evening we shot a klipspringer from behind the tamarisk trees near the water-hole, and so we had fresh meat again. Otto was even more pleased than we were and wagging his tail he licked our blood-stained hands clean. He didn't care for fish.

Together we explored the canyon as far as the Goagas mountain chain, and found more water-holes full of carp. But we saw nothing of the cow and her calf; she seemed to have left the neighbourhood.

One day Hermann stayed behind to repair his boots and Otto and I made a trip towards the southern plateau, where we thought there might be more game than on our side. Every day we had looked over to the broad, light plains below the purple face of the Roststock. In our direction they ended in a white scarp, the counterpart to our Carp Cliff. Below the shining scarp lay a sort of frieze of red sandstone scored by hundreds of small gullies, from which long rocky ridges with dark ravines between them stretched as far as the edge of the canyon. It didn't look very far but it was hard going.

First we went down into the canyon and tramped through loose, heavy sand. Then came a precipitous side gulch with threatening overhanging walls and innumerable boulders. The wind had formed the low sandstone walls into fantastic shapes: columns, holes and caverns. It would have made an ideal town for cave dwellers, and I couldn't rid myself of the impression that they were man-made; half the time I was expecting to see a bearded face peering out of a hole.

Then to my satisfaction I spotted old clumps of grass in the sand, and the game tracks became more frequent. Three zebra were the first sign of life. Their bold stripes merged almost completely into the rock behind them, shimmering in the heat, and in fact it was only when the stallion began to snort that I noticed them at all. The stones crunched and rattled under their hooves as they disappeared over the ridge. For hours I strolled across wide plains and through the shallow valleys which lay behind the chalk ridges, and finally I made my way back with the good news that I had seen forty-seven gemsbok and two springbok.

Hunger was no threat for the time being, but the barren landscape constantly reminded us that it was only at arm's length and we therefore continued experimenting in order to make our food supply more secure and more varied. In particular we were anxious to stretch our flour supply as far as possible, so we tried concocting a sort of meat meal out of crushed biltong. We then baked biscuits made of half flour, half meat meal, and we produced a tasty dark-brown biscuit — 'biltong bread'. We had to be very careful in baking it because if only the least bit burned it tasted horrible. We ate it all the same; we couldn't afford to be fussy.

There were small, finger-long carp in far greater quantities in the pool than would ever grow up and it worried us that we couldn't make any use of them, so we started to smoke them as though they were sprats. We also discovered that jellied with vinegar they made a very piquant dish.

Materially we had little to complain of, but unfortunately we had too much time to think and brood, and before long a feeling of uncertainty and insecurity came over us. Hermann, with his rapidly changing moods, was less affected than I was.

Looking back on it this period seems strangely vague and detached. To some extent this may have been due to the enormous breadth and depth of the landscape itself; it rolled up to and surrounded our bastion like a great ocean. But in addition there was the strange contrast of our new experiences in the wilderness with the war news that came to us through the ether. The lunatic, suicidal struggle in which the civilised peoples of Europe were engaged almost destroyed our belief in man's whole culture and civilisation. Centuries of development seemed to lead us only towards progressive destruction and disaster. Perhaps in the circumstances it was a good thing for us to be cut off from this civilisation and to fight the primitive fight of endurance for mere survival. Perhaps we could build up something new on the hard rocks of the desert? But for the moment a feeling of instability and uncertainty was uppermost — old doubts as to the meaning of man's existence — and vague feelings and half-formed ideas were swept along like loose blades of grass over the parched earth.

63

Taking root in the barren soil of the desert was a slow and difficult job.

I must have got on Hermann's nerves quite often in that period, but again and again he shamed me by setting an example of deliberate and purposeful activity, and from time to time he would jerk me to my senses with a dry and pointed remark. At that time we were busy building a wall to protect our 'living-room' from the west wind, and also a sort of veranda in front of it with a low stone parapet and a stone table where we planned to spend our evenings.

When these jobs were done we began our scientific work, exploring the landscape, identifying the geological formations, and cataloguing our results. Here too the start was difficult and quite often we squabbled and harsh words were spoken. But I like to think back on this period. The weather was sunny and the sky was blue. Individual incidents appear and disappear like white clouds in the summer sky.

I see three inquisitive klipspringer perched on a glistening stone slab, their thigh muscles bunching in the clear morning light. Near that slab is a moringa tree with a squat trunk and silvery bark. Clearly defined black shadows fall on the rock face.

What extreme forms of adaptation those two forms of life represented! The graceful, speedy antelope, built for swift and powerful jumping to escape danger; and the squat, shapeless tree rooted firmly in the ground, able to store up moisture in its trunk for the dry years and to defy evaporation with its firm, glistening bark.

I can see the cave town with its fantastic gramadoela gulches cut deep into the red sandstone, as close together as the ridges on a washboard. The black shadows of the holes contrast with the hot, ochreous glow of the barren slopes and bright light falls on the pale, twisted branches of dead balsam bushes. It was here that we shot our first gemsbok. We had stalked it for hours and that evening we were so tired that we almost cried.

Cruel and Beautiful

We had always known that life was a hard and bitter struggle and that those who survived did so only at the expense of others. But until we went into the wilderness to live, that knowledge was abstract, theoretical, a reasoned conclusion; and sentiments of a sheltered childhood told us that it was really all quite different and much nicer. Now the truth was hammered into us pitilessly. We had to kill in order to live — and our supply of ammunition was limited, so that more than once we dared not waste the bullet to give a wounded animal the *coup de grâce*.

I can remember one hot still day when I set out on my own, leaving even Otto behind — much to his disgust — to search the area to the north for game. We had left our lorry in a ravine there, and we hadn't been near it since. I hadn't far to go. Right on the edge of the plateau I startled three springbok which had been concealed in a small gulch. Two does fled towards open ground in long, graceful bounds, followed more slowly by a splendid buck. He was not more than fifty paces from me and there was no cover of any sort. I had fallen to one knee. The buck stopped, snorted and looked at me with mingled curiosity and alarm, still snorting and whistling.

He was a magnificent beast, the lovely lines of his tense body were clearly defined in the sunlight. The great head sat firmly on a graceful but powerful neck and lyre-like horns shone like polished bronze. I took all this in without thinking about it; my whole attention was concentrated on one thing: food! I was armed with the pistol and still kneeling, I took careful aim and fired. The shot seemed to have no effect; the buck just stood there and looked at me. I aimed again, and I could feel the wild beating of my heart. I fired and missed a second time. The buck now turned to go after the does, turning his scut towards me. It was my last chance. I aimed and fired a third time. After a wild leap the buck collapsed, but he was up again in a moment, making off with difficulty on three legs, blood running down the light fawn of his hindquarters.

I could have kicked myself for forgetting in my excitement that the adjustable sights of our parabellum tended to slip sideways and had to be checked at each shot. How often we had told ourselves that we mustn't forget that! And now at the critical moment I had forgotten it.

I went after the limping beast as quickly as I could, fearing to lose it from sight in the broken landscape. When I came up with him again he was lying in a small pit in the sand. As soon as he spotted me he clambered to his feet and made off, disappearing from view in the slaty gulch. If only I had Otto with me! For a while I managed to follow the trail, but then I lost it for good, but he suddenly loomed up again. I got in another shot. Through the field-glasses I could see the wound high in the shoulder blade before he disappeared behind the next ridge. I followed slowly and cautiously in order not to frighten him up should he have crouched down again.

He lay in a small gorge, his head up looking around. I went as near as I could without being seen and lay down on the hot rocks to wait. The sun was a pitiless weight on my shoulders and the air trembled in the heat over the schist slabs. It was a long wait and the handsome beast still kept his head up and I could see the alert eyes through my field-glasses. The constant flicking of his ears showed that the poor beast was being tormented by flies. I was sorry for him but I was waiting eagerly for his end. Quite close to my hand were two drops of dried blood on the grey stone.

Another hour passed before that head slowly sank down. It rose again for a moment and then sank until finally it lay on the ground motionless. I made a wide detour to come up from behind, but when I was within twenty paces the dying buck scented me, staggered to his feet with difficulty, and stood there on trembling legs. He tried to flee but he only swayed; he was too exhausted to move now, and rushing up I seized his horns and forced him to the ground. He just had time to utter one frightened bleat and my knife sank into his neck.

I drew the entrails at once, carefully removing every scrap of fat. I had hoped to carry the carcass back whole, but it was too heavy — it was only later that I learned the knack of balancing a heavy buck over the shoulders. I needed assistance so I hurried back to fetch Hermann.

We had already decided that at some time or other we would climb the Roststock, which was the highest mountain in the area. Every day we looked at its purple slopes across the canyon, and our attention was attracted by a gleaming white patch on its rear summit. Could it be an auriferous quartz vein? Or perhaps a pegmatite vein with rare minerals? Such speculations made the climb attractive to a geologist. We had enough fresh meat for a few days and so we could afford the time for a scientific expedition.

The very next morning a garland of cirrus clouds in the southern sky announced the approach of cooler air. That meant a few clear days. We roasted a leg of springbok to take with us and at about midday we shouldered our packs and set off. Before we left the canyon to clamber up to the south plateau we filled our water-bag, a five-litre can and a field water-bottle at the last water-hole, then with this extra burden we tramped along in the shadow of an overhanging rock face. From a projecting ledge higher up a pair of klipspringer watched us inquisitively. A zebra track zigzagged over a steep schist ridge onto one of the long ribs cut out of ochreous sandstone. By the time we came to the west side of the plateau the sun was almost touching the horizon.

A little further away there was a patch of red sand between low chalk rims. We had just reached its edge when a group of springbok came galloping in our direction, dancing in line over the sand. Their graceful bodies glistened in the slanting rays of the sun and little purple clouds of dust sprang up under their slender forelegs. Suddenly the leading buck paused, stopped for a moment, hesitated and then sprang away at a tangent in great bounds. The others followed and galloping at full stretch they reached a small summit which was already in shadow and disappeared behind it one after the other.

The landscape seemed very still when that calvacade of dancing jumping life had vanished. I was glad that we had a roast haunch in our pack and did not need to shoot. Otto chased after the disappearing herd and looked very hurt when Hermann called him back and put him on the lead.

After an hour's march we came across several dead ebonywood trees in a dried-out river bed. The black wood provided us with fuel that burned well and glowed for a long time during the night. We made tea in an old jam tin and ate cold venison for supper. Then we scooped out sleeping places in the soft sand near the fire and turned in. Despite our warm sleeping-bags and the good fire it was bitterly cold and we slept little. When Orion appeared in the sky we were already up drinking tea and warming ouselves at the fire, and as the stars paled we hid our water-can, cooking-tin and what remained of the meat under a rock and went on.

There was a grey bank of mist over the desert to the west as we set off, and travelling light we made rapid progress, reaching the foot of the mountain shortly before sunrise. An hour later we were on the summit. Our first glance was to the south, for that was unknown territory. Wild, precipitous walls of red granite disappeared into broken depths, and on the far side the rear summit rose just as steeply. Now we had the explanation of the white patch we had seen: a colony of vultures had settled on that vertical mountain face, and had probably been there for thousands of years, using it as a nesting and observation place. Many vultures were wheeling around in the sky. It was the only mountain summit we had ever known to be used in common by them like that. Their choice was understandable though. This mountain was a forepost of the uplands overlooking the desert, a sort of watchtower affording a magnificent view over the grey stony wasteland, the white chalk cliffs and the maze of summits and gorges.

Emerging from the deep shadow of the mountain a small bird rose singing into the light, let itself fall back into the shade and then rose into the light again, singing in full-throated joy. With rising spirits I watched that tiny symbol of joyous life as it wheeled towards the blue sky. Then we looked eastwards into the glaring sun which burnt over the wide sweep of the African uplands. 'The first morning after the creation of the world,' said Hermann quietly.

And I too experienced an indescribably reassuring

feeling of belonging to the wild, beautiful and cruel life of this vast country. It was as though the fresh wind from the south were dissipating all doubts and uncertainties and a feeling of peace and security came over me.

We stayed the whole day on the summit, taking photographs, making sketches and measuring, for its exact height was of great importance for our calculations.

When the sun reached the bottom of the deep Gaub canyon a circling vulture peeled off with a great flapping of wings, gliding downwards silently. Two others followed. Then three more ceased circling and dived too. And finally we heard the swish of air as all the vultures dived swiftly to the bottom in one great swarm. We followed their descent through our field-glasses and saw them disappear one after the other into the jet-black shadow of a ridge. Was some animal dying there? Had a leopard pulled down a zebra on its way to a water-hole during the night? Death had certainly struck there in one form or other and the vultures were busy picking the bones.

In the afternoon we took a siesta in a niche in the rock. Whilst scratching himself a place to lie down in, Otto dug up a beautifully worked stone blade of brown chalcedony. The hunters of the Stone Age had obviously used this summit as a vantage point for game, and we now followed their example. Again and again we scanned the game tracks with our field-glasses, seeking to impress their pattern on our minds, memorising where they led down into the ravines. On one path we spotted five zebra, and we saw two gemsbok under a lonely camel-thorn tree. But no matter where we looked, all we could see was ochreous or greyish patches; nowhere a yellowish tint to indicate the presence of last season's grass. It was just as well that we had the carp safely swimming in our pond!

The sun gradually sank away in the west and the red dunes began to glow. Slowly the shadows gathered in the ravines and gorges and rose up the steep sides, flooding over the top into the depressions like dark water. The flat spaces were like vast carpets with heavy folds edged with the lace of spidery schist ridges falling away in all directions.

Night was falling and we hurried down the mountain slope.

The East Wind

I awoke abruptly. The wind was booming, the stars were flickering in the sky like wind-blown torches, sand was running into my ears, and my mouth and nose were dry. Every new gust of wind poured fresh sand over us. Hermann woke up too. 'An east wind,' he muttered and snuggled deeper into his sleeping-bag. Half awake I could hear the gusts of wind becoming more regular and finally developing into a rhythmic soughing.

When the sun rose we were half buried. Our hair, eyes and ears were full of sand and at breakfast the springbok meat crunched between our teeth. The wind had become noticeably warmer and on the chalk plateau it was so strong that we could lean against it. A red veil of sand rose from a small dune into the blue sky. To the south a sandstorm was raging and the dunes were covered with a reddish mist.

When we entered the canyon the grey sand was whirled into our faces and we could hardly distinguish the other side. A few hundred metres further on we unexpectedly came across a sheltered spot, but that made the tremendous concert all around seem even louder. Waves of sand lashed up the sides like the sea beating against the shore, and the rock face was scoured and polished five metres high in many places. Tiny particles of mica seemed to be raining from a blue sky.

When we clambered back again to our quarters we had to carry a full load of water and we were thankful when we were at last sheltered from the wind. Panting we put our loads down and Hermann made coffee. We celebrated our return with an extra teaspoonful of jam and a small piece of chocolate each, including Otto. The wind continued to roar and howl across the rocky ridges and the air was so full of sand that we could hardly see the Roststock across the canyon. It must have frozen hard in the uplands and the east wind would certainly blow for at least three days.

This winter east wind of the Namib belongs to those great movements of air which maintain a changing equilibrium between the air masses over land and sea. When, as a result of one or two frosty nights, the air over the uplands grows colder than the air over the Atlantic then this colder air begins to brim over the edge of the uplands, rushing like a waterfall over the mountains, gaining speed and growing warmer as it sweeps unhindered over the broad smooth plains of the Namib, until it finally races out over the sea. The wind that began as a cold blast in the uplands finally ends over the Atlantic as a hot, sand-laden storm which flattens the great breakers until the sea laps the sandy edge of the desert as a lazy blue swell.

Owing to the great volume of air involved it usually takes three days for a new equilibrium to be established between land and sea. In summer the same process takes place but in the opposite direction. The suction of the warm air rising above the land draws in cooler air from the sea which rushes inland as a west wind. For these reasons the prevailing winds in the Namib are east in winter and west in summer.

Due to the warmth of the sun during the day the east wind fell a little towards evening, but in the cool night air the strength of the wind increased and we could hear it roaring again. The following morning it was still whistling and howling amongst the rocks and caves of the long cliff ridge, and clouds of whirling sand covered the floor of the canyon like mist.

At breakfast we discussed our game chances, for we hadn't seen much from the Roststock. 'We mustn't let those loose sights waste any more ammunition,' I said. 'We can't possibly afford to use four bullets on one springbok. At that rate we'd soon have no ammunition left at all.'

Hermann agreed. 'It means we must solder it in one position, but then we shan't be able to adjust for range, that's all. In any case we never had much luck at long ranges.'

We therefore heated up our soldering iron and soldered the sights for a range of fifty-five metres. For our target practice we sacrificed four cartridges, but at least it gave us some idea of how the pistol behaved with the fixed sights.

The storm had charged our battery to the full and we were able to listen to the radio as much as we liked. We found that a Beethoven concert fitted in perfectly with the howling of the desert wind; they seemed to be made for each other. Then a German announcer came through with a summary of the week's events, and we learned that 'reprisal raids' had begun against Britain two days previously. We were depressed. Was it the preliminary to an invasion? And how long would it be before there were reprisals for the reprisal raids?

The wind blew strongly all that night and it was not until the following afternoon that it dropped a little. We went down into the canyon to fetch water and at the water-hole we had an unpleasant surprise: the level of the water had sunk by about eight centimetres; obviously less water was filtering through the gravel of the river bed than was being lost by evaporation. If that were already happening now, what would it be like when it got really hot?

Our garden had been protected from the worst of the storm by a bush, but it was half buried under sand, and the leaves of the mangelwurzel were drooping because the ground water had sunk. If this went on we should have to water the beds every day. Whilst we were drawing water Otto was sniffing at something in the soft ground near the carp pond; it turned out to be a half-covered hyena spoor. Apprehensively we counted our carp and discovered that two were missing. We did our best to protect the pool from such depredations with branches and stones, but we weren't very optimistic about the result.

The Fish Poacher

The next time we came down to fetch water we could see how right we had been. Our barricade had proved useless; it had just been forced aside, and another fat carp was missing. I swore vengeance and decided to lie in wait with the shot-gun during the night. Hermann tried to dissuade me, saying that they certainly wouldn't come whilst I was there; in any case it would be a moonless night and I probably wouldn't be able to see them. But I was determined to do something in defence of our valuable fish suppers, so when darkness fell I took up my position on a soft patch of sand above the water-hole near the foot of the rock face. I scooped out a hollow and clambered into my sleeping-bag, consoled by the thought that a soldier on guard at any of the fronts would probably be much less comfortable than I was. The loaded shot-gun leant against the wall ready to hand, and during the day I had put the rough-shot cartridge in the sun to increase the explosive effect.

Gradually darkness swallowed up the rocky ridges and ribs; the sky above was still light and between the rocks shone the white sand of the river bed like a faithful reflection. Then the sky turned dark blue and the two brightest stars of Centaurus appeared as infinitely distant specks of light. Quite suddenly the Southern Cross was there too. The river bed was now only a faint glimmer between the velvet black of the canyon sides. The sand had already yielded its warmth to the desert night and it had grown cold. A variety of smells imperceptible in the heat of the day pervaded the air. There was the thrilling smell of mud from the water-hole, and a delicate aroma of vanilla from the three small tamarisk bushes at the upper end of the hole.

The first noises of the night became audible. There was a rustling in the bushes by the garden; the cry of an owl sounded loud and clear between the canyon walls, and from somewhere further away came an answering call. I was wide awake and strangely excited. The sound I could hear from the bushes was probably being made by a mouse; after a pause it began again. Then came a few moments' silence followed by a little squeak which stopped almost as soon as it had started. Something scampered across the sand. Stones rolled down a slope into the valley. Then everything was quite still. Some marten had perhaps just pounced on its supper.

The waiting and listening both soothed and excited me far more than a thrilling film or interesting book had ever done, and it occurred to me that probably ten thousand generations of men had lived from the chase, whereas only the last couple of hundred or so had abandoned it for cattle breeding and agriculture, thus laying the basis for our civilisation, a civilisation which, in addition to films and books and a good many really marvellous things, had given us horribly bloody and senseless wars.

The stars glittered as they do only over the desert and the mountains, and the two bright Centaurus stars swung slowly round the pole like a giant clock hand. The air was quite still. It seemed to me that hunting peoples, like Bushmen, Red Indians and Eskimos, must be happy and contented so long as they were untouched by civilisation. They certainly knew danger, sudden death and cruel enemies, but who could say in this year of grace 1940 that modern civilisation spared civilised man any of those things?

On the contrary it had increased the dangers; it had enormously increased violence and senseless destruction, and in doing so it had deprived the individual of all independence. But the old instincts of the hunter were still alive in civilised society, and millions of men felt elated at the thought of war. The old killer instincts were awake again, but surely they could not give that deep inner satisfaction that this vigil in the night gave me, because operating under civilised conditions they had been robbed of their original significance; they no longer served to defend and sustain life.

My thoughts were suddenly interrupted by the sound of rattling stones. It came nearer and I could hear the softer thump of hooves in the sand — zebra. It came still closer and I felt my heart beating harder though I was not lying in wait for them. The noise was right in front of me now, hooves crunching on gravel. Then suddenly a loud snorting and blowing sounded right ahead. Their leader had scented me, and the sand and gravel was churned up violently as they swung round and galloped away. I heard the short, explosive rattle of their hooves and then the sounds suddenly ceased. But I could sense they had not gone far and after a while I heard soft, almost imperceptible sounds as they stood rubbing flanks and probably wondered what to do. I was sitting up and staring into the darkness, but I saw nothing; although they could hardly have been more than thirty metres away, the striped pattern on their flanks completely merged into the surrounding darkness. Once again the stallion snorted, and the group fled again for a short distance. But after a while they came slowly back again. This happened several times. They were inquisitive and they were behaving as though they knew perfectly well that their stripes made them invisible in the darkness.

I got a bit tired of the game and I waited until they were once again quite close to me and then I hurled a stone at them. As it struck there was a tremendous snorting and whinnying, a mad clash of hooves which made sparks fly from the quartz shingle and a swift pounding as they made off down the canyon. The sound gradually faded away and there was once again absolute silence in the canyon. The star clock had moved forward quite a bit in the meantime.

My hands were cold and I put them into my sleeping-bag between my knees to warm them. I realised that I should probably have to sit through a good many of these vigils, but the thought did not dismay me; and because I was not dismayed it meant that I was gradually slipping into the habits and manner of life of the Bushmen as a man slips into an old shoe. It occurred to me that it would be worth while to study the process and mark the attending emotional and mental phenomena.

Was it possible that our whole civilisation was a perversion of man's proper development, being fundamentally irreconcilable with the instincts and feelings he had inherited from his Stone Age forebears? But if that were so then why had such a development taken place at all? At least there would be a good many starry nights in which to think all these problems over at leisure.

It was late now and I was beginning to feel sleepy. Once a short gust of wind came whistling down the canyon, a small layer of cold air from somewhere in the mountains swept along between the craggy sides of the canyon for a few minutes and was gone. In the silence that followed I heard the sound of zebra hooves in the distance. But there was no sign or sound of the hyena for which I was lying in wait.

It looked as though Hermann had been right.

By the time the eastern sky grew a little lighter I was shivering with cold. Slowly the stars faded and the higher ridges and crags of the canyon began to loom up in the first light of the morning. Then suddenly I spotted a pair of klipspringer on a small ledge. They were standing perfectly still as though cast in bronze, looking towards the east where the sun was about to rise.

As I got up and stretched myself I noticed a movement on the gravel a little distance away. A small animal was making its way across the river bed with sedate bearlike movements. I ran up to see what it was. It heard me coming, stopped, looked round, and then continued its way calmly. Its lower parts were dark, but across its back and forehead there was white. It was about the size of a badger, in fact it was a badger — a honey badger. I was surprised to find that it was able to live so deep in the desert.

An old Boer once told me that the honey badger was the most courageous and tough little beast he knew; he wouldn't go out of his way even for a lion. Three big dogs were not enough to account for it, and it was not easy to kill even with an axe.

I went closer still, and when I was about ten paces away the honey badger stopped again and looked round at me over its shoulder. Then it turned right round and made a couple of deliberate steps in my direction, looking at me challengingly very much as a schoolboy might when he stands with straddled legs and demands: 'Well, do you want to start anything?'

No, I didn't want to start anything; I just wanted to look at him. Apparently satisfied, the honey badger slowly turned and went on his way. The incident was so comic that I was still chuckling to

81

myself while fetching a carp for our lunch.

When I got back to the cave Hermann had a good hot cup of coffee ready for me, and this civilized amenity gratified me enormously. After that I turned in and slept until midday. That evening Hermann wanted to know whether I was going to try again. I could see his lips twitching and I knew that he was pulling my leg. I had to admit to myself that it wouldn't be much use. That zebra stallion had scented me at once and I had not been able to see a thing. It would hardly be any different with the hyenas. But Hermann's ill-concealed mockery roused me, and then, to some extent, I was counting on the amazing insolence of the hyena, so I answered that 'of course' I should watch again.

But a second night in ambush is never so exciting as the first, and before long — as Hermann had prophesied — I found myself dozing off. I was roughly shaken out of my sleep by an infernal and ear-splitting noise. With trembling hands I reached for my gun. The noise died down and ended in a rattle of screeching laughter. Only a hyena could howl like that and the brute was probably sitting quite close in the river bed. No doubt it had scented me and was now venting its feelings about human beings who wanted all the carp for themselves. I couldn't see it, of course, and its dirty brown spotted hide was just as good a protective colouring as the black and white stripes of the zebra.

A new howling started up with notes reminiscent of a giant owl. Slowly I lowered my gun and aimed in the general direction of the noise. The pale starlight shone faintly on the steel barrel before me. When the brute had gone through his solo and come to the final burst of infernal laughter I felt that I more or less had a bead on him and I fired. A spurt of flame stabbed the darkness, and the roar of the explosion rolled round the rock faces like thunder. And immediately after, like music to my ears, sounded a short, distressed yelp followed by snorting and whining and the furious sound of scratching claws. I'd hit the fish poacher and I could hear his crippled progress as he crawled away through the sand and gravel. I grinned with satisfaction, rolled myself up in my sleeping-bag and slept until the early morning chill awoke me.

As soon as it was light enough I went to see the result of my lucky shot. About twenty metres beyond the carp pond I found a spot where the sand had been churned up by great paws. From there a wide trail showed where the hyena had dragged itself towards the far side of the canyon. The brute was obviously badly wounded and it ought not to be difficult to find him. On the other side I saw where he had tried to clamber up the slope but had fallen back each time. After that the trail went down canyon. You could distinctly see the marks of the powerful front paws as they dragged the helpless hindlegs along. The front legs of a hyena are considerably stronger than the back legs and the wounded beast had been able to drag itself much further than I would have thought.

I was just wondering whether to go back and fetch Hermann and Otto when I heard a sound ahead. About a hundred metres further on lay an uprooted acacia tree with a wide spread of bare roots. Something was moving beneath it. I looked more closely and then I saw the bullet head with the rounded ears. It was my hyena and it slunk further back into the tree as I came nearer. It was an ugly brute, as big as a mastiff, with a great black naked belly, a shaggy spotted coat and a broad loathsome head with round black ears.

I was wondering how to finish it off. I certainly had no intention of wasting another cartridge. I threw a heavy stone at it and it drew back growling. Then I poked at it with a thick stick. With a swift movement it snapped at the cudgel and bit it in two. It was soft wood, but even so the swiftness with which the big stick was cut into by those strong teeth made it seem advisable to keep well out of their range.

I now collected some heavy stones and began to pelt the brute's head at close range. After several direct hits there was a pitiful bleating and the hyena dragged itself from the tree and tried to reach me. The bleating angered me, and easily avoiding its feeble attack I furiously bombarded the back of its head with stones until the sweat ran down my face. Then it collapsed. I looked round for a heavy cudgel to finish it off with. It sat up again, but it was obviously almost finished. I got in a heavy blow across its neck and that made it turn furiously. The powerful neck muscles offered good protection to the spine, but in the end I succeeded in beating it to death. By then the sun was already shining into the canyon bed.

It hadn't been a very glorious victory, but I wanted to take back some trophy so I whetted my knife on a piece of quartz and skinned the carcass. I could see now just where the hyena had been hit. A lucky shot indeed! Only three pellets had hit it and one of those had lodged in the spine, crippling its hind legs.

Proudly I entered our cave dwelling and tossed the hyena skin into a corner as though it were a daily occurence. Otto approached cautiously, sniffing and growling, his tail between his legs and the hairs on his neck bristling. Hermann said nothing, but to acknowledge my triumph over both him and the hyena he gave me a teaspoonful of his own jam to

84

go with my breakfast porridge. Whilst we ate I told the story. Below us lay the fantastic world of gorges, ravines, ribs, ridges and crags, and a fine blue smoke rose peacefully from Hermann's pipe into the still air.

The news that the water in the drinking pool had dropped even lower was disagreeable. The soil of our garden, which had at first been moist was now dry and dusty. Only daily watering could keep it going at all, but for that the way down into the canyon and back was too laborious — we should have to abandon it. The frog pool grew smaller too and it was now divided into two by a sandbank. We decided to try a new and bigger garden on this sandbank.

The next day we sadly stripped our old garden of all it contained: eight radishes of varying sizes, a few mangelwurzel leaves, several stalks of parsley and a dozen carrots not much bigger than matchsticks. In the damp sandbank which had emerged from the frog pool we now laid out a variety of small beds and sowed radishes, carrots, mangelwurzel, kohlrabi, onions and tomatoes — and Hermann insisted on a bed of tobacco plants. I pointed out that the water would have dried up long before he'd get a chance of rolling himself a cigar, but he said there was such a thing as fantastic luck — my hyena episode had proved that. I raised no further objections to his tobacco-growing efforts. By the time we had set up a thorny barrier of young acacia trees the midday sun was beating down.

It was a hot day and eminently suitable for a very necessary bath. Once in the water we decided to extend the operation and wash our shirts and pants too, and having done that we sat around naked in the shade of the overhanging rock face and ate biltong, cut into thin strips.

A jutting crag hid the lower part of the pool from

sight. Suddenly Otto began to sniff excitedly and he looked as though he were about to dart off. Hermann held him back by a hind leg and I leant forward cautiously and peeped round. A gemsbok was standing not ten metres away from us, quietly drinking at the pool. At a sign from me Hermann came forward cautiously and we both looked at the animal. We had never seen an uninjured gemsbok so close. At that moment it raised its head and looked round. We both remained quite still, but I could feel my heart beating. Its long horns glistened like bronze in the sun, its dark liquid eyes looked calmly out of its black-and-white face, and beneath it the delicate legs with their black stripes and white socks were reflected in the water of the pool. Although we were so close the gemsbok seemed unable to realise that we were dangerous and the strong neck muscles rippled under the grey coat as it lowered its head again. The black-and-white face approached the surface of the water, the muzzle broke the mirror picture in ripples as though in a kiss, and then the reflection vanished in countless ripples as the beast drank.

It was an ideal opportunity for a sure shot in the head, but the pistol was up above in our cave. Hermann fought a silent battle with Otto until the gemsbok had drunk its fill and trotted off out of reach down canyon.

That little incident taught us something important: we had always supposed that gemsbok came down to the water-holes only at night, like zebra, but that obviously wasn't true, or not exclusively true, and we wondered whether it would be worth while to sit up at a water-hole now and again.

The Gramadoelas

We were never able to discover whether the word 'gramadoelas', the description for barren, broken and fissured terrain, derived from the Portuguese or from some local dialect. But it always struck us as very suitable. The word seemed to express just the bleak desolation of those grey-capped masses of rock and the wild labyrinth of those innumerable gorges and ravines.

Gradually we became at home in this rocky underworld and we learnt where the more readily accessible game paths were leading from the big canyon along the main watersheds. And in the process the unknown lost none of its attractions. After all, the most desolate ravine could hide a bees' nest or a vein of ore with valuable crystals. It was highly improbable of course, and we knew that, but it wasn't impossible and so the attraction remained.

How unimportant hunger, thirst and cold nights can become when you're out to wrest the secrets from an unknown landscape! In fact it's just those experiences that require the last ounce of determination and physical effort which deeply impress themselves on the mind.

How can I convey the richness of those sights and experiences? I remember one evening on the southwest plateau. The chalk plains stretched away to the horizon, unbroken and as flat as a table, an age-old, petrified river bed. When the sun sank all the game tracks around, narrow grooves in the hard chalk debris, suddenly began to show up as blue shadows! From all sides they led towards the few shallow depressions dotted over the plateau, depressions which a few gnarled old trees and bushes turned into arid oases in the barren chalk desert.

That night the trunk of a dead tree provided us with a wonderful fire. Whilst we were already rolled up in our sleeping-bags the red flames still licked up the gnarled trunk and danced around in the branches like elves in the silver moonlight. The next day we woke to a sunrise resembling a menacing conflagration against a red and hazy horizon. The north wind came in warm gusts under a grey-blue sky which grew heavier and heavier from hour to hour until it swallowed the horizon and wiped away the outlines of the distant mountains. By midday even the Rost-stock was no longer visible.

The phenomenon probably meant that the rolling grass steppes away to the north were burning and that the wind was blowing clouds of smoke from the conflagration into the desert as a leaden-coloured haze. Even the living beings of the endless white desert now took on strange and unreal forms. A herd of springbok crossed our path, dancing through the flickering haze like ghostly, dreamlike demons.

Towards evening it seemed as though the canyon was fooling us, as though it had disappeared in secret windings so that we should never reach any of its water-holes again. The bare rock-ribbed mountain looked almost near enough to grasp though it was on the other side, and yet we could see no sign of an entrance. It confused us and made us apprehensive. Suddenly the rock ridge under our feet came to an end. We held our breath and stared into a wild abyss, an apparently bottomless pit which had opened up beneath our feet like the gates to the infernal regions. Down below in the narrow depths the shadows of night were already gathering fast, but the last rays of the setting sun blinded us and we could neither see the bottom nor estimate its depths, so that our relief was mingled with an uncanny feeling.

Then the sun sank low below the horizon and the gloomy depths turned into a fairylike blue twilight in which a few water-holes glimmered like mysterious eyes. At this point the canyon narrowed down, and the vertical walls looked as if they had been hewn by some giant axe. It was almost unbelievable that water alone could have done that.

The next day we followed a steep breakneck zebra path down into the canyon and it was not long before a sweetish smell of carrion told us that the way down from the arid desert plains to the cool waters below was not altogether safe even for such sure-footed creatures. The path led over a narrow rib of rock, and below this rib, caught between two slabs of rock was the carcass of a half-grown zebra. The greater part of the chest and the haunches had been torn away and on a grey rock slab close by we saw the bloody imprint of a leopard's paw. Had the leopard jumped on the zebra risking the fall himself, or had he merely scared it so that it fell?

What can be more heartening than cool, clear water after a long tramp through the hot desert? At each gulp a feeling of well-being floods through the body and all trials and troubles are forgotten as though they had never existed. Looking up from the water-hole we could see the sky far away above our heads, a narrow strip of light between dark walls. Here and there the overhanging sides of the canyon were no more than ten metres apart, or about one-eighth of the width of the canyon at Carp Cliff. When rain storms in the uplands sent the river running down valley in full spate this narrow gorge would become a roaring, swirling, froth of gushing water. We wondered how high the level of the brown, sandy waters would rise up those steep walls, and we saw the answer quickly enough: about twenty metres up was an uprooted tree trunk wedged into a fissure in the rock face, where the flood had left it high and dry. The sudden arrival of the waters in such narrows might be fatal to anyone caught there, for the walls were scalable only in very few places.

There was a pool here almost the width of the canyon and behind it overhanging walls formed a kind of dark archway before which a small castor-oil plant bathed its glossy green leaves in a shaft of sunlight. A great silver-grey heron swept through the arch on silent wings. Its plumage gleamed in the sunshine over the still water, and then it disappeared into the shadow, sweeping noiselessly away between the high walls.

It was a wearisome journey up the canyon through the loose, deep sand and as we trudged we counted our steps in turn and noted the changing direction with our compass so that later we should be able to record its windings accurately on our map.

Even on this wintry day the air was dry and warm, how dry we only realised when we came across water dripping steadily from a ledge: like most of the springs in the desert it was salty, and from the ledge hung delicate stalactites of white crystals, resembling icicles, whilst where the drops fell broad white stalagmites had grown upwards. The small basin in which the water collected was full of salt too, and there was no outlet; the dry air of the canyon drank all the water. Our salt supply was at low ebb so this discovery was opportune, and with our knives we hacked off the massive stalagmites and took them along.

How had this gramadoela world come into existence? What had formed the white chalk bastions and the plains of chalk that lay like a broken lid over this underworld? Had the river scoured out this deep canyon in a relatively short space of time when the climate was more humid than it is now? Or had it done its work in present climatic conditions taking many thousands of years? The answers to these questions were to be found in the river bed and in the canyon walls.

Everywhere, even at the narrowest points, the course was covered with sand, and the rushing waters could therefore no longer leave their mark on the rocky bed. The process of erosion could not have been continuous, since the ridges formed various levels whose individual steps were at the same height. They could only be the remainder of old river beds, stony witnesses to a pause in the work of scouring out the canyon; periods when the river had widened its bed instead of deepening it. Thus the canyon must have been formed under alternating wet and dry climates whilst in the course of millions of years the continental land mass had gradually risen. But here in the Namib the climate had probably always been drier than in the uplands, as indicated by the gouged, waterless falls of the gramadoela gorges, which had failed to keep level with the Kuiseb valley as it bit its way into the earth. The thick network of gorges pointed to the same conclusion, because lack of rain can lead to the formation of such serried valley systems only where the topsoil is not protected by vegetation.

And the stretches of chalk? They were undoubtedly the remains of old petrified river levels built up by the Kuiseb in the Tertiary period when the continental land mass was not so high, and the river, having a shallower fall than today, had not the strength to scour its way deep into the earth.

We could read what had happened along the high walls of Carp Cliff as though in a book. At the base of the bevelled mica schists was a layer of white chalk mixed with debris and rubble, evidence of a steppe climate in which long periods of rain had alternated with long, dry, warm weather during which the ground water in evaporating had left a residue of lime.

Then came the great masses of red sandstone scoured deep by the wind and made up for the most part of washed-down dune sand. This long desert period had probably been even drier than the present one, but not dry enough to prevent the growth of trees and bushes in the broad river courses, which received water from the uplands, and there we found petrified roots embedded in the sandstone in regular lines. Each line indicated the one-time level of the land surface, and the long series of lines showed how the broad valley had gradually filled up with sand. The whole process had probably lasted for millions of years. After this desert period the climate must have improved again, and great floods had spread boulders and gravel over the area; in the subsequent steppe climate white chalk had cemented the gravel forming it into a solid cover over the whole landscape.

So far all our observations dovetailed neatly — with one exception; a crater-like formation amongst the chalk stretches to the south of the canyon. We had first spotted it from the Roststock and we had racked our brains over it again and again. Measured in human periods that chalk layer was age-old, but in the history of the earth it was still young. No such young volcanoes were known anywhere in South Africa and it therefore seemed unlikely that the crater was of volcanic origin. But what else could it be?

Only a visit could solve the problem, and one evening we found ourselves at 'our crater', which was crowned by a red sandstone ridge like a hat with upturned brim. Along its edge we could see glistening chalk, the confirmation that it could not be of volcanic origin, which disappointed that adventurous curiosity which is the mainspring of all scientific investigation, but at the same time satisfied that true cataloguing scientific spirit which by nature dislikes any exception to the rule. What it actually was we still didn't know, and we didn't find out that day either, for the sun went down soon after our arrival.

When the first rays of the morning sun fell across the long ribs of rock making the face of the Roststock glow purple and violet we were standing on a small rocky mound in the centre of a chalk basin about two hundred metres across. It rested on red sandstone with petrified roots, and the conical peak on which we were standing was also of sandstone, crowned with a remnant of the highest chalk layer. The depression itself was made up of several layers of hard white chalk neatly lifted out by the erosion of two gorges. There was no doubt that at one time the sandstone had completely covered the chalk basin.

How could such a basin have formed? We hadn't to look far for the answer, for we soon came across a bank full of calcified stems of rushes and similar plants, surrounded by a fine network of petrified utricular algae. Rushes and algae! In other words, open water. At one time this chalk basin had been a lake with rushes growing round its edge. A petrified lake in the desert! Or was our deduction that the red sandstone originated from a desert age false? Even today there are deserts with oases in which ground water rises to view, and the sandstone must have been an excellent water carrier before it was broken and drained by gorges. The floods of the uplands had probably drained into it. The presence of petrified roots in a desert deposit was thus more understandable. Those trees and bushes had lived from shallow ground water. We now saw far more clearly how this landscape, and thus the whole countryside, had come into being.

Every expedition we made brought us new experience, new knowledge and new devices. On one occasion we dredged an almost dried-out water-hole for fish, and afterwards, smeared up to the eyebrows with clay, we sat round a small fire and roasted carp on a grill of green twigs. In a quarter of an hour they were beautifully soft, succulent and slightly smoked, and we realised that by accident we had lighted on the right way to smoke fish. The importance of this discovery was enhanced by the fact that on our expeditions we had found so many water-holes with carp in them that there was enough to feed us for a year at least. Or so we thought at the time; actually the future was to disappoint us.

After spending days in the gramadoelas it was always like a liberation to climb back to the brighter world of the plains, put our rucksacks down at the edge of the plateau and take deep refreshing breaths of the cool west wind.

At this time a thick haze usually hid the distant mountains from view, but towards evening the west wind would often bring up fresh air from the sea. On the western horizon a clear strip of sky would then appear and rapidly gain in height and breadth as the cool sea air drove the warmer air upwards. The foot of a distant mountain would become clearly visible, though its peak remained hidden. Slowly the haze would rise, its lower edge sharply defined like a theatre curtain, until one by one the western mountains appeared. It was an astonishing sight; the interplay of land and sea air masses, the visible breathing of a great continent. We watched this extraordinary phenomenon many times until the first storms cleared the smoke haze from the distant steppe fires.

The Daily Round in the Desert

The arrival of the west wind brought us cooler days again. We smoked the carp, spent a day entering up the results of our survey of the canyon, and noticed with elation that the radishes were beginning to sprout in their new bed.

Our stomachs were demanding a change of diet, but the potatoes were all gone and the onions too, and all that was left of the oranges was the dried peel, which we used to give our morning porridge a little flavour. We had eaten nothing fresh since picking over our old garden and both of us began to suffer from frequent headaches; and the feeling of hunger was ever-present, even after a meal. We both realised that this was due to a shortage of vitamins. What we needed was raw meat, and perhaps now and again fresh blood. All carnivorous animals drink blood, and Nansen has described how during the winter he spent in the Arctic he kept himself fit by consuming polar bear blood in the form of pancakes. Perhaps we could try our hand at sausage making?

One day Hermann shot a gemsbok on the big south plateau game track and returned with a field-bottle of blood. We fried the blood with a good deal of salt and pepper. It rose like a frothy omelette and it was so filling that we could hardly finish it. As a casing for the sausages we squeezed out the gemsbok's larger intestines, washed them carefully, turned them inside out and then soaked them in salt water.

We celebrated Hermann's bag with simmered tongue and kidneys for breakfast, and then we got down to sausage-making. We put a goodly quantity of

96

meat and a little fat through our small mincer and seasoned it all with salt, pepper, paprika and a pinch of sugar. The sugar was Hermann's idea; he was always particularly interested in culinary matters. Now and again we ate a mouthful or two of the raw, well-flavoured mixture. It wasn't easy to stuff it uniformly into the skin, but we did our best, and when we sat down to liver dumplings and sauerkraut that evening we could look with satisfaction at long rows of sausages both large and small festooning our wall. Two tins of fat stood out on the rock to cool and Otto gnawed contentedly at a bone.

We did the smoking in the night — short, intense and warm, as we had learned from the carp. After an hour of this we took the strings of sausages out of the smoke chamber and hung them up to cool. The rest of the meat had to be attended to quickly, for the days were warm and there were a good many blow-flies about, and so the next day Hermann cooked it all. When I brought up our water I also brought back tamarisk branches, and with these and an old mosquito net I built a fly-proof larder, making the doors from the weatherbeaten sides of an old wooden provision chest we had found under the plateau together with the remains of a mule cart. We wondered who the chest had belonged to. Perhaps a German patrol during the Hottentot war? Or some lonely prospector? In any case the remnants were as valuable to us as the remnants of the stranded ship were to Robinson Crusoe.

A swarm of predatory red ants had chosen our cave dwelling and they lived in a crack in the rock face in our living-room. After that we found them everywhere and if we forgot to put the cover firmly on the sugar tin or on the jam jar, it was full of ants the next day. We squirted petrol into the crack to discourage them, and several times we tried to stuff it up, but we never entirely got rid of them.

We were more amused by other guests, a pair of tiny mice with huge whiskers and pink ears. They would scuttle around after dark looking for scraps, and sometimes they would sit quietly on our stone table, their shiny eyes following us. With their long silky whiskers, which reminded you of a cloak, they looked like dwarfs.

We were always short of kindling wood and occasionally we had even tried to cook with zebra dung, so we now decided that whenever either of us returned to the cave he should bring at least one piece of wood with him — if there was nothing else to carry.

Sanitary arrangements belong to any house, even the most primitive, and ours were attended to under an overhanging ledge a little distance away where we had shade during the day. A long natural slide ran down from this convenient place into the depths. The powerful sun and the drying winds removed all odour and very soon the various kinds of dung beetle, which are to be found even in the desert, turned up. Animals naturally avoided our immediate neighbourhood, which smelt of man and dog. Only very rarely did we hear zebra in the night now, and they were probably new herds unacquainted with the lie of the land. Sudden wild snorting and trampling would betray their excitement as they unexpectedly caught our scent.

But there was one exception: a small family of klipspringer who didn't seem to object to us as neighbours. There was a buck and two does, and the three of them would stand and watch us from a jutting ledge when we went down to fetch water. Sometimes we would see them gnawing away at the sparse bushes growing on the rock face. They were like people you meet constantly in the street without knowing their names, and we soon began to look on them as neighbours and we certainly wouldn't have dreamt of shooting at them; we even stopped Otto from chasing them.

The great adventure was now becoming everyday life, and we soon felt ourselves thoroughly at home in our cave dwelling. It was the day-to-day life of the bushmen and other primitive peoples, and it revolved around hunting and eating. It was therefore no small matter for us that our efforts at sausage-making proved successful — only one or two of the bigger sausages went off and had to be thrown away.

But it used up a lot of salt. Quite generally we found that we had considerably underestimated our salt requirements. This wasn't a very serious matter because salt belongs to the desert as sand belongs to the seashore. Most rocks in weathering produce salts, and when there is not enough rain to wash the salts into the sea the ground becomes salty. Salty ground water and salt springs are the consequence. But not all this salt is suitable for cooking; for example micaceous slate gives off a high percentage of sulphate of magnesia which tastes horrid and has a most upsetting effect. There was plenty of this kind of salt around but the only cooking salt we had come across was the stalagmites and stalactites in the canyon. It soon became clear that we should have to organise a proper salt foray.

Years previously we had noticed great accumulations of salt and a profusion of game around a spring near the Goagos mountains, a good fifty kilometres away. But why shouldn't we organise a salt foray and hunting expedition combined, and go there by lorry? We hesitated for quite a while because a lorry track fifty kilometres long meant taking a certain amount of risk. Further, we knew that an old *pad* passed by the spring in question, and that wasn't a particularly pleasant thought either — we weren't keen on coming anywhere near our fellow men.

As our main topic of interest was hunting and eating, that quite naturally included our weapons. We were very conscious that our shot-gun was not a very efficient weapon and finally we got the bright idea of casting bullets from the shot, so we cut open two cartridges, melted down the shot in a tin and poured the liquid lead into two round holes we made in the wetted sand. The result was a couple of irregular lumps, but with our hammer we soon gave them a reasonably spherical shape, and we then jammed them back into the cartridge cases between solid wads of paper. After that we eagerly tried out our innovation at about twenty metres distance, using a board as a target. We scored with both shots, and the holes they tore in the board were satisfactorily large. I then made five more such missiles.

Hermann was suffering from the monotony even more than I was. At first he turned to his violin which up to now had remained in its shabby old case tucked away in a niche. Sitting on our stone table he would often play on far into the night. The wilderness around us could never have heard such melodies before, and as the high rock roof resounded to the deep-toned longing rhythms it seemed almost as though the warm depths of the earth were answering. But I would sit there and listen a little sadly because I knew that the music came from a troubled heart.

Sometimes he played for so long that I would fall asleep, and after such concerts he would be taciturn and a little disagreeable the next day. Then one Sunday, when we were both having our weekly treat, a bit of chocolate, I saw Hermann give Otto a piece bigger than our two put together. He glanced at me as he did so and I knew that he realised his action would irritate me; in fact I felt fairly certain that this was the real reason why he had done it. It was a dangerous sign; the loneliness was getting on his nerves. I said nothing, but that evening I raised the proposed salt-gathering expedition. This time we didn't discuss the matter in theory but practically, and that night the violin was silent. The next morning we drove our lorry out of its hiding place.

Desert Source

Before sun-up we were moving forward slowly over the sharp chalk debris of the plains. The air was cool and refreshing and in the distance we could see the upland slopes shining like blue silk. When we came to a stretch of sand we drove faster. There wasn't a blade of grass or a game track to be seen anywhere. In the first light of the morning sun the sand was like red damask, and the wheels of our lorry cut out a long and endless pattern that would be readily visible for months to come. After that we had to drive round a widespread system of dried-out river beds whose steep gorges might have been clawed out of the chalk ground, and again and again we were confronted by vertical cliff faces and had to make wide detours to the west.

Before long a heat haze covered the dazzling plains. In a shallow pit with a few chewed-off tufts of grass we came across a herd of zebra standing with inquisitively pricked ears. As soon as they caught our scent they galloped off in a cloud of dust.

Soon after we had negotiated the gorges we crossed the old *pad,* a mere track in the rubble of the plains, and we were relieved to see that there were no tyre marks anywhere, not even old ones. On the other side of this track we turned towards the northern end of the Goagos mountains, driving over a rolling stony plain covered with a thin layer of quartz and chalk rubble. Here and there we saw the remains of small tufts of old grass, and a little further on we came across a shallow sanded-up river bed with a few lonely camel-thorn trees.

In one of these sandy beds we got stuck. At first we tried to save ourselves the trouble of letting air out of our tyres, but laziness of that sort is rarely rewarded and after a good deal of swearing and shoving on our part the lorry slipped sideways into a sand hole up to the axle. In the end we had to let air out after all, jack it up and collect some stones to put under the wheels. As soon as we started up the engine the wheels just flicked away the stones like bullets and we had to start all over again, jacking up the lorry and collecting still bigger ones to make quite a longish path. The sand was hot and the sun was beating down relentlessly as we worked, but we got the lorry moving. After a couple of metres or so it slid off sideways into the sand again. This happened two or three times, and each time we were ready to try again, we first had to shoo Otto out of the way; he was always underneath the lorry — it was the only patch of shade in sight.

It took us two hours before we got ourselves out of that patch of sand and were able to pump up the tyres again. Although we felt parched and were covered with dust we dared not take more than a drop or two out of our water-bags, for we didn't know when we should find drinking water again.

A little later we came across large game tracks, and after we had crossed several of them we saw that they radiated from a black rocky hillock; obviously the water source must be there somewhere. We went on in the same direction for a while in order to keep away from the track. The stretches of debris were barren and there wasn't a blade of grass anywhere, not even in the river beds.

Then we spotted six gemsbok trotting peacefully along a large game track which followed a shallow watershed. They were obviously on their way to drink, and they looked neither to the left nor right. We got up fairly close to them before they heard the lorry, and then they darted off snorting wildly.

Behind the hill the ground descended more steeply and became even stonier. Then we came to a slope armoured with gleaming slabs of rock. Below lay a shallow valley dotted with three big bushes, spreading a shadow like a dark carpet. Several graceful springbok were standing at a small source between a clump of grey tamarisks. A number of ostriches had spotted us at once and were disappearing up the far side of the valley with long loping strides. Their flight alarmed the springbok and they too bounded off into the west wind.

What clumsy and awkward creatures we seemed in our lorry! I had to walk in front to find some way down between the rocks, and now and again we had to shift boulders out of our path, but finally we got to the bottom. We didn't dare to go as far as the three bushes, because we knew that the old *pad* passed close by. We camouflaged the lorry as well as we could between the tamarisks and then went down the valley to examine the spring. The sand round about was full of game spoor. Where the bare rock was visible water welled up through small cracks forming pools here and there amidst grey stretches of stone. Each of these springs had its own particular taste: one was bitter, another salty, a third sulphurous. But the water in all of them was so bad that we didn't dare drink. Finally we found a spring that we thought might do and from this we drank, though it still left a rather bitter taste in the mouth.

There were a good many birds around the biggest pool, and a shot at the Namaqua quail which were present in large numbers looked tempting. In the evening twilight they would probably be wheeling around in their hundreds. Below the pools was sand and rubble crusted with salt, and a number of rocky gullies and depressions were also covered with layers of salt, which was what we had primarily come for, but we couldn't yet tell the percentage of magnesia sulphate it was likely to contain.

Within the next few hundred metres there were more and more springs rising between clumps of tamarisks. The effect of evaporation was clearly noticeable, and the lower-lying pools contained the most salt. The last ones, those nearest to the old *pad*, were practically concentrated brine. The *pad* itself showed only the spoor of game and it was well over a kilometre from where we had hidden our lorry.

By the time we got back to the lorry the sun had gone down and the west wind had risen and got so much colder that we had to make ourselves a wind-break with an old tarpaulin. Whilst Hermann prepared the supper I went back to the pool to try my luck with the Namaqua quail. We hadn't eaten anything since the morning and I was so tired that my legs almost refused to carry me. Sitting with my back to a rock I had a clear view over the pool and hardly had I settled down when I heard the quail begin to call. Before long the air was full of the whirr of their wings, and in the half light I could see birds the size of pigeons coming in to the water. More and more flocks of them wheeled in out of the sky, calling melodiously as they dropped to the ground. Then a soft cooing and clucking betrayed where the various flocks had settled in the sand or amongst the stones.

When there was no further sound of wings in the air I heard a general movement beginning towards the water. Then the glimmering surface of the pool broke into countless ripples as the first birds paddled in.

The crack of my shot faded into a wild flapping of many hundreds of wings as the birds rose panic-stricken into the sky. I bagged no less than twenty-two, enough for at least five meals. After supper when we turned in the wind was still cold and strong.

I awoke in the first light of dawn and everything around looked strange and unreal. The west wind had blown up mist from the sea over the desert, and the rocky slopes of the valley were out of sight. The light was a colourless grey and the silence was heavy and oppressive. The air smelt damp and mild, the tamarisks looked unusually green and waterbeads hung from each branch like seed pearls. I turned to look at Hermann and for a moment or two I was startled to see two heads of hair peeping out from his sleeping-bag. I had to look twice until I realised that one of them was Otto's hairy rear end. Both their faces were buried in the sleeping-bag and they came to light only at my hearty laughter.

In the meantime the sun must have risen, for a delicate rosy light diffused the fluffy veil all around, and the dewdrops on the tamarisks were glistening like iridescent opals. After all those months of harsh light reflected from hard rock faces we felt as though transported to some milder and more friendly climate. But the illusion was soon dispelled; I was about to make breakfast when I discovered fresh traces of hyenas a few yards from our sleeping quarters. It was a bit of luck that Otto had crawled into Hermann's sleeping-bag.

As the sun grew stronger it soon dissipated the mist. The tamarisks looked grey again and each drop that had fallen from their branches onto the lorry was now a white spot of salt.

Hermann found a niche in the rocks where he proceeded to pluck the quail — we didn't want the feathers to blow about in the neighbourhood. Whilst he was doing this I cautiously went to the edge of the clump of tamarisks and saw six gemsbok drinking at the pool. They were those we had seen the day before; I recognised them easily because one of them had a broken horn. This time there was no need to disturb them.

Hardly had their long horns vanished over the edge of the valley than seven ostriches appeared making their way towards the water. And before the birds got there a herd of springbok followed, and immediately behind them another group of gemsbok. After that there was a coming and going of birds and animals like peasants at a fair. It was such an astonishing sight for me that it was some time before I realised that it was nothing out of the ordinary here, but an everyday occurrence. As far as we knew, this was the only water source which did not lie in a narrow gorge — favourable hunting ground for beasts of prey — and at the same time it was easily accessible from the broad plains of the Namib. In the dry period this source meant salvation for many hundreds of animals. Life here was bleak enough — just sand and debris, bare of all vegetation, and a few pools with salty water — yet every movement of these drinking animals proclaimed strength and triumphant beauty.

It seemed unlikely that we should ever come across a better opportunity for observation and photography, so we decided that both the salt and the chase could wait for a few days. But if we proposed to stay here for a while we should have to find some place more sheltered from the sun, at least during some part of the day.

A little higher up the valley the river bed narrowed between rocky bastions and there we found an overhanging ridge which offered us a convenient hollow to camp in. Whilst we were clearing away dead branches and rock scales which had fallen from the roof above we came across bones, small stone blades and many white beads artistically formed from ostrich eggshells. The hollow had obviously once been the home of Bushmen, and indeed a more favourably situated spot for the little hunters could hardly have been imagined. There was water in the immediate neighbourhood and a profusion of game and wild-fowl. From the rock on which their camp had been you could see over the whole valley and the water sources. The game paths led to the springs from all directions so that no matter from where the wind blew, they could always find somewhere to sit up without immediately being scented.

That night we slept by the lorry again, but this time we shut Otto up in the cabin to make quite certain the hyenas didn't get him in the night, leaving the window open to give him sufficient air. The stillness of the night was broken by the stamping and snorting of herds of zebra, the howling of jackals and the horrible cackle of hyenas, and I was suddenly woken out of a nightmare by a violent thump in my back. I started up with a wild shout, expecting the sharp teeth of a hyena to snap into the back of my neck, but it was only Otto who looked at me innocently, wondering what all the bother was about. He had leapt out of the window of the cabin. Hermann, awakened by my shout, thought it very funny.

Days brimful of hot sun and fascinating experiences followed. To the east and west of the water sources we had built ourselves small stone shelters from which we could observe and photograph the animals coming in to the springs. During the night there were only zebra and beasts of prey. One leopard came regularly, but we never saw anything of him beyond the round imprints of his paws the next morning. And once in the early twilight two horribly ugly hyenas slunk down to the cover of the deeper ravines. As soon as the sun was up the first herds of springbok would appear on the edges of the valley, but they never came down to the water at once. They would wait around for a good hour, going a few steps here and there, looking down into the valley towards the water and gazing around again, presumably to make quite sure that no big beasts of prey were in the neighbourhood. And often just about this time a jackal would cross the valley, sniffing to right and left. At first we thought that the springbok were waiting for the jackal to pass before coming down into the valley, but we were soon to realise that they were quite indifferent to its presence.

It was usually about half-past ten when the first group of springbok began to move in single file down the most open part of the valley. Once at the water the groups broke up, each antelope going to the spring it fancied, and after they had drunk their fill they always lingered for a while.

At about ten o'clock the first steppe quail arrived, but they came and went in small groups, and not in the large flocks of the evening hours. Ostriches came, and then more herds of springbok. They all drank peaceably together and wandered around, each kind undisturbed by the presence of the others. It was a unique experience for us to observe all these animals at close quarters; usually we saw them only in swift flight.

By eleven o'clock the coming and going was at its height. Animals were trotting up and down the sides of the valley and groups were drinking at all the pools. Towards twelve the throng subsided and between half-past one and three o'clock there was rarely

109

an animal at the water. But one midday was particularly busy. The place was crowded with ostriches, and we counted no less than one hundred and fifty-six of them at the pools, a great mass of feathers and a forest of sinuous necks and wedgelike heads. In the afternoon other herds would arrive, but never in such numbers as in the morning. The everyday round of the animals was well regulated by the heat of the desert sun.

There were occasionally amusing surprises. We discovered that if we remained quite still neither zebra nor antelope were able to make us out even if we made no effort to hide. Often we would notice that a gemsbok or a springbok was looking straight at us from only a few metres distance, and always the animal would just turn its head and move towards the water. Ostriches behaved very differently; their ability to see and recognise things verged on the fantastic.

In our stone shelter we had left three narrow slits each about forty centimetres long. When we were sitting in wait early on the first morning a male ostrich came down the opposite side of the valley with a couple of hens. The cock-bird was still about four hundred metres or so away when suddenly it stopped and stared towards us. Was it possible that he had seen something at that distance? Some movement through the small slits of our hiding place? This would have been difficult even with powerful field-glasses. But even if the ostrich had seen something move how did he know it wasn't a rock dassie or one of the many rats which lived in the cracks and crevices of the rock face? We couldn't guess, but something had obviously upset him. The two hens stayed where they were whilst the cock-bird patrolled to and fro along the valley slope, and it was quite clear that he was examining our hiding place from every angle.

During this inspection we sat as still as mice, but the ostrich remained suspicious and refused to come any nearer. He moved a few steps in this direction or that and then stopped again, but he never took his eyes off us. Finally the two hens got tired of waiting and they squatted down. We were amazed and spoke in whispers, almost without moving our lips; but something even more astonishing was to follow.

About an hour later five more ostriches came down the valley along the same game track. Seeing so many springbok and gemsbok at the water they probably assumed that the coast was clear and that there was no need for special caution. But then suddenly the first cock-bird stepped into their path with out-stretched wings, obviously barring their way, like a policeman halting the crowds. The gesture was un-mistakable. The newcomers stopped and they too looked over towards our hiding place, whilst the first cock-bird joined his two hens still sitting in the sand.

Hermann and I looked at each other, speechless. Not only had these strange birds incredibly sharp eyes but they also obviously had something like a sense of responsibility even towards strange birds belonging to other flocks. The ostriches did not come down to the water at all that morning, and at about midday they all marched off.

In the afternoon a large flock of them arrived, but in the meantime we had reduced our peepholes by half and this time they all went down to drink.

One day the jackal appeared later than usual and there was already a herd of springbok at the water. We rather expected the jackal to slink up to them, but not in the least: he approached quite openly and without the slightest precaution. And the springbok made not the slightest effort to move off; they just stood still and did not even turn their heads when

111

the jackal threaded its way between them to the water like a sheep dog between sheep. This incident taught us something new. Obviously the springbok had no instinctive fear of the beast of prey or of its scent. Animals seemed to know each other and their mutual reactions. The jackal, which would have attacked a sick or wounded springbok at once, knew perfectly well that it would have no chance against a vigorous animal. And what seemed even more astonishing, the springbok obviously knew that the jackal would not attack them.

Unfortunately the distance was too great to take a photograph of springbok and jackal drinking together at the same pool, but a few days later we did succeed in getting such a picture.

Every day there was something new and interesting. On one occasion ten great white vultures soared into the valley in line and went down to the water one after the other in rapid succession. Had the leopard brought down some beast in the neighbourhood during the night? And one morning as they were waiting around for the usual hour or so before coming down into the valley, two herds of springbok mingled. After a while two buck began to fight. They had gone up to each other slowly and then as they met the heavy curved horns began to clash. Three or four times the clashing sounded, then the horns locked and each buck tried to force the other to the ground. After a while one buck tired, and with some difficulty he managed to free his horns; then he humbly retreated behind the others, leaving the field to the victor.

A fight between two male gemsbok was a more serious affair. One of them was licking salt when the other approached, and only the alert attitude of the first buck indicated that it was not to be a friendly encounter. For a moment they stood silently facing each other, their long and dangerous horns glistening in the sun like drawn swords. Then they lowered their heads and put forehead to forehead. We could see the powerful neck muscles bunching under the skin, the sunlight brushing the straining haunches. We watched the pushing and shoving with some astonishment. Perhaps they didn't use their dangerous horns against each other? At that very moment one of the buck swiftly moved its head to one side and tried to bury his horns in the other's flanks. But the lunge was parried in an instant and followed immediately by a counter-lunge. It was a fierce struggle, and each combatant stood his ground well. Feint, lunge and parry followed each other in rapid succession, punctuated by the sound of clashing horns. Ten, fifteen seconds passed, and then the two were again pressed forehead to forehead, snorting, their nostrils close to the ground. Once again they released themselves and a new battle of thrust and parry began. They seemed very evenly matched and each thrust was so quickly parried that neither could gain the advantage. At last one seemed to be tiring. His hind legs began to give way and he was forced back. Then suddenly he gave up the struggle and dashed off at full gallop, the victor chasing him with triumphantly slashing tail — but only for a short distance and then, satisfied with his victory, he abandoned the pursuit.

On another occasion we could hardly suppress our laughter at what we saw. A flock of about thirty ostriches had drunk their fill and were standing in the sand by the pool. One or two of the hen-birds were squatting down, others were preening their feathers. Suddenly the male birds came together in a loose circle. One or two began to sway on their great white hips and then others took up the movement. Two of them then bowed to each other in a slow, deliberate tempo, at the same time flapping their wings. More and more movement developed amongst the group and soon they were all taking part in this strange dance. They swayed this way and that, fanned each other with their wings, waved their long necks and hissed loudly with wide-open beaks.

It was a kind of ostrich ballet, complete with short black feathered tutu, powerful white thighs and what might have been arms in a feathered veil of wings. They might easily have been a *corps de ballet* except that in place of smiling faces and neat hair there was a weird forest of waving necks topped by wedge-like ostrich heads. It was a fantastic and ridiculous ballet performed by birds in the hot sand of the desert, a sort of surrealistic pantomime under the broiling sun.

The hen birds took no part in this performance and seemed quite uninterested; they just stood or squatted to one side indifferently. When it was all over the whole band marched off slowly and solemnly in single file. What was the meaning of this grotesque performance? It was obviously not the nuptial dance. Was it just for the sheer joy of living — in a merciless and barren wilderness where nothing grew for kilometres around?

There are misanthropes in the animal world too. One day a solitary zebra arrived late at the pool and hurried down to the water. Whilst he was drinking a gemsbok bull approached from the other side. There was plenty of room and usually the various animals drank peacefully side by side, but this gemsbok seemed to resent the presence of the zebra. He looked at it from the other side of the pool for a moment or two and then he came round towards it, his dangerous horns lowered menacingly. The zebra just looked up and then trotted off to another pool

114

to continue drinking. Satisfied, the gemsbok lowered his head to drink but noticing a female ostrich near by he galloped towards her with lowered horns. She staggered awkwardly to her feet and made off with flapping wings, though she didn't seem very upset, for she soon stopped. The gemsbok stared around challengingly, observed that he now had the pool to himself, and at last began to drink.

The male and female of the gemsbok lived separately at this time of the year, and the bulls went about together in groups. We saw one group of five magnificent fellows which we christened 'the heavy-weights', for they were easily the most powerful bulls in the neighbourhood, and recognisable at quite a distance because the leader had horns set very far apart, whilst those of another were very close together. They were wonderful beasts, and strength and confidence was in their every movement. The other gemsbok bulls all took good care to keep out of their way. From our observations of these 'heavy-weights' we noticed that gemsbok came to water only every four or five days. We shot none of them; nothing but urgent necessity could have made us; they were too beautiful.

In the morning most of the animals came down into the valley with the east wind; and in the afternoon with the west wind. This contradicted earlier observations which had suggested that animals preferred to graze against the wind and to move into the wind, a very understandable preference since the wind would warn them at once of any danger ahead. What was the explanation for this very different behaviour when they went to the water-holes? It was simply our presence. One afternoon I scanned the district with my field-glasses. Animals were coming and going in considerable numbers, and two herds of gemsbok were approaching from the east. They were about two kilometres away when the leading beasts pulled up suddenly. As though directed by some invisible hand the first herd now turned in its tracks and made off. The second herd saw what had happened and it too stopped, turned and galloped back. I carefully searched the area ahead of them with my glasses to discover what had frightened them, but there was nothing to be seen. Then I realised what had happened: they had stepped into the wind which swept across our camping place! Naturally, we knew that all big mammals have a very keen sense of smell, but it was a revelation to us that our mere presence could keep them away at such a distance. It was an important discovery; after all, we relied on the chase to keep alive, and the range of our pistol was no greater than that of the little bushmen's poisoned arrows.

By carefully observing the behaviour and habits of animals we naturally learnt a good deal about them. We learnt to recognise their mood and intentions from the way they held their heads, or set their hooves, or from the swishing of their tails or the flicking of their ears. We got to understand them and their behaviour as you get to understand your friends without the need of speech.

But our eyes were not the only ones to watch their movements. High up above the vultures circled constantly; they too lived on the animals, and as they soared slowly around waiting for sickness, injury and death, their keen eyes missed not the slightest thing that happened below. One day we shot a springbok and carried it back to our camp, and when we had cut it up we laid its head under a bush. A quarter of an hour later the head was gone.

The days passed swiftly. Life seemed new, splendid

and exciting, particularly because of the startling contrast between the dead, arid, sun-parched rock landscape all around and the swift and beautiful animals that lived in it. Death was always at their heels, but they defied him gaily and lived their lives with obvious gusto.

After dark the red glow of our fire shone comfortingly. A great owl would swing silently across our sight; down there in the dried-out watercourse the sand would crunch under the paws of some prowling beast of prey, and alert eyes would gleam out of the darkness. Life other than our own was always near us, and finally the very conception of life took on a new significance. It was reflected in our talk. It seemed a miracle that life, which had at one time been confined to the sea, should have spread throughout the bleak and cruel wilderness. For us it was an illuminating experience to learn at first hand that nature was not a unity. What greater contrast could there be than that between the old desert with its slowly crumbling rocks and the eternally renewed life which day in and day out joyfully defied the relentless contradictions of dead matter?

Living and dead matter were so obviously at variance here, and the living matter so obviously triumphant in its adaptability over the dead elements and their rigid laws that the barren wilderness seemed to us more essentially alive than green trees rustling in the wind.

How was it possible that for over a century scientists should have regarded nature as a harmonious whole, in itself so divinely complete that it needed no god? As long as the word nature conjured up the green woods and the flower-strewn meadows of our childhood that was understandable and in line with our own feelings. And even long scientific expeditions into the desert had done very little to correct this impression. It was only now, when the desert had become our home, that the old impression slowly began to fade.

And we looked at the wilderness and the world with new eyes. New questions were written in the skies, and the spirit of intellectual adventure filled the barren mountains and the gloomy gorges. This revelation itself was surely another astonishing proof of the marvellous capacity of life to transcend, even under the most stringent conditions, the realm of mere existence? We were able to identify ourselves with the animals and the plants that snatched beauty and joy from the barren desert. We were no longer alone.

Two weeks had passed. The salt-encrusted sand of the dried-out river bed was covered with our footprints and we decided that it was inadvisable to stay any longer. It didn't take us long to scrape a goodly sack of salt together; it was not pure cooking salt and we could only guess at the various unsuitable salts it probably contained. The meat that we had cooked in the water of the source had always become brick red in colour whilst sinews and skin had blanched. We should just have to re-crystallise it, that was all. So far it seemed to have done us no harm.

With our home-made bullets I bagged two plump gemsbok at twenty paces. We left the meat to cool during the night and the next morning we packed it in its own hide and covered it up with our sleeping-bags and blankets. And when the first herd of springbok came down to the water to drink we bagged a buck. Then we set off and by midday we were back in our own cave.

Hard Work

A small mountain of meat lay under skins and bedding on the lorry; it meant weeks without having to bother unduly about food. But first of all a good deal of work had to be done and done quickly to prevent its going off. We even had no time to put the lorry back in the gorge where it had been parked previously, so we camouflaged it as best we could with a tarpaulin and a few dry balsam bushes. Our bedding, cooking impedimenta and more than two hundred and fifty kilograms of meat, hides and bones had to be carried for over five hundred metres along the rocky path from the lorry to our cave. By the time we had got everything up, our shirts were as hard as boards with dried blood and sweat; meat was on the ground, on the table, and hanging up along the wall.

The first problem was to find sufficient containers to pickle the meat in. We just hadn't enough empty petrol cans for the job. We couldn't pickle it in the hides as we had done with the bull because there was no sand here in which to dig a trough. We thought of looking for a suitable hole in the rock when we remembered the tropical metal-lined trunk we were using as a table. We cleared everything out of it and discovered that it was split. I soldered it whilst Hermann cut up the meat and separated the fat.

Our smoked beef had been too salty, and yet some of it had gone off. But now the weather was warmer and therefore the danger was greater. We remembered having heard that lymph and blood went off first, so perhaps we could squeeze out the liquid, pickle the meat dry, and then smoke it quickly and intensely as we had done the fish? It would be just too bad if the experiment didn't come off, but on the other hand, salty smoked meat on its own would be very difficult to get down, so we decided to try the experiment. We packed the best pieces of meat in layers in the tropical trunk, sprinkling only a little salt between them. Then we laid wooden boards from the old food chest on top of the meat and weighted it with heavy boulders.

When this had been done the springbok had to be skinned and cut up, and it was dark by the time we were ready to turn in. We hadn't even had time to carry up our battery so we couldn't switch on the radio to hear the latest news.

The next morning the shaft of our mincer broke and it took us almost all day to repair it. Hermann reduced the marrow fat and started the meat extract going, and we smoked meat until midnight, so when we went to bed we still didn't know what had happened in the outside world in the meantime.

We left the smoked meat out in the night to cool, and in the morning we packed it back into the trunk, weighing it down again with the wood and lumps of rock and pouring away the blood that had been pressed out. During the day we drove the lorry to its hidden parking place and brought up the battery. In the afternoon we continued to boil down the extract, and the cooked meat we put through the mincer and then dried it. Considering the poor grazing it was astonishing how much fat the meat had yielded: a tin and a half of marrow fat and about two kilograms of other fat.

We again smoked meat until far into the night and as we worked we listened to the radio, London reported air battles over Britain, and Berlin enthusiastically described the spectacle of burning British towns. Was this the decisive battle of the war?

Actually a more urgent question for us was the water situation in the Kuiseb valley. Had the water sunk even further? Was our little garden still a-growing and a-blowing? After breakfast we went down into the canyon. The first sight of our water-hole shocked us. The fish pond was little more than a muddy puddle in which a few carp lay rotting. The level of the drinking water had fallen below the rock bed sub-stratum. In one spot a small trickle of water still seeped through the gravel down into the rock basin, but it looked as though it might give out at any moment.

It was even worse than we had feared. The whole water supply could fail any day now. Should we try digging a well down through the gravel? If that proved ineffective should we have to fetch our water from one of the more distant larger water-holes? But supposing they dried out too! The gloomy rocks seemed to tower above us more threateningly than usual, and the sun beat down cruelly. At home we had so often heard the sun glibly called the source of all life; here in the desert it certainly wasn't.

The garden wasn't in too bad a state and the water level there had not sunk a great deal. We were even able to pull a few radishes. The two beds with carrots and mangelwurzel showed feathery foliage and fresh green leaves, and the tomato plants were already eight or ten centimetres high. We looked proudly at the result of our efforts, and Hermann thought he could see the shoots of three tobacco plants. The state of the garden cheered us up a bit and we climbed back to our cave in better heart.

The next job was to cleanse the salt we had brought back with us, for our old supply was almost exhausted. Our idea was to dissolve it and then let

121

the liquid slowly evaporate in the sun, after which we would collect the cooking salt before the rest of the solution evaporated. In the little gorge beneath our cave we cleaned a shallow hollow in the rock, dissolved the salt in a petrol tin and passed it through a cloth into this hollow, which held about half of the liquid. The following morning the first small crystals of salt were visible and the morning after the bottom of the hollow was covered with salt, but the liquid over it was oily and bitter. However, when we had cleaned and dried the salt we were quite satisfied with the result.

Altogether we had cause to be satisfied. Our cave dwelling was comfortable. The long festoons of brown smoked meat promised good food; in our fly-proof larder stood tins of fat and meat extract; and the meat meal we had made had dried out well. And Otto was now the undisputed possessor of so many bones that he didn't even consider it necessary to bury any against a rainy day.

Footprints in the Sand

There is never enough rain in the desert to produce a complete covering of green, and even after the rainy season the grass tufts are few and far between amongst debris and loose sand. The sand retains the footprints of all the different animals, and after living in the desert for a while you learn to read the writing of hoof, claw and pad. In fact before long you're reading their message almost subconsciously. From time to time a strong wind obliterates them all and leaves a clean page of sand to take the next chapter.

One morning, soon after we had returned from our exploration of the petrified lake Hermann stopped dead on his way to our garden with a look of deep concern on his face. 'Blacks' he said quietly and pointed at traces in the sand. Yes, the white sand clearly showed the imprints of human feet. Three men had gone down the canyon. Were they sent out by the police to track us down? If so they must have seen traces of our presence. And they could hardly have missed our garden.

We stared at their footprints with as much dismay as if we had discovered the traces of cannibals. They were long and narrow, and obviously those of Khoi-Khoin. We knew that Khoi-Khoin lived on the lower Kuiseb beyond Walvis Bay. Perhaps these three had worked on one of the outlying farms and were going back? They might themselves be on the run. But that didn't help us! Even if they were they wouldn't fail to talk about what they had seen in the dried bed of the Kuiseb; white men were living there and they had even made themselves a garden. The news would soon come to the ears of the police.

We went on our way rather depressed. The trail had not touched our garden but kept to the centre of the valley; nevertheless, with its protective fence of acacia trees it was just impossible to overlook. And then there were our innumerable footprints everywhere in the valley. Our gallant little tomato plants no longer cheered us. We sat silently in the shade of the rock and each of us knew what the other was thinking. Finally Hermann spoke:

'We'll have a bath before we go. Who knows how long it may be before we will find enough water again.'

Back in our cave dwelling we brewed ourselves a strong coffee. We felt we could do with it. Whilst we sat there drinking it we discussed the new situation. Where could we go from here? There must be water-holes somewhere in the wild gorges fringing the Swakop valley, but there were also human settlements, which meant that someone would always be prowling around after lost cattle or honey. The Gaub canyon was more suitable, but the entrance was barred to us by the Kuiseb. Perhaps we could go to the Ugab west of the Brandberg? But there wasn't likely to be much game there and our petrol would hardly take us that far. The neighbourhood of the Goagos source was rich enough in game, but it was too exposed for us. On the eastern side of the Goagos mountains there were probably a few smaller water-holes, but how to find them? And it was not at all certain that we should be able to get there with the lorry.

Another important question was how much time had we got. If those people had been sent out by the police then the sooner we made ourselves scarce the better. But why hadn't they gone back to report as soon as they spotted our garden and our tracks? Perhaps they had been cunning enough to go on down the canyon and climb out there so that they could look for us unobserved. In fact they might even now be watching us from some hiding place. On the other hand, they might really have gone straight on down the Kuiseb. In that case it would probably be three or four weeks before the police got to know about us. Well, at least that was easy enough to find out; we would just follow their tracks and see.

We decided that Hermann should bring up a good supply of water, because if we really had to clear out we should need plenty of it. In the meantime I put on my hat, took some biltong for the journey and started off down the rocky path into the canyon to follow the trail of the strangers. I picked it up near the garden and followed it as rapidly as I could in the soft sand. I knew that behind the next bend in the canyon there was a place where it was easy to climb out, and it was there that I should probably find out what they had actually done. With beating heart I approached the spot and then to my relief I saw that they had kept on down the centre of the canyon. That made it seem very unlikely that they had actually been tracking us, but I wanted to make quite certain. For a while the trail went along the left side of the canyon and from there it led to a muddy water-hole. At this spot one of the three had gone down on one knee and scooped a hole in the sand. Obviously he had drunk from the muddy brackish water.

Why on earth had he done that? A little distance away on the other side of the canyon there was a water-hole, its clear surface sparkling in the sunlight. And then with a tremendous flood of relief the answer dawned on me! They had passed down the canyon at night. They had come across this almost exhausted hole by accident and in the darkness they had not seen the good water source on the other side of the canyon; which meant that they had not seen our garden either, or our tracks.

With a lighter heart I clambered up the western face of the canyon, and on the plateau with the broad heavens above me I consciously enjoyed the wide sweep of the landscape. I was so relieved I even sang aloud. When I got back Hermann and Otto were still below and I ran down to meet them to give Hermann the good news. As a special celebration he made a wonderful rice pudding which we ate with some of our carefully rationed dried fruit. We were certainly relieved to know that the danger was not acute, but we didn't feel altogether safe. For one thing the track of our lorry would remain visible for a long time and if a police patrol came across it and followed it they would certainly find us. Where we had gone another car could go. We discussed the situation at length and finally we decided to set a booby-trap.

Shortly before sun-up the next morning we were on our way with our water-bags. We went to the gorge where we had parked the lorry and we measured the exact distance from the front wheels to the oil sump beneath the engine. Then we tramped over sharp chalk rubble until we came to the first dried-out river bed ten or eleven kilometres from Carp Cliff. The track of our lorry was clearly visible. We soon found a suitable spot, where the bed narrowed down and passed between rocky banks on either side so that a car would have to keep on right in the centre. Further, the sand in the river bed was so loose that any driver would go through it at top speed. On this we had built our plan.

Where the slope rose on the Carp Cliff side we dug

a hole in the track of the right front wheel. Then we looked for a slab of chalk which was just as long as the distance between the front wheel and the oil sump. This took us quite a while but at last we found one. We set it in the ground in such a fashion that it lay like a seasaw over the edge of the hole we had dug. When the right front wheel of a car bore down on the free end of this slab the other end would spring up and inevitably smash the oil tank. After meeting with such an accident no one would be likely to continue following a chance car track even if he succeeded in repairing the damage on the spot. And it would probably look like a sheer accident; the sort of bad luck which is quite common in stony parts without proper roads. To camouflage the trap still further we covered the hole with a tuft of grass, and whilst we were setting the trap we took good care to tread only on stone so as to leave no footprints.

When we had finished we didn't exactly feel proud of our ingenuity, but we consoled ourselves with the thought that a driver in South West Africa is used to trouble and canny enough to get himself out of almost any jam. And further, a lunatic war was going on in the outside world; that was why we had fled into the desert in the first place, and now we felt ourselves entitled to keep the line drawn firmly between us and that global hysteria.

Summer

September was over. For the first time clouds hung above the blue mountainous line of the uplands. Distant thunder had already sounded like a wonderful promise over the parched land, but so far that promise had not been fulfilled. Once more the south wind was driving a feathery web of icy cirrus clouds over the sky. Once more in the morning the thermometer stood at just under 5 degrees. Grey banks of mist lay over the red dunes to the west, but the arc of the sun was rising inexorably higher and higher in the heavens and the shadows grew shorter daily.

Finally came the long-threatened day on which our water-hole was dry. We thought it too laborious a job to carry water from the garden pool through the loose sand, so we decided to try our luck with a well. About a hundred metres or so above our water-hole the shape of the valley suggested a basin filled with gravel and there we began to dig. As the upper layer was of very loose sand we had to scoop out a wide funnel-like opening to prevent the surrounding sand from sliding down into the hole as we dug. Below the sand we came across big stone slabs, and one of them over a metre long had to be prised out. Beneath it we found black smelly mud with dark sulphurous water welling up. The sweat was running down our faces and we were so hot and thirsty that we drank some of the water. Afterwards we both had head-aches. However, we took two cans of it up to the cave in the hope that in time the sulphuretted hydrogen gas would be given off or could be boiled away. This hope was not fulfilled and the next morning we found ourselves without drinkable water. Then we remembered that charcoal absorbed gases and so we picked charred pieces of wood out of the ashes of our fire and used them for filtering. After that it didn't stink so much but it had become salty. In the end we had to fetch water from the garden pool. But later on, round the next big bend in the canyon, we discovered a dried-out water-hole, and digging through mud to a depth of about thirty centimetres we found clean sand and drinking water.

We were not the only ones after water. The zebra were searching for it too, and they were better equipped than we were because their keen sense of smell helped them to find it under sand or gravel. They could dig too, holes often more than a metre deep. One night, when the full moon hung almost vertically above the canyon and we were walking along in the soft light, we suddenly heard extraordinary noises ahead: the crunch of sand and the rattle of earth, thuds, stamping and the clinking of stones. It was like the clatter of heavy excavating machinery, an astonishing noise in the desert. We stopped, listening with a creepy feeling at the nape of the neck. After a short pause the noise started up again, echoing from side to side of the canyon. We walked on slowly and cautiously and Hermann put a cartridge into the chamber of our pistol — we had no idea of what might lie ahead. Then we saw a cloud of dust, and immediately afterwards we heard unmistakable snorting and whinnying: zebra! It was amazing how their black and white stripes made them practically invisible even in the bright moonlight. At a distance of thirty paces we could hear but not see them, and we came within ten paces before we could make them out properly.

A big stallion was standing knee-deep in a hole

pounding away with his front hooves at the hard rubble and flinging it far and wide. Beside him a second stallion was waiting. The mares and foals looked on from a little distance. Just as we came up the waiting stallion relieved the other; they took it in turns. For a few minutes we watched them silently. Then one of them snorted again and Otto, who was on the lead, was no longer able to restrain his excitement and he barked. At that the scene dissolved into a wild flailing and thumping of hooves, shrill whinnying, snorting, stamping, and the crunching of sand and stones, and the zebra were gone.

Summer came and from day to day the face of the desert looked more parched and cracked, more cruel and pitiless. It was already difficult to stand the midday sun, and at that time of day even the gemsbok and the zebra abandoned the open plains and took refuge in the shade. Only after the west wind had cooled the air a little did they go back to their impoverished grazing sites.

There was almost no growth in our garden now. We pulled a few radishes and picked a few leaves of the mangelwurzel, but that was all. Neither the tomatoes nor the carrots could stand the blazing sun. And Hermann's tobacco plants turned out to be young and vigorous acacia trees!

We had already removed the oven from our livingroom, and now we had to heighten the stone wall we had set up as a protection against the cold winds from the west, but this time in order to protect us from the scorching rays of the sinking sun. Our smoked meat dried out quickly and we brushed it with hot fat to keep it from drying out altogether, but that didn't help much. Our luck was out too. Again and again we hit an animal and then lost it after tracking it for hours. As we learnt much later the broiling sun was largely responsible for this.

But our chief worry was the rapidly sinking level of the water everywhere. The sun and the dry winds drank up water with invisible but greedy mouths. You could read the menacing process along the sandy banks of the water-holes as though on a water-gauge. In the afternoon the surface of the water was ruffled by the west wind and the little waves bit a step into the sand, and at nights the sinking water left a smooth shallow strip below the step. In this way every sandy bank was now a miniature staircase, each step marking a day's evaporation. Every day the water-level sank by perhaps a centimetre. Only those water-holes which were supplied from larger sandy beds kept their level a bit better. For us the steadily increasing number of steps in the sand was a disturbing warning that we must not rely too much on the coming rainy season, for, after all, what is more uncertain than rainfall in the desert?

We did not take kindly to the thought of leaving our comfortable cave, though since the appearance of the Khoi-Khoin footprints we had no longer felt altogether safe there. We could have given up the garden, though with heavy hearts, but we couldn't possibly efface all our tracks.

One morning early we were on our way to explore the gorge which ran from the north-west between the Goagos mountains and Carp Cliff and ended in the Kuiseb. The air was cool and refreshing and the Gams mountain was a clearly defined blue silhouette against a crystal clear eastern sky. But we had hardly passed the gorge in which our lorry was parked when the sun surprised us. It moved over the eastern face of the rocks, fell hotly on our cheeks and began its scorching daily course.

Bare and monotonous, the ribs of the old desert

131

spread out before us in a maze of gorges. Like the ridges of a giant file, the rock ribs ran dead-straight over the edges and down into the depths. Where spreading veins of quartz showed in the dark rock and covered the slopes with gleaming white boulders they merely heightened the general impression of barren hostility. Yet we knew that it was only in this grim underworld that water could be found. In times of need the proudest life up there on the plateau has to descend deep down into this underworld to seek the sources which alone can keep it alive.

The harsh and pitiless nature of the landscape did not depress us, for we were out to explore the unknown, and round every corner some new surprise might await us. Hour after hour we plodded over level rubble or through loose sand, and our rucksacks weighed heavier and heavier.

Suddenly we heard a loud whistle ahead of us and high up a rock face we saw a spot of green and beside it a pair of klipspringer. It was a pity we hadn't seen them before, because we had very little food left. The buck whistled again and then the two of them leapt up the slope in swift bounds. The green patch was a tuft of palmetto grass, and that meant water, and in fact a trickle was coming from a fissure and running down into a hollow the size of a fingertip. The klipspringer had been licking it. We used to call these tiny water sources bee holes, for it was there that the bees usually preferred to drink.

The sand was so hot now that it burnt our feet through the leather of our boots. We were just thinking of stopping for a rest when tamarisks and tsawi bushes came in sight. Near them we found a small pool overgrown with rushes, but the water was warm and sulphated and tasted horrid. We spat it out and went on. The lower water-holes are always the worst because evaporation greatly increases the salt content.

To come across water and green plants in the desert is always tremendously exhilirating. Small birds were chirping and a flock of starlings rose up before us with a great flapping of wings and flashes of white under their flights. And then we saw larger pools of water with high rushes and palmetto grass growing beside them. The tail of a black snake disappeared silently into a clump of old undergrowth. Pigeons were cooing, and all around we saw the tracks of zebra, gemsbok, klipspringer and beasts of prey.

Unfortunately all the water was muddy, bitter and salty, but finally we came across a source which needed cleaning out but the water looked as though it might be drinkable. All in all it didn't look a bad place for our new home if we could get the lorry up.

During the midday hours the grey rock face radiated intense heat and the sun reflected in the sand of the dried-out water-course was so bright that it hurt our eyes. The sun itself was like a heavy ball of fire, and yet this was still October, only the very beginning of the hot season.

Sitting in the shade of the rock face that had been scooped out by the river we took off our heavy boots, wiggled our toes in the warm sand, ate dried fruit and dried meat and drank a little water from our waterbags. Tracks in the sand indicated that animals were also in the habit of sheltering here. And as usual in shady places where game takes refuge from the sun, there were sand ticks in large numbers. They were round, ugly, khaki-coloured insects with a wrinkled leathery skin and yellow legs, and some of them were so small you could hardly see them. Their bites cause itching festering sores. Fortunately you usually notice their presence in good time and you can pick them off with your fingers — not so the unfortunate animals. But even with the plague of sand ticks the cool shade was preferable to the burning sun, and this time we were lucky enough to keep them off. We weren't so fortunate next day when we again sought the shade, after having discovered that we couldn't reach the place with the lorry.

We were lying there dozing when suddenly Hermann started up and with a jerk threw off a fat sand tick. The insect had bitten him in the palm. He sprang to his feet and began to scratch himself all over, declaring that the clouds of small flies which surrounded us had bitten him everywhere. I was about to point out that those particular flies didn't sting when he became giddy, tried to support himself against the rock face with one arm and slid down into the sand. His skin was covered with little bumps as though from a nettle rash. I looked for the tick he had flung away. It was black and swollen from old blood, and it seemed clear that this infected blood had got into the wound and caused acute blood poisoning. I cut open the bite and put a crystal of permanganate of potash into the wound. We always carried a small supply of these crystals with us for use against snake bites.

The poison spread rapidly. Hermann complained of a terrible headache and after a while his sight began to fail. The mucous membranes were swollen and he vomited. He looked in a bad way but I didn't know what on earth I could do for him. He lay there on the sand groaning and in my impotent rage I took a thorn and killed all the ticks I could see.

After about an hour, when the sun drove us away, I had to help him up over very rough ground to another little cave. He was half-blind now and unable to stand alone. I got him to a bed of dust and rock rabbit dung and he lay there whilst the west wind

134

blew sand over him. I sat beside him and stared at the dry water-course and the cheerless rocky slopes and had plenty of time for oppressive thoughts. At least it was a good thing that it had happened near a water source and not in some arid desert. The water we had brought with us was used up and there was no knowing when Hermann would be fit to walk again.

The dismal afternoon passed and I made some tea with the sulphated water. It tasted horrible. Hermann was very thirsty but he couldn't keep even water down. However, the next morning he felt a bit better. I shot a klipspringer at the water source and when I was skinning it I found seven fat glassy blow-fly maggots under the skin of its back; the graceful little beast must have suffered agonies.

In the afternoon Hermann managed to get up and he declared that he could walk back to our cave. I carried both rucksacks and we set off. We went up a side gorge and we had to pause and rest many times. It was quite dark when we finally reached home, and our hollow in the rocks had never seemed more comfortable and more homely.

A terrible year of drought had now begun and even on the distant farms cattle and sheep were dying in their thousands. After his misadventure Hermann was weak for a few days, but he was feeling more and more at home in the wilderness and he didn't play his violin so often — just occasionally in the evenings and never for very long. He spent a good deal of the day filling in our map and now and again he got out his paint-box to try his hand at springbok and gemsbok. 'My palaeolithic soul feels at home here,' he said with a grin.

The First Rain

For months there had hardly been a cloud in the sky except occasionally a high web of icy cirrus. But on October 26th the first real clouds appeared. They sailed swiftly over the blue mountainous line in the east, rolling along like great balls of cotton wool in a deep blue sky, bellying upwards, twisting and turning and lending an unusual touch of drama to the desert sky. We sat together at the southern end of our rock shelter and watched the performance eagerly.

Before long the bigger clouds became darker in the centre and their edges glistened like silver. Large and small black shadows like splashes of ink now rolled across the gorges, plains and mountains, and the whole landscape was turned into a dazzling chequerboard of moving light and shade. The light by contrast was more intense and much sharper, reflected and magnified by the silver clouds. Sitting in our cave without a shirt I got sunburned merely from the light reflected from the clouds as they came over the uplands in long shining processions. They were the first of the rainy season and they rolled over our heads into the Namib. But before long the west wind halted their progress and the warm, dry air swallowed them up.

Would it rain? All our work was suddenly forgotten as we stared and waited and wondered. Behind the silver clouds rose great shining white towers which made the mountains look like low hills. One of them rose over the Gams mountain and another to the north over the Komas uplands. Their glistening crowns spread outwards and they increased in size, particularly the Komas tower until it spread out like a threatening wall and its blue velvet shadow swept down over the mountains.

After a few puffs the west wind had dropped, and the whole of nature seemed to be waiting with bated breath. But the cloud came no nearer; it remained as though tethered to the mountain-side and brooding in dark-blue shadow. For hours it bulked there, gradually becoming darker and darker, and then towards evening it burst and there were long stabs of brilliant light and peals of reverberating rolling thunder. Where the rain fell the rivers would come down in spate.

After about half an hour a bitterly cold gale reached us; it was swiftly cooled air rushing away from the storm centre, sweeping great clouds of dust and sand into the grey evening air, driving away the sultry heat of the day and bringing sweet-smelling humidity.

We knew that rain storms in the Namib usually lasted three or four days so we waited anxiously for the following day to see if the performance would continue. Even heavier clouds rolled up and by the afternoon there were grey, gold-tinted curtains of rain hanging down in the sky. Warm shafts of iridescent sunlight occasionally broke through, and between the curtains of rain glistened fairylike stretches of plain bordered by the deep-blue slopes of shadowy mountains. The colours were clear and brilliant, the light changed constantly and protean clouds surged and rolled. A rainy day in the desert is something so marvellous that you never tire of watching it. Unfortunately, however, the long, colourful fringes and the moving curtains were not heavy rain, but just light showers and most of the rain evaporated before reaching the ground.

Towards evening a darker bank of cloud put the Hakos mountain into blue shade. Long, grey fringes began to fall away from the edges of the cloud and curtains of rain swept over the gorges and the mountain sides in a spinning pelting downpour. The mountains appeared in the sun again but now the gramadoela gorges were cloaked in a grey haze of rain which extended over the south plateau, our hunting ground. That meant game and good hunting for us and we jumped up in delight. For a moment or two the Roststock was hidden from view, then the last curtains of rain swept over the ground and the west wind tore the thinning cloud into silver shreds. A radiating sun sank over the western edge of the desert and in the sky dove-grey clouds with purple edges battled against the wind whilst to the south red and gold curtains hung down across the Nauchas highland and shafts of lightning pierced the black cloud bank over the Gams mountain.

Shadows rose out of the gorges and extinguished the rosy glow, and the grey twilight over the Gams mountain darkened into the blackness of night. Now and again isolated flashes of lightning lit up the sky. A moment or two before, the mountain had appeared as a blue mass against the black sky, now a flame licked up suddenly at its foot and then ribbons of fire ran up a ridge, spread out, sprang from ridge to ridge and rose to the summit like torches. A flash of forked lightning had set light to the dry grass and undergrowth on its slopes. Outlined in flickering flames the great mass of mountain stood out in the darkness, a glowing landmark over the Namib. For a long time the smouldering fires could be seen on its ridges, and here and there flames still sprang up, but finally the last glow disappeared and a dark starless night covered everything.

On the third day the west wind got the upper hand, the sun established its reign again, and a hot, light-blue sky spread out over the thirsty wilderness. It had rained, but we hadn't received a single drop.

In the next few days there were fresh spoor on all the game tracks. The animals had smelt the rain and now they made their way to those few lucky spots where rain had fallen and fresh grass was beginning to grow. We were hungry; for several days we had had to go without a midday meal. Otto was obviously bitterly regretting that he hadn't after all buried any of the wealth of bones that had come to him from our Gaogos journey; hyenas had carried them off and eaten them all.

We hoped to come across game along one of the nearby tracks, but we were unlucky. The fact was we still didn't know enough about the habits of animals. Every day with our glasses we searched the fissured south face and the limited area on which rain had fallen. Gradually animals began to show themselves there. Amongst them were some with lighter patches and we couldn't make up our minds whether they were zebra or gemsbok. The smaller animals were certainly springbok and every day there were more of them. On the ninth day after the rain we went over.

The balsam bushes were now shooting delicate green leaves and young tufts of fresh grass were growing amongst the chalk rubble. Green, delicate but vigorous new life was sprouting in the grey, ochreous gorges and the sight elated us.

For a long time we searched through winding gorges and over stretches of hot red dune sand beneath the abrupt edge of the plateau. We stalked one gemsbok and risked a shot, but we didn't get him. Others we stalked without even getting a shot

139

in at all. Soon we were so tired that our legs almost refused to carry us, but then when we had practically given up hope we bagged a fine springbok.

It made a wonderful supper and its liver was particularly delicate. Altogether its flesh was incomparably better than any meat we had had so far. Seven days good grazing had done that.

The Bushmen's Water-hole

The Bushmen's water-hole was the biggest in the neighbourhood. It lay in a narrow bend of the canyon below the southernmost peak of the Goagos chain about an hour and a half's journey from our cave. Even in November its water was deep enough to come up to our chests. Rank wild tobacco shrubs, tamarisks and thick salvadora bushes grew on its banks. The wind was blowing pieces of pierced ostrich-eggshells from a sandbank over the water; they were Bushmen's beads, and because of this find we called the place the Bushmen's water-hole.

November was a hot month and the white chalk walls gave off a tremendous heat. The gramadoela gorges were like long ovens, and at midday you could burn yourself on the stones and in the sand as though on hot metal. The tremendous ball of fire, the sun, had almost reached its zenith, and in the evenings its fiery course swung far over to the south-west.

The cool morning hours passed all too quickly, and later in the day it was difficult to look out into the glaring heat. Worst of all were the days when a light wind brought hot air from the burning dunes. But usually just when the heat became intolerable, when the air rose trembling from the ground as though from an oven, a cool, fresh breeze from the sea would bring us relief.

When we had eaten almost all the meat of the springbok we decided we could stand the heat and loneliness of our cave dwelling no longer. We knew that it was hotter than ever in the canyon, but the pool with its moist banks and its narrow strip of vegetation drew us like the seaside in summer. Our accommodation there could hardly have been simpler: two slabs of rock which had been hurled into the canyon by some landslip had fallen one against the other to form a sort of roof, and this offered us protection from the sun and from the sand-bearing wind. Two hollows in the sand were our sleeping quarters 'within sight of the sea'. Three stones placed in a triangle represented our hearth. But it satisfied us and we were as cheerful and high-spirited as a couple of youngsters playing truant — except that our hunting, trapping and fishing plans were all dead serious. From the long hairs of the gemsbok we plaited several dozen small running snares, which we now fastened along a stick and buried in the sand at the edge of the pool, with the snares emerging above the surface. We hoped that the steppe quail waddling down to the water to drink would get caught in them. Our supplies of ammunition were not inexhaustible and if we could catch quail without depleting them, so much the better.

The early morning hours at the water were delightful. The growing plants and the ground gave off a fresh, earthy smell and the surrounding bushes were full of chirping, cooing birds. The sides of the canyon still threw long cool shadows over the valley, and perched around on ledges and jutting rocks were flocks of pigeons. Little grey warblers flew busily to and fro between the bushes and the pool, and birds with two dark rings around their necks, whose name we didn't know, strutted up and down with darting heads pecking up insects. A small sun-bird with curved beak held itself suspended in front of the yellow flowers of the tobacco plants, carefully inserting its beak deep into each flower. A busy mouse sat beside the rushes and nibbled away, and the end of its long tail twitched gently. A flock of black starlings were chattering loudly by the edge of the pool, and the sun made dappled patterns through the leaves. There was so much life and bustle all around that it was almost easy to forget that we were in the desert.

But we weren't sitting there merely to enjoy the scene; we were hoping that some thirsty animal would turn up to drink, and one of our home-made bullets was already in the chamber of the shotgun, which lay beside us ready for instant use. But we waited in vain. No larger form of life showed up all day. However, we didn't let that depress us; we were gradually beginning to develop the patience that life in the desert demands of its inhabitants.

But when the twilight began to fall we became very eager to see whether our snares would work. We were hidden in the bushes, and the mosquitoes had woken up. We ignored their bites as the quail began to move in large numbers towards the water. Had we made the snares the right size? And if birds got caught in them would they stay where they were or struggle wildly and frighten all the others away? We heard a soft fluttering of wings. Were some of the birds already caught? Impossible to say, and the quail were still making their way towards the water. Perhaps they had just trodden the snares down? After a while the birds had drunk their fill and then suddenly the flock rose into the air with a great whirring of wings. Hermann and I ran down to the water's edge to see if we had caught anything. The snares were empty. We lit a match and discovered that five of them had been torn; they had worked, but the gemsbok hair had not been strong enough for the powerful wings of the quail.

143

We were very disappointed because our hopes had been high, and in anticipation we had already seen ourselves eating quail. If only we had horse hair, or waxed thread, or thin wire! At least we had once again learned that we still had a lot to learn.

When Hermann had finished breakfast the next morning he got up purposefully. 'If we can't have quail it'll have to be carp,' he said. But we found it wasn't so easy. We hadn't our dragnet with us and after an hour of trying to grab them with out hands — with the loud encouragement of Otto from the bank — we had caught only one small fish. We cooked and ate it at once, but the exercise had made us hungry and that fish was hardly big enough to take the edge off our appetite. We discussed whether to expend a charge of shot on the rock doves, but in the end we decided that we should be lucky if we bagged a couple that way, whereas we could reasonably hope for a dozen quail in the evening for the same cartridge. So the rock doves were left in peace.

But our hunger didn't leave us in peace. Perhaps we could spear the carp? A fallen slab of rock jutted out over the water and provided an ideal spot. At first we tried with sharpened tamarisk branches, but they weren't sharp enough and they just slipped off the wriggling fish. Then we got the idea of using needle-sharp porcupine quills, of which we had found a heap in a hole in the rock. We fastened four quills to each tamarisk pole and then took up our position on the rock slab again and waited — clad only in our hats — for the shadows moving in the water below.

After a while I was lucky. I had hurled in my home-made spear and as the water pushed it upward from the centre of the many ripples there emerged a fine fat carp waving its tail feebly. With a gleeful shout I jumped into the water to retrieve it, and in

144

his excitement Otto jumped in with me and clawed me down the back. But I got the carp. Again and again we hurled our spears into the water, and again and again there was booty for us to spring after. All in all it was a wonderful occupation for a broiling hot day in the desert, and by the time we had finished we had caught seven big carp and we cooked and ate the lot.

That evening one charge of shot brought us in sixteen quail. As I was washing the drawn birds in the pool there was suddenly a good deal of movement in the water and unseen mouths dragged at the birds and at my fingers. I called out to Hermann and he came up with a flaming brand from our fire, and in its light we saw perhaps fifty blood-thirsty frogs scrabbling for every vestige of entrail that fell in the water.

The sixteen cleaned quail just fitted into our cooking-pot, and we closed the lid and let them simmer all night on the ashes of the fire, and the next morning a wonderful breakfast was ready for us. When we had finished we decided to explore the canyon higher up along the Goagos mountains. It was to be a three-day trip and we took the pot of quail with us in a rucksack. It was so hot that at midday we were ready to give up and go back. But then we came across a narrow rocky entrance to a side canyon. That could only be the dry course of the Nausgomab, a tributary of the Kuiseb.

We entered it and suddenly we were breathing, humid, tropical, Turkish-bath sort of air. Wet sand was crunching under our feet, and there were brown pools of water all around. The Nausgomab had obviously had a flood during the storm. But where had the water gone, and why had we seen no sign of it in the Kuiseb? We turned back and then we saw that a thirty centimetre flood from the tributary river had been absorbed by a two-hundred-metre stretch of loose sand on the floor of the canyon. No wonder the water-holes had dried out so quickly.

Although the fresh water was brown and unpleasant to look at we were elated at the sight and determined to walk on. During the afternoon we sweated freely in the humid air between the high, narrow walls of this side gorge. The following day when we explored another side gorge which ran parallel with the Goagos mountains the air was just the opposite, dry and arid. Our sweat evaporated before it even formed liquid, and by evening we were covered with a crust of salt.

There was no way down into the gorge from the uplands and the only water it ever received was the rare desert rain. We clambered over dried-out waterfalls like hot broken stairways and made our way round great boulders until the bed grew shallower and broader. Early in the afternoon when the heat was almost intolerable we found a 'rain-hole'. Salt water dripped down from an overhanging rock and we sat back in the shade of the small cave behind it and breathed air which had been wonderfully cooled by evaporation and watched the drops as they fell like sparkling diamonds against the tremendous glare of the sun beyond and disappeared in small round funnels in the sand below. A row of tamarisks like a dusty garden hedge protected our eyes from the glaring sand in the river bed.

We thought it was wonderful and in our minds we were enumerating the advantages of a water-cooled home, but of course we knew that it was mere fantasy, since first of all the place could be reached only on foot and secondly heavy thunderstorms could put the river in spate so suddenly in this narrow gorge that we could be drowned like rats in a trap.

146

The desert is a landscape of extremes: on the same day you could die of thirst or be drowned. But that didn't alter the fact that what would have been a wretched damp little hole, was a heavenly oasis in this burning gorge.

After our rest we went out again rather unwillingly into the torrid heat. If we had known what the next day was going to bring we should have been even less willing. For days there had been no wind to speak of, but now the hot air which had collected over the dunes came into movement and spread out scorchingly over an area which was already too hot. It was as though some giant had opened an enormous furnace door, and the blast caught us during the midday hours. The first puffs of air were so hot and dry that several times we had to stop and gasp for breath like fish out of water. We had only one thought now: to get back as quickly as possible to the Bushmen's Water-hole.

We had about an hour and a half to go and it was the hottest journey we ever made in the desert. We had to bend forward almost double to drag our feet out of the hot clinging sand, and the air was so dry that our eyes smarted. Otto seemed to find the going even worse than we did and he adopted an unusual method of progress. If he found a bit of shade anywhere he would lie down in it and pant, letting us get a good way ahead of him; then he would jump to his feet and race after us to the next spot of shade beyond us and spend the time of waiting licking his sore paws. They were actually burnt so badly that after a few days the whole skin peeled off and for a week he could only limp around.

The next day Hermann and I discovered that the soles of our boots, which were only a few days old and which had been well dubbined, had cracked and we had to tear them off and put on new ones.

At last we could see the welcome green of the wild tobacco plants ahead, and when we got there we waded into the pool just as we were in our sweaty clothes and drank as though we wanted to drink the pool dry. We spent the rest of the afternoon in and out of the water and we speared a few more carp for our evening meal.

The next day we had a look at our garden and, as we had feared, we found everything scorched, although the roots of the plants still reached down to the ground water. We ate a few carrots which were little more than matchsticks, and those were the last fresh vegetables we were to see for a whole year. Then we effaced the whole garden, abandoning all hope of tomatoes or onions.

During the next few weeks we often visited the Bushmen's water-hole. We tried to catch quail with snares made this time of waxed thread, but they fell over as soon as they got into the damp sand and they proved ineffective. Then we tried our luck with thin electric wire, but this was too rigid and the birds were easily able to get their feet out again. We also ate the remainder of the carp in the pool. In all the others they had died or been eaten by hyenas or jackals. According to our calculations they should have lasted us for at least a year. We were sorry now that we hadn't eaten more of them.

Evenings at Home

The starry nights were magnificent after the burning hot days and we often spent the warm evenings sitting at the stone table in front of our living-room and our thoughts had plenty of time to roam at leisure under the slowly revolving stars. As most of them arose from a similarity of experience very few words were necessary to make ourselves understood. Again and again our thoughts went back to that profound impression we had received at the water-source visited by so many animals; it was the tremendous contrast between the parched and arid world of stone and rubble and the magnificent high-spirited animals of the plains. Over both of them circled the burning sun, and around both of them moved the same arid winds, and yet they obviously developed according to different laws. For inanimate matter adaptation meant continuous passive decay, but plants and animals actively and triumphantly surmounted the same conditions. What particular characteristics gave living matter its obvious superiority? For us the problem was so intimately connected with our present life that it could not be denied, and we felt that our proximity to nature ought to have simplified it a little.

'The secret must lie in the fundamental characteristics of life,' said Hermann.

'Hunger,' I suggested. That was an idea never far away.

'No. Hunger is a feeling with complicated psychological conditions.'

'But feeling? Mere feeling?'

'Perhaps. But what is feeling? Joy, hunger, fatigue, fear ... What have they in common? What's their basis?'

'A warning. And what about thirst? Thirst is a warning of the body that it needs water.'

'What about joy?'

'Joy in its simplest form probably means that man or animal is in full harmony with his or its surroundings.'

'Is there any fundamental difference between positive and negative feelings? Or is there some superior conception which embraces the two? But with that we seem to be back to where we started.'

'Not quite. Perhaps feelings are judgements which tell a living organism whether a situation is favourable or unfavourable. In that case the capacity for forming judgements would be one of the basic attributes of life.'

'Really basic?'

'Yes. Life is essentially characterised by activity as compared with non-animate nature. Even a unicellular creature is able to avoid unfavourable conditions either by flight or by sealing itself off. But before it can do so it needs feelings, or in other words the capacity for judgement. How otherwise could it know what was favourable and what wasn't?'

'True. But if each feeling involves a judgement isn't the human understanding with its capacity for forming judgements merely the further development of that primitive instinctive capacity for judgement which belongs to all forms of life? So why shouldn't the unicellular creature contain within itself, in a most primitive form, of course, the potentialities of the highest intellectual capacities reached by man?'

Hermann's pipe glowed, and our midget mice scuttled to and fro between the kitchen and our stone table like little dwarfs.

'Those mice are certainly developing too quickly for our poverty-stricken stores,' he observed. 'Incidentally, do you realise that we've just upset the whole Darwinian theory of evolution by natural selection? Natural selection replaces intelligent judgement, killing off everything which isn't suited to its environment. Wouldn't adaptation to new conditions result quite passively and mechanically as soon as in the course of procreation a species had provided sufficient numbers of mutations amongst which selection can operate? After all, it's quite certain that in the millions of years of development millions of generations have been available for the process.'

'You mean that the activity is apparent only? And that with the numerical increase of any particular form of life sufficient mutations will take place for the process of selection and adaptation to take place quite passively and mechanically? In that case why has no crystal ever learned to fly?'

'Because the possibilities of change in a crystal are too limited. But for albumen with its great variety of atoms there are a thousandfold, or a millionfold more possibilities. Isn't that perhaps the fundamental difference between living and inanimate matter from which all else stems?'

'Just a question of statistics in short? And hereditary changes arise by chance, damage done by radiation, by poisoning, and so on. Evolution by accident — wouldn't that be very unfortunate?'

'Perhaps, but just turn on the radio and then tell me that evolution has in fact been fortunate?'

'That's good repartee, but it doesn't get us much further. Why, for example, if everything is settled automatically should feelings develop at all? They would be quite unnecessary and their existence an

151

inexplicable anomaly.'

'A good argument, but no proof.'

It wasn't easy to philosophise even in the desert, but the subject gave us no peace. The senseless war in the outside world had made us doubt the significance of all evolution, yet somehow we had the feeling that the solution of the great questions involved was almost within grasp. Again and again we came across marvellous examples of adaptation. The praying mantis for example; it waited ready to pounce on its victim, and in the meantime it was almost indistinguishable from the twigs and leaves of the bushes in which it lived; in fact it was so perfectly adapted to its surroundings that you noticed its presence only by chance. And then there were the grasshoppers, though here they ought to have been called the stonehoppers because they so closely resembled the stones amongst which they lived that you could recognise them only when they jumped. On the chalk plains they were white like their surroundings; amongst the slate they were a greyish brown. And you never saw a white grasshopper anywhere but against a white background.

And what about the little rock dassie, remote relative of the rhinoceros? It lived in nooks and crannies in the rock and it could go without water for months, even years at a time. To make this abstinence possible it was provided with a large double appendix or caecum so that the moisture in its food could be utilised to the utmost, and was in fact utilised to such an extent that the little animal exuded a viscous urine only about once a fortnight, leaving white marks on the rocks everywhere. Could such things really be merely the result of blind chance?

The days were long and hot now and the new grass

on the south plateau was scorched, and in consequence our hunt for game was often unsuccessful. We usually took it in daily turns so that one of us could rest whilst the other was on the prowl. We were gradually developing the infinite patience of beasts of prey. On one very bad day I shot a springbok in the leg and followed it for two hours before finally losing it. Then I shot and wounded a gemsbok and lost that too. And on the way home I shot a klipspringer and lost that as well. In all I wasted seven cartridges and brought home nothing but an even bigger appetite. On another occasion I was crawling along to get within range of a gemsbok. I had grazed my knee and crawling over the sharp rubble was painful. Then a stone slipped and the gemsbok escaped. Thereafter, on similar expeditions, we padded our knees with old stockings.

Despite lack of success our hunger drove us on to try again and again, and we learned why primitive peoples who live from the chase have so much more patience, persistence and self-control than civilised peoples. We also learned that the chase with primitive weapons was one of the most difficult ways of keeping yourself alive.

We crawled around in the narrow gorges like beasts of prey intent on nothing but killing, and there was clearly a danger of becoming dull witted, but fortunately our evening discussions after the day's hunting helped to counteract that. If we had not succeeded in keeping our mental faculties alert I think the loneliness would have destroyed us in the end.

One evening we discussed the feelings we experienced when we were after our prey. 'I trembled with eagerness like a dog when that gemsbok came near,' Hermann confessed. 'It was only when I raised the pistol that the trembling stopped.'

And I had felt the same thing myself. When you go out hunting after food with an empty stomach you find yourself tremendously keyed up, and when you've bagged your game the release of tension is correspondingly great.

On another occasion when we were sitting together talking in the evening Hermann exclaimed: 'It's actually not surprising that Red Indians and Bushmen leave all the work to their women, occupying themselves only with hunting. I could willingly laze around now and see a woman do all the work: I shouldn't turn a hair. And I'm not tired; just completely satisfied.'

'I think the town dweller misses that quick change between tension and relief,' I remarked, 'though to some small extent active sport makes up for it, particularly dangerous sport such as climbing and so on.'

'That's true. And when life becomes unbearably dull people begin to run after every loud-mouthed demagogue, and when war or revolution comes they feel a sense of relief.'

'Small wonder,' I agreed. 'After all, thousands of generations of our forefathers lived just as we're living now, and I don't suppose the past few hundred generations have made a great deal of difference to our fundamental instincts. In short we've still got the soul of a Stone Age man.'

'What you're saying is that modern man doesn't feel himself in harmony with his own civilisation and you may be right. A Bushman who had to live in a town would probably die of it. But we're living quite reasonably here as Bushmen.'

Despite frequent hunger and despite all our troubles we quite liked the life, and we discovered that despite all the harshness and cruelty a feeling of almost childlike innocence remained — as though the whole thing was a game instead of being deadly serious. The theory of the Stone Age soul didn't seem to fit all the facts.

'Do you think that's because we're living outside human society and doing no one any harm?' I asked.

'At least there are no commandments we can break,' replied Hermann.

'The innocence of Man before the Fall. Without social life there can be no laws. But is that quite right? Otto had a bad conscience every time he went anywhere near the mouse cage which we had built because we'd forbidden him to kill mice. But any cat would have killed them without the slightest hesitation despite our prohibition.'

'That's true, but a cat isn't a social animal, whereas the forefathers of the dog hunted in packs. They learnt to subordinate themselves to a leader and suppress their own desires. For that reason you can train a dog, but a cat walks alone and you can't train it. Our forefathers were physically so inadequately equipped for the chase that co-operation was absolutely necessary to secure food. But co-operation involves give and take and in particular subordination. Whoever is incapable of that, whoever in short is ineducable, must starve.'

I had to laugh: 'Conscience as a substitute for sharp teeth and powerful claws.' But Hermann was undismayed. 'Why not?' he demanded. 'Conscience has made such a degree of co-operation between men possible that tonight thousands of people will be blown to pieces by bombs. The fact is that man's educability first enabled him to be a beast of prey, but it also created the possibility of going beyond that stage. There aren't only bombs in the world; there are also cathedrals. All progress increases man's possibilities, for good and evil alike.'

155

'But if conscience is a mere product of education who's to say what's really good and what's evil?' I objected. 'None of the big religions would admit that for one moment.'

'Religion hasn't been able to prevent a situation in which — tonight for example — several hundred men will go out with a good conscience and drop bombs and blow women and children to pieces. Could there be any better proof that conscience is a social product and not something absolute? Whether a man has a bad conscience in a given situation depends on how he's been brought up. Conscience can urge one man to wage a blood feud, and it can nag at another man because he has inadvertently violated some trivial rule or other, for example, that he mustn't eat jugged hare. I don't think there's anything too trivial and absurd for it not to have been a matter of conscience for some religion at some time or other.'

'And yet the commandments of the various big religions are extraordinarily similar, which suggests that they must be in accordance with some fundamental spiritual characteristics or requirements of man.'

'Maybe, but what? And how did they develop? Perhaps we can find the key in our primitive, pre-social life. Religions all developed from more or less similar conditions. All the religions, philosophies and moral systems put together haven't prevented civilised man from plunging into this fratricidal war. We must get rid of all the overgrowth and get down to rock bottom no matter how barren and comfortless it may appear at first.

'Agreed. So let's ask ourselves in what respect the life we're leading here is untypical of the primitive and original condition of human life.'

'First of all we're not a family. Our earliest, almost

pre-human, forefathers pretty certainly lived together in families or in some blood-relationship group.'

'Then the first steps would be to educate a child in some such original-type family. The education and upbringing of a present-day Bushman probably does not differ fundamentally from that.'

In this fashion we felt our way forward; and each discussion provided some new subject for other evenings. We became more and more convinced that man can be understood only from his development, and it seemed to us that the fundamental error of philosophy was to regard him as something fixed and given. Religions on the other hand have always insisted that man must develop towards perfection, and that demand recognises at least indirectly and unconsciously that he has developed. If he had been created ready-made why had God created him imperfect?

The red dunes still lay beneath the western sun like molten metal, but finally the sun sank beneath the horizon and mild night rose up out of the gorges. Using towels as loin-cloths we sat there and tore apart the ribs of an antelope which we had bagged with difficulty, and gnawed away like carnivorous beasts. But our thoughts were freer and less oppressed than they had even been, and later that evening Hermann's violin sang triumphantly into the dark night around us.

Christmas

For months the sun had risen higher in the heavens and now it had crossed its zenith, and the pole of our wind generator cast a short shadow towards the north at noon. For fourteen hours the relentless sun dominated the sky, and even in sinking its rays were still scorching. Once again we had to raise the west wall of our living-room, this time to give us a little shade in the evening.

Our clothes, always stiff with blood and sweat, were torn and frayed from crawling over the sharp hot rubble; and the material was faded and rotted by the glare of the sun. After a while we gave up wearing trousers and stockings, but we continued to mend our khaki shirts because they protected our skin from the sun. All we wore now was a felt hat, a shirt, boots and a belt with a bag for tobacco, knife and cartridges. Now and again we trimmed our beards with a pair of scissors, but we looked like scarecrows. We both kept a reasonable rig-out to one side for the day we returned to civilisation.

As the new grass on the south plateau had shrivelled up, the visiting game had disappeared and the remaining animals grazed as well as they could on the year-old stubble. By this time we knew the game tracks so well that we could easily follow them through the maze of gorges and ridges even on moonless nights. But we hadn't much luck and we were always hungry. And again and again even those few animals we did hit got away. This puzzled us a good deal. Finally we found the explanation.

A shoulder shot with our pistol was rarely enough

to bring down a gemsbok. When cutting up a carcass we had carefully located the position of the heart, but it was well protected by ribs and they were very tough — so much so that when a bullet hit them it was invariably deflected and instead of lodging in the heart it penetrated the lungs. But a shot in the lungs wasn't enough to disable a gemsbok, and once for six hours on end I had watched a buck with such a wound; it behaved as cheerfully and vigorously as all the other animals in the herd.

On another occasion Hermann was stalking a gemsbok and I was watching his progress through my field-glasses and holding Otto on the lead. There was no cover and Hermann crouched forward slowly and carefully over the sand until he thought himself close enough for a shot, and then he half raised himself and fired. The gemsbok was hit but it made off towards a pass between two chalk ridges. Hermann sprang to his feet and made after it. At that moment a whole herd of gemsbok, no doubt roused by the shot, suddenly appeared from a gorge. I counted eight animals and I started to run forward. Hermann crouched down again but the gemsbok spotted him. The first was not more than thirty metres or so away and he swept round followed by the others until Hermann found himself surrounded.

He followed them with his pistol as they circled round, and then the leading animal swerved inwards with lowered horns. Hermann fired and the antelope swung away again. But a second buck now lowered his horns to attack. Hermann fired again and this one also retreated. But they were still circling round him and now a third attacker left the circle and moved inwards. Another shot sounded. I was running to-wards Hermann, shouting at the top of my voice and waving my arms, though I had the feeling that I was

159

hardly moving. There was a fourth shot, and then the gemsbok saw me running up. The circle broke and they galloped off. When I got to Hermann he was still crouching in the sand holding the pistol, but the magazine was empty.

And we didn't get a single one of the animals that had been hit. After considerable thought and discussion we decided that generally speaking we should aim only at the head, and specifically at the relatively small mark between the eye and the ear, because a bullet glanced off the sloping forehead of a gemsbok only too easily. But for such a small mark the outside range was not much more than fifty metres. With heavy hearts we sacrificed another five target bullets at that range. The markmanship was good, though even after that we suffered inexplicable failures.

We had certainly learned to stalk animals, though it was far from easy to approach them crawling through the hot sand. When there was no cover you dared not move a muscle the moment your prey raised his head. And that wasn't so easy if you happened to be in an uncomfortable position, perhaps kneeling on a sharp stone, or with flies buzzing round your nose or ears. And as soon as you had fired there was a moment of tremendous tension, followed often enough by bitter disappointment when your prey galloped off instead of dropping. Even if the animal were hit there was little chance of coming up with it once it had bounded off.

Again and again we asked ourselves miserably why we aimed so badly. Sometimes we wondered whether the bow and poisoned arrow of the bushman were not more effective than our heavy parabellum pistol, and we seriously considered poisoning our bullets, but we didn't know of a poison which wouldn't spoil the meat, and it so happened that at that period we never came across a snake from whose fangs we could have extracted poison. We were hungry all the time now and talking of nothing but food. And of course it's when you're in difficulties that accidents happen.

We had baked ourselves a loaf from a whole week's ration of flour, and it had turned out well, crisp and wholesome. Before we went out on the prowl that night we each cut ourselves a couple of wretchedly small slices to take along. But unfortunately we left the bread tin in the kitchen. The following evening when the sun was sinking we returned — empty-handed — to find that our lovely loaf of bread was green, slimy and completely ruined. The sun had beaten onto the bread tin all the afternoon. To make up for the loss we now had to reduce our breakfast flour ration by fifty percent for the next fortnight. We felt so miserable over this mishap that we allowed ourselves a few currants to cheer us up.

The following evening we were very hungry and we used two shot cartridges on the quail at the bushmen's water-hole and returned in triumph to our cave through the darkness with twenty-one birds.

Christmas was approaching, and we weren't feeling very Christmassy, but then we received a wonderful present. On December 18th white billowing clouds appeared in the sky and the following day two showers fell on the south plateau. And in the afternoon of the 20th a shining white monster with a dark belly appeared behind the Goagos mountains. We dropped everything and sat on the plateau trying to hypnotise the clouds, told each other what we could see, and discussed each new stage of development.

Then the first flashes of lightning rent the sky and a grey veil was drawn across the Komas uplands. After that everything went very quickly. A chain of

161

ragged clouds swept over the sky, the precursors of the coming storm. The thunder was louder now and we counted the time between the flash of lightning and the subsequent roll — forty-five seconds: about sixteen kilometres. And before long it was only ten seconds. Then the last of the sun on the Goagos mountains disappeared and the furthermost peaks were hidden in rain. Ridge after ridge was blotted out by the slanting curtain of the storm. There was no doubt about it now: rain was coming!

A roaring and drumming like the sound of great breakers came up from the gorges as the storm thrashed down on thousands of rocky ridges. The rain was spinning on the plateau now and a cold wind hit our faces. And then a higher note in the roaring of the storm announced the rain as it swept forward over the gloomy gorges. Yet quite close mountains and plains were still in bright sunshine.

Our hair began to stand on end and with long bounding strides we ran from the plateau. We were hardly under the rock face when a blinding, hissing, stone-splitting fork of light dazzled us for seconds and the first great drops fell on our heads. We laughed and danced with delight — the first rain for nine months!

Swiftly we detached the wind generator from the battery, drew a tarpaulin over our sleeping quarters and weighed it down with stones. There was a rushing sound like a waterfall now and slanting grey clouds of rain sluiced from heaven to earth. Suddenly each small rock rib wore a kind of milky transparent aureole as the rain fell on its hot surface, bounced off and evaporated into fine steam. Every detail stood out as though sketched with light chalk, and the smell of wet earth was intoxicating. We were beside ourselves now and we tore off our clothes and danced

162

around naked in the rain, letting it splash over us from the rocks, shouting with joy.

Then a new sound was added to the symphony of falling water. Brown streams carrying earth were gurgling in every gully now and from the high rock face near our cave poured a small waterfall.

'Collect some!' shouted Hermann, and we rushed to put out anything that would hold water. The downpour was already subsiding and gradually it resolved itself into individual silver droplets. For a few moments a brilliant rainbow hung in the sky and across the dark dripping rock face, and then it was all over.

The whole downpour had lasted perhaps seven minutes, but we measured about a centimetre of rainwater in a tin canister though the outer edge of the storm had only just reached us. We scooped out the water from all the pools and puddles around and filled our receptacles to the brim, and when we had finished we had water enough for a fortnight — a truly heavenly Christmas gift!

The next day the west wind arrived early and clouds remained over the uplands. All around us the short shower had awakened life. Within twenty-four hours the new grass was showing, and within another twenty-four hours the ground bore a shimmer of green if you looked across it at an angle, and the buds of the balsam bushes swelled almost as you looked at them. Five springbok appeared on the plateau and after stalking them for hours we managed to bag a young one. The first bowl of raw meat dissipated our gnawing hunger, and from our full stomachs a wonderful Christmas peace crept up into our souls. We spent the whole evening thinking out our Christmas menu.

Bread was a rarity for us and therefore a great

delicacy, and the baking of bread became almost a religious ceremony. In the morning I would knead the prepared dough in a wash-basin and then cover it up with a cloth to be put in the sun to rise. When it had begun to swell it would be kneaded again. Our bread mould was made out of a petrol tin. Fire had to be prepared in good time because only the hard camel-thorn wood and the blackwood of the tsawi bush would glow long enough to bake a fair-sized loaf of bread. We were always keyed up when, after about three hours, we carefully lifted the hot tin out of the earth as though it were a buried treasure; would the bread be brown and crisp or burnt?

In the meantime Hermann was making chocolate macaroons from oatmeal, cocoa, sugar and gemsbok fat, and marzipan sweetmeats, each with a currant in the centre, from toasted flour and sugar. We also proposed to allow ourselves three pieces of real chocolate per man and dog for Christmas. With dried fruit and gelatine we did our best to make a pudding, but we failed — it wouldn't set. But Hermann certainly succeeded in producing a wonderful strawberry cup. He dissolved four spoonfuls of strawberry jam in water and left it long enough for a slight fermentation to develop and give the thing a little fizz. The necessary strength came from a cup of brandy, of which we had two bottles in all. The aroma soon attracted a cloud of bees, and when a puff of wind lifted the cloth that Hermann had cautiously put over the mixture all the bees disappeared into the pot like dive-bombers.

Hermann rushed to the rescue and got several stings for his pains; Otto, hearing his far from Christmaslike curses, scampered up to help and got stung on the nose; and I trod on a bee with my bare foot. In the end we saved our drink — at a price — and

Hermann tucked it carefully away in his bed.

But where the devil had those bees come from so quickly? There must be a nest quite close. We started to look for it at once and before long we found it, for the bees were still flying in and out. It was high above our cave and in all the months we had been there we had never noticed it. It would have to wait till after Christmas now; in any case there wouldn't have been time for honey-cake. What we did need was a Christmas tree. We found a small balsam bush that didn't look too bad. But where could we get candles? Then we had an idea: weren't there so-called Bushmen's candles on the plateau? The yellowish wax covers which protected the plants from drying out were lying around everywhere amongst the chalky debris. I collected a quantity and fixed the little wax tubes onto the balsam bush. Hermann cut a moon and a few stars out of some silver paper we possessed. Looking at the result, I decided that we needed a few red apples. 'Don't mention it,' said Hermann, 'you can have 'em.' I thought he was joking but coming back from some errand I found shining red apples hanging on the tree. I had to look very close before I discovered that they were dried-out zebra droppings which Hermann had lovingly painted.

Evening fell and the sun went down, burning hot to the last moment, and the tension created by the intense heat of the day was relieved. Solemnly we ate our Christmas dinner. The bushmen's candles gave only a dull flame and a good deal of soot and they went out at the slightest puff of wind, but our strawberry cup was exhilirating beyond all expectations. With full stomachs and quiet minds we sat together and our thoughts wandered off to other climes and other people; to our families and friends, none of whom had the slightest idea where we were.

Bees and Gemsbok

There seemed to be a lot of bees in the swarm, and they flew in and out across the blue sky in an uninterrupted stream of transparent wings. And there was probably a good deal of honey in the nest. At the thought we began to lick our lips; like Otto when he hears us sharpening the carving knife.

Our rope was long enough, but we had to search for half an hour before we found a fissure amongst the rubble of the plateau into which we could ram a wedge to hold it. I put on my only pair of trousers, thick woollen socks, a pullover and a jacket with the sleeves tied at the wrists, almost ready for glacier-climbing. And over my hat and face I fastened a piece of mosquito netting. The rope went round my chest in a loop so that if necessary I could use both hands, and a long cord was fastened to my belt so that I could draw up all the tools I needed.

The first thing to be hauled up as soon as I was suspended outside the entrance to the nest was a smoke pot — an aluminium saucepan containing glowing embers, Bushmen's candles and pieces of bark. Under cover of the smoke I dangled in front of the hole in the rock, my foot in a previously prepared sling. Many bees, benumbed by the smoke, now swarmed around and crawled over me, and inside the nest I could hear what sounded like the throbbing of a powerful motor. Slowly I inserted my hand and arm into the hole right up to the shoulder. My hand was covered with bees now, but they didn't sting me. I could feel the rock at the end, but there was a passage leading upwards to the comb, and it was so narrow I couldn't even get my finger into it. Hermann sent me up a wire hook, but also that was too large and the bend of the passage too sharp. Suddenly Hermann shouted: 'Your pants are on fire!' I looked down, and sure enough they were: little flames were licking up my trouser leg from a glowing brand that had fallen into my turn-up. In my haste to beat out the flames my mosquito net slipped. A bee stung me behind the ear, and my sudden movement upset the smoke pot and sent the burning embers down in a shower onto Hermann's head, and in his wild leap to escape he barked his shin badly. Those bees were too clever for us. We didn't get any honey, and my trousers were ruined.

We opened the New Year by scouring the sandstone gorges below the south plateau for game, but after the rainfall the animals seemed to have gone further afield. There were very few fresh spoor, and only once in the distance did we spot a herd of zebra. But we did find a hole full of rainwater in the rock and we decided to spend another day in the area. We ate biltong for supper and we drank rainwater. We slept in the sand, and when we woke up next morning our stomachs were rumbling. By midday we felt as though there were lumps of lead tied to our feet. So far we hadn't seen any game at all.

But when we turned into another gorge Hermann suddenly stopped and raised his hand in warning. Silently he dropped to one knee. Under a wind-scoured ledge a little distance away sat a gemsbok chewing the cud. The direction of the wind was unfavourable for us and we couldn't go round. But Hermann decided to try his luck. I held Otto on the lead whilst he crawled forward over the sand. Then I felt a puff of wind at the back of my neck and at that moment the gemsbok must have scented Hermann, for it sprang to its feet and galloped diagonally away from us. Hermann jumped up, sprang onto a rock and fired twice. For a moment I spotted the gemsbok again between two rocks and it was obviously hit.

We raced over the rocks, Otto straining at his lead and almost pulling me over the sheer drop into the next gorge. The gemsbok was squatting on its haunches down below and shaking its long, sharp horns wildly; obviously it couldn't get up any more. Hermann killed it with a bullet in the head.

Whilst we were skinning and cutting it up we ate small pieces of the warm red flesh and wondered how to cook ourselves a meal without pots and pans. In the end we cleaned the intestines and turned them inside out, cut the liver up into small pieces, seasoned it with salt and pepper, put it inside and made a large sausage of it, which we cooked on glowing wood embers. After about twenty minutes the thick sausage was brown and crisp. We cut it open on a flat piece of rock and ate the pieces of liver with our knives, looking at each other with shining eyes and smacking our lips. We ate the lot in one go and went to sleep until the cold of the evening woke us. Then we cut the fillets and cooked them in the same way for our supper. After that, replete and contented, we went to sleep again. When the first pale light of the morning was putting out the stars we started for home, each of us carrying a heavy load of meat on his shoulders.

Dental Treatment and Summer Holidays

Throughout January the burning sun ruled the heavens without even a small cloud to dispute its sway and provide a little shade. Yet the gnarled balsam bushes covered themselves with green leaves and the armoured Bushmen's candles unfolded their delicate red blossoms, but the young grass between the stones was already scorched. Our Christmas water was all used up now and we had to go down into the canyon for more, and make our water-hole deeper and deeper to reach the sinking surface.

For some time we bagged nothing at all, for the animals had left the scorched grazing grounds. Our last boot leather was gone now and we made ourselves soles from old tyres and fixed them on with wire. Henceforth we always carried a little wire in our rucksacks for any small repair.

Then one day a big stopping came out of one of my back teeth. Only a little while before Hermann found that he had bitten through the top of a gold crown. We were now faced with a serious problem; supposing our teeth decayed and the roots became inflamed: could we pull teeth with the small pair of pincers we had? Hermann made a face. Quite apart from the pain we should probably just break off the crown and leave the roots in the gum. Then Hermann had an idea: we could dissolve a piece of celluloid in acetone. It wasn't soluble in water and it would quickly get hard. After some deliberation we decided to try.

I had a go at Hermann's tooth first. With a needle I scratched the hole under the bitten-away crown as clean as I could, then I stuffed a small piece of cotton wool soaked in pure alcohol into the hole to disinfect it. I left it there for twenty minutes then dried out the cavity with a hot wire and rammed a piece of cotton wool soaked in the celluloid solution into it. Hermann sat there patiently with his mouth open for half an hour and by that time the stopping had hardened. Then it was my turn. The experiment was a great success and it was a year before those stoppings came loose, and even then all we had to do was replace them.

Most of our time was still occupied in the laborious search for game. It was easy enough to get within a hundred paces of a grazing animal, but to get within the fifty paces we required demanded concentration, persistence and skill — and on top of that a good slice of luck! We failed so often that we were sometimes in despair, but the determination with which we overcame our despair and disappointment and tried again and again gave us self-confidence and strength. It made us realise just how much modern civilised man misses any real test of stamina and ability, and we felt that to some extent this might encourage an unconscious desire for wars and revolutions; at least they did give a man an opportunity of demonstrating his manhood and bravery. The conditions of civilised life were dangerously unbalanced; they demanded primarily an antlike co-operation, yet in man there was a subconscious urge to live the life of a beast of prey. It seemed quite likely to us that one day our whole civilisation would be destroyed by this contradiction.

But as far as we were concerned at the moment, there just was no game, and so all the persistence, patience and skill in the world was of no use. The chase necessarily involves a nomadic life and as the month with its burning hot days came to an end we realised that we must follow the game to its new grazing grounds. We knew that somewhere beyond the Goagos mountains there had been two good rainfalls. We should just have to go there. We had at least one advantage over Bushmen: we could take our lorry and load as much household impedimenta on it as we liked; so one morning, after careful preparations, we set off. The way from the plateau to the Goagos mountains was already familiar to us and in sandy places the tracks of our tyres were still clearly visible from our salt expedition.

Suddenly on the way Hermann reminded me of the car trap we had set and it gave me such a shock that I braked hard and Otto squashed his nose against the windscreen. I had forgotten all about that trap, but it wasn't far ahead, and to be hoist with our own petard would have been a wretched misfortune.

The sun rose quickly and before long hot air was rolling over the level plains like smoke, distorting the outlines of the distant mountains and turning them into swaying pyramids and columns. But sometimes it lay still in the hollows and depressions almost like blue water, then, as though at a magic word, receding like a silent ebb-tide and turning once again into flickering breath-taking heat. This silent play of light, air and colour only heightened the impression of cruel emptiness in a dead landscape from which all life had fled. On the way we had not seen a single blade of grass nor a single animal of any kind.

At about midday our lorry rumbled over the stony slopes down to the Goagos source. Nothing moved; not a zebra hoof sounded on the stones, and not a springbok darted off in the distance at the sight or scent of us. Clearly no rain had fallen here. We crossed the valley and drove over switchback stretches of rubble towards the mountains in the north-east. The

171

river beds carried white granite sand and glistening feldspar crystals and their courses were loosely lined by gnarled camel-thorn trees. Then the plains ended and we found ourselves looking into a shallow hollow which spread before the mountains like a broad trough. Rounded ridges lay together like the fingers of an outstetched hand and between them were many dried-out beds with steep sides. Rocky mounds rose here and there but none of them jutted beyond the level of the Namib plains. The hollow shape of the landscape here was clear proof that the mountain foothills received more rain than the plains in the west, and the slopes were dotted with bushes. Hermann raised his field-glasses.

'The bushes over there are green,' he said, indicating the middle distance with his hand. 'It must have rained there recently. I can see zebra and gemsbok, and behind them ostriches.'

There was no obvious way for the lorry so we clambered up a rocky mound to look for a passable route. We found a way down into the first valley, but we had to shift a good many boulders and dig away a sandbank before we could get the lorry into the dried-out bed. On the other side of the valley the terrain was passable, but in the meantime it was growing dark and we camped amidst young springbok grass. Whilst we were gathering wood for a fire we came across many fresh traces of game, and this encouraged us to use a double portion of macaroni which we flavoured with biltong and a tin of tomato purée.

A silver moon sailed over the blue mountains. From all sides we could hear the howling of jackals, and now and again the distant barking of wild dogs. There was life around us again and the empty wilderness lay like a half-forgotten dream under the western

172

stars. Early the next morning we looked up into a deep-blue sky across which delicate tatters of golden cloud were sailing. The sun itself was as yet invisible but its rays were already shooting into the sky from beyond the dark mountain peaks. Otto began to sniff eagerly and following the direction of his nose we saw a gemsbok standing quietly on a mound and looking down at us in astonishment. But first of all we needed water. We set out on foot. The further east we went the longer grew the grass and the richer grew the green of the bushes. Having clambered to the top of the next ridge we could hardly believe our eyes: the valley below us was full of grazing springbok.

There were perhaps three to four thousand of them, though it was impossible to tell the exact number. We stared at the graceful filigree of delicate feet, the thousandfold rhythm of arched backs, the lovely necks lowered to the ground as they cropped, the bronze-like horns and the warm fleeces. Those nearest to us raised their heads and cautious ears were pricked. Hesitantly and doubtfully the buck retreated with graceful leaps. The doubt and misgiving spread like ripples over a pond until a forest of horns rose everywhere over the tensely poised bodies. Long lines of brown backs glistened in the sun along the bed and up the slopes. Here and there was a dense concentration of bodies like a whirlpool of water when a dam is opened, and we could see white bellies shining like silver fish in a net. The whole valley was in movement now. The first small ripples had given way to rhythmic flight, and like a flood the whole vast herd swept over the ridge and away.

When the last stragglers had disappeared we stood staring at the empty valley and feeling almost surprised that the bushes and rocks were still there. We recalled the stories old Boers had told us of lions finding themselves in the middle of big herds of springbok and, unable to extricate themselves, being compelled to pad on swiftly until they sank to the ground from sheer exhaustion. If only we had had a cine-camera! And even our Leica was back in the lorry.

We decided to separate in the hope of finding a suitable camping place. Hermann was to take one valley and I the other. We met again in the afternoon. Each of us had seen herds of zebra of thirty and more animals, and gemsbok herds of sixty and more, as well as smaller groups of springbok. This narrow stretch of fresh grazing ground seemed a paradise. Both river beds had water-holes, and Hermann found one which we could easily reach by lorry. We pitched camp between a few thorn bushes along what had been the bank, and spanned our tarpaulin, for the bushes gave little shade, particularly at midday when their leaves turned vertical in order to offer as little surface as possible to the scorching rays of the sun. It was a fine place to sleep in, and the stars were reflected in the cool, brown water, and at any time of the day or night we could wade out into the water up to our waists. Our drinking water we obtained from a hole we dug in the sand near by.

In the light of the early morning I went some little distance up the river-bed and found a rock face under which the sand was encrusted with salt. Numerous spoor indicated that animals came here to lick the salt. I sat up out of sight with our pistol and waited. I hadn't been there more than ten minutes when eleven springbok came up in single file. The first one disappeared behind a bush, but the second came right into my sights. After the shot they disappeared as though they had been wiped off the landscape.

Had I missed again? No, behind a bush I caught a glimpse of white and there lay my buck with fading eyes, shot through the heart. He was only a youngster and I was able to carry him back across my shoulders. The sun was just rising over the horizon when I got back and Hermann was still asleep. He awoke to a breakfast of fried liver brought to him in bed — to his surprise and pleasure.

A succession of sultry days followed and the skies became alive. Every midday clouds came sailing over the mountains and every evening the west wind drove them back again. By this time we had scouted the whole grazing area. It was only about ten kilometres by five, and the grass in it would soon be nibbled away. It was therefore all important for us to know whether it was going to rain again, and when and where, so we were constantly climbing up some hill to look around.

On the fifth day the rolling of thunder was heard over the mountains and there was no west wind. The grey clouds hung in the sky like wet rags and the following night was as hot and oppressive as a Turkish bath. But we didn't mind, and our rising hopes were not disappointed: the next morning a thunderstorm burst about twenty or twenty-five kilometres away. The sun looked pale and watery through serried windows of cloud banks and at two o'clock in the afternoon it began to rain again and went on until four, wonderful, steady rain. We caught the rain which poured off our tarpaulin and filled four bottles for our battery, and then we sat and listened with delight to the rain beating down, splashing on the bushes and pattering into the pool. Hermann smoked and sketched and I whittled away at the stock of what was to be a small crossbow.

Suddenly Otto got up and stared down intently at

the ground and there we saw hundreds of small brown frogs on the move; they were leaving the pool and making towards higher ground. What did that mean? We thought about it but came to no conclusion and finally gave up. Water was flowing down from the rocks into the river bed but the rain was not heavy enough for it to run down from the sides of the valley, which was a pity because we had hoped that the pool would fill up again.

The rain left off and Hermann lit a fire, using wood which we had kept dry under the lorry. Then he put water on for tea and prepared some oatmeal. After a while we heard a distant rushing sound above the singing of the kettle and it came rapidly closer. It wasn't wind. Suddenly we realised: the river was coming down. Hurriedly we jumped onto a ledge of rock. As far as we could see from there the river bed was still empty, but the roar of the approaching flood grew rapidly louder. It was like an express train in a tunnel. The empty sand-filled river bed under the quiet grey sky and the threatening roar were quite incongruous.

I think we both shouted involuntarily when we first spotted it. A frothy brown mass of water boiled and gushed between the rocks, overbrimming the narrow channel and pouring itself over the wider bed with a hissing roar. We ran down to see it at close quarters. It was already gurgling under the ledge where we had just been standing. It seemed to fall back for a moment and then it rose again with foam-flecked back to pour on, a roller of water perhaps two metres high, churning around tree trunks, branches, great boulders and other debris and then overwhelming the pool. For a second or two the wild rush valley-wards ceased; the water rose again, spreading outwards in all directions, overbrimming the banks with foaming ridge-like waves and hissing up to our feet.

We retreated. We could hear a louder roaring in the distance now and on the back of the first rolling flood came still higher waves like screaming riders urging their rushing steeds forward, and before we realised it we were standing in water.

'Quick, the beds!' exclaimed Hermann, for the water had almost reached our encampment. Not a moment too soon we snatched up our bedding, the chairs, the boxes and our cooking utensils and ran with them to higher ground. There was a sharp fierce hissing as the water put out our fire. The pan with the oatmeal rose on a wave, tipped over and disappeared. I leapt at it, and measured my length but I just managed to get hold of the handle of our precious pan, whilst our breakfast floated away on the tide. In the meantime Hermann had rescued our pump. At that we looked at each other and not a word was said, but what a disaster it would have been if we had lost that and been unable to pump up our tyres!

When the roaring had died away in the distance and everything was calm again we sat on our bedding and talked. A dead lizard and a thorn bush floated past. The thing had happened quite without warning. There had been no thunder and no fierce wind to announce it. But somehow the frogs had known. Or did they always leave the water when it rained? Three days later it rained again and this time they didn't leave the pool, and there was no further flood. Had the frogs some highly developed sense which gave them warning of such danger? They had certainly all saved themselves, and later that day when everything was quiet they had returned to the pool, and that night and the following nights they held simply fantastic nuptial concerts, forcing us to stop up our ears to get a little sleep.

All the water-holes were now full, and for a few days a small stream of clear water ran down the river bed amidst the sand and stones. After all those dry, waterless months on the barren desert plateau it was wonderful to have water in plenty for a while. There was intense life all around us now. The wood pigeons cooed from morning to night, and within the space of a week one weaver-bird built no less than four ingeniously woven nests amidst the sparse foliage of the hawthorn tree above our heads. We didn't see the vast herd of springbok again, but there were plenty of smaller ones, and all we had to do to spot gemsbok and zebra was to climb on to a hillock. Naturally there was no shortage of beasts of prey and in the other valley we frequently saw traces of a leopard. Then early one morning before the sun was up we spotted him squatting on a rock at a little distance, but as soon as we moved he disappeared with a single lithe spring. On another morning I came across seven big spotted hyenas going through a small valley like riflemen in extended order. Woe betide the weak or the wounded if they came within reach of those jaws!

Again and again we observed how well the animals knew each other's ways. For example an ostrich watched the approach of hyenas with indifference, but as soon as it spotted me, although I was still a great distance away, it fled. I had a similar experience with a gemsbok. At midday a strong buck stood half dozing in the shade of a camel-thorn tree. I approached cautiously with my Leica at the ready, but unfortunately I dislodged a stone, whereupon three hyenas rushed out of a hole in the rocks and made off, one of them falling with a loud splash into the water. The buck turned its head disapprovingly towards the disturbance of his peace, but it was not until he noticed

178

that they were fleeing that he too made off. That gemsbok had stood in the wind of the sleeping hyenas without bothering his head about them, apparently knowing that they would treat his long horns with respect.

Herman told me of another encounter with hyenas. He was out after game with Otto and he was resting at midday in the shade of an overhanging rock face when he heard a loathsome cackling. Otto's hair began to bristle. Three hyenas came up the river bed together. Hermann got up and put Otto on the lead. As the hyenas continued to advance in line, Hermann shouted and waved his arms but they took no notice of him and their wicked little eyes were fixed on Otto. Hermann now raised his pistol, and at about six paces he shot the leading beast right through its ugly head. It fled across to the other side of the valley and collapsed between the rocks. The other two also fled.

After the rain more and more animals came in for the grazing and we had meat in plenty for very little effort. One steel-blue morning before the sun was up I was sitting by a salvadora bush and before me the sandy river bed was covered with a crust of salt. A late-walking porcupine trotted along, and when I whistled it immediately put its head between its front legs and arched its back to form a ball of prickles, rattling its tail angrily. As I made no further move it relaxed and hurried on its way.

When the golden light of the sun flooded over mountain, bush and rock, a springbok appeared apparently from nowhere. With raised head, twitching ears and blinking eyes it looked up into the air. Other springbok now joined it, emerging from the shadow into the sunlit river bed. There were about twenty of them, all young bucks, with smooth hides, powerful

179

muscles, and strong, fluted lyre-like horns. They licked at the salt crust, walking delicately here and there to try out different spots. Then suddenly there was a sharp sound. Two pairs of horns had clashed together. Two buck stood head to head with straddled legs and lunged at each other, parrying the blows, engaging their horns and testing their strength with lunge and pull. It seemed to be catching, for soon another pair was just as vigorously engaged, and then a third. The clashing and rattling sounded like salvos now, salvos of joy in the morning sun. Finally there were five pairs of them fighting with shining horns, rippling muscles and gleaming eyes. And then it all ended as suddenly as it had begun and the whole herd moved off in perfect amity. But in the sky above the vultures had circled lower, looking down the whole time with keen eyes for death which is so often the companion of young and high-spirited life.

Not all our experiences were exhilirating. On one occasion Hermann and Otto returned under a cloud-covered sky from a tramp towards the north. They had come across a stony area swarming with termites, and on almost every stone sat a scorpion with outstretched claws, whilst ugly reddish-yellow centipedes slithered around between the stones. There were so many of them that Hermann had had to pick Otto up and carry him. After the rain the termites were making their nuptial flight; for a short period they left their gloomy quarters in the earth to rise into the sky on diaphanous wings. But when they returned to earth they were received by poisonous death.

Those predatory insects were like killing machines; perhaps because they had such a long period of development behind them. There were scorpions and spiders in the world long before there were mammals, and they had had plenty of time to adapt themselves to perfection to a certain form of life. Hermann's experience gave us a good deal to think about. Was there a danger that in time the use of machinery would turn men into automatons too? But at least man had developed consciousness and it was therefore possible for him to recognise any danger inherent in his development.

Once the frogs in the pool had calmed down sufficiently for us to hear ourselves speak, our evening discussions turned again and again around these problems — and our arguments were punctuated by the hooting of owls and the howling of jackals.

Man's Evolution

We had slid so readily into the life of primitive hunters that we came to the conclusion that underneath the veneer modern man still had a 'Stone Age soul', which was difficult to reconcile with the civilised life he was leading. Could that contradiction be resolved? In view of man's steadily increasing powers of destruction it was a vital question. It was quite certain in our minds that man was, in fact, the product of development, and the stages through which he had passed formed the basis not only of what he was but of what he might still become. How much did we know of the development through which he had already passed?

Clearly, man owed a good deal of his evolution to his physical build. How could he have become a man at all without hands that allowed him to grip and hold. 'We'll have to go back a long way,' said Hermann. 'The very first vertebrates had five-boned paws and they crawled on to land something like two hundred and fifty million years ago. That's sound confirmation of the law of evolution which says that simple and not specialised forms have the best chance of survival and represent the only basis for further evolution. All animals with four-and three-boned claws, the cloven-hoofed antelopes and the solid-hoofed zebra, represent specialised types. They have all developed from five-boned fore-runners in adaptation to special conditions of life, and with that they have largely put a stop to further possibilities of evolution.

'Almost all the organs of the human body show a

striking absence of specialisation,' I pointed out. 'For example, man hasn't enlarged canines like carnivorous animals and apes; he has no serrated teeth for tearing; and no excessively pointed teeth like those of the insect eaters. Man's teeth are more or less of a size; they're a sort of general-purpose set for eating practically anything. Man's arms are not excessively long like the arms of climbers. And his nails are no good for digging or even serious clawing. Further, his digestive apparatus isn't specially adapted to any particular kind of food.'

'All very true,' Hermann agreed, 'and you take the human foot. It's just made for walking and moderate running and for nothing else in particular. If it were made for speed the main stress wouldn't be on the big toe as it is, but on the central or outer toes. And it isn't a foot made for climbing either; the heel is too well developed for that. But what are you getting at?'

'I'm anxious to shed some light on our genealogy if possible. From everything we know about development a simple organ can't develop from a specialised organ, whereas the opposite can and does take place. For example an arm can develop into a wing, but a wing can't develop into an arm. That means that none of our predecessors can have had more specialised organs than we have. In other words, there's nothing whatever in our genealogy similar to the anthropoid ape of our day; and there can be no creatures in it with big canines, bony skull ridges, long snouts or prehensile feet. You can come to the same conclusion in a different way: for example the young of anthropoid apes and their embryos have heads which look more human than those of the apes themselves, which suggests that they must have developed from unspecialised forerunners, that is to say from more human stock. Have there, as far as you

183

know, been any fossil discoveries tending to support that view?'

'Well, there's the *Australopithecus* skull found in South Africa which has more characteristics in common with a human being than with an anthropoid ape.'

'There's one big difficulty though. We human beings make up for our lack of natural weapons only too successfully by inventing weapons, firearms, bombs and so on. But how did our forerunners manage to survive before they discovered what they could do with sticks and stones? We've just deduced that they were no better equipped by nature than we are: no long claws or sharper teeth than we have, for example, and that they couldn't run very fast, like hares or springbok; nor climb trees easily, like monkeys. Well, how did they manage to get food and stay alive?'

'Perhaps the problem isn't so difficult as it looks at first sight. Take baboons for example; they live alongside leopards and hyenas, and they live most of their lives on the ground. It's true that the old men of the tribe have canines a leopard might envy, but how often do they have to use them for fighting? They have very keen eyes though, and when they make any kind of sortie they invariably set up a whole system of watch-posts first. In other words, they protect themselves primarily not by their natural weapons but by their intelligence, and they do it so efficiently that they could probably survive even against the long-range rifles of the Boer farmers. And if they had just a little more intelligence they could probably survive quite well even without their canines, particularly as they live on more or less edible fruits, larvae, beetles and scorpions, and manage to get by even in an inhospitable neighbourhood like this.'

'Splendid! Now let's go a step further. Our human forerunners probably didn't live in the tropical jungle at all but in a region of wooded plains, which constitute the ideal environment for a creature with prehensile hands and unspecialised feet, for it doesn't demand any particular adaptation, for example either swift running or powerful climbing. Climatic history suggests that the greater part of Africa has been wooded plains for millions of years.'

'So now we've got our forefathers on wooded plains. But how did they get there? And how does it come about that their intelligence is above the average?'

'We must think back even further. The main evolution of mammals began about fifty million years ago. At that time they were all still very small; for example, the fore-runners of the horse were not much bigger than a terrier, and those of human beings and apes were no bigger than squirrels. I once took part in the excavation of fossils from that period. The bones we came across were all small and delicate, and the differences between the various orders were only very rudimentary. In those days the forerunners of both human beings and apes must have been primarily insect-eaters.'

'There are a good many indications that the first mammals were actually insect-eaters, and that all the others — the beasts of prey, the ruminating animals, the rodents and the pachyderms — branched off from the insect-eaters and developed according to their mode of life. Does that help us at all?'

'I think it probably does. Insect-eaters must have lived chiefly in trees and bushes. Such a life encourages the use of the forefeet as hands; think for example of mice and squirrels. And once the hand is used for grasping there is no need for the develop-

185

ment of the long snout. Perhaps the common fore-bears of all mammals were short snouted. In any case it's interesting that the embryos of all mammals show strikingly human skull forms. Perhaps the shape of our head is more like the original shape of the mammalian head than we think, apart from size. Perhaps not only the head, but other parts of the body too, have retained a good deal of their original characteristics.'

'Something else: to what extent would evolution be influenced by the use of the hand for holding food, in place of a snout? It means that sight would become the most important sense, more important even than the sense of smell; in other words, the eyes would develop at the expense of the nose; and at the same time they would tend to move closer to-gether because stereoscopic sight makes it easier to use the hands. Instead of the development of a spe-cialised sense of smell, association centres would be formed, and the development of the skull would not be hindered by a long, heavy snout and powerful jaws. Thus the use of the hand leads to the develop-ment of the eye and the brain, the two exclusive specialisations of the human body.'

'Exclusive did you say? Aren't you forgetting the upright stance? But certainly those specialisations must be connected with it. Whatever takes its food in its hand and carries it to its mouth must adopt a more or less upright position. Think of the mouse and the squirrel. Further if an animal uses its eyes to detect its enemies then it will raise its head as high as possible to do so. The small ground squirrels sit bolt upright as soon as they're alarmed. With the develop-ment of the hand into the sole tool and the eye into the most important organ of the senses the tendency to adopt an upright position must necessarily increase.'

'But the upright stance can have developed only in the environment of the tree savannah, and thus it would seem to be the original environment of man.' For a climbing animal without any special protective weapons it was ideal. It is the only form of landscape in which alertness and intelligence offer any real protection. In the open savannah alertness is no protection against a swifter enemy, and in the dense growth of the tropical jungle its value is very limited.

'The next step was, of course, the invention of weapons and the hunting of bigger animals. This must have greatly encouraged the development of intelligence, because now it was more than ever necessary to be alert, to plan and to outwit other animals. At the same time a carnivorous diet allowed man to penetrate into all parts of the world, and new conditions constantly gave his brain new problems. Without the transition to the life of a hunter preying on other animals our further evolution is inconceivable.'

'Let's see how far we've got. Man is less subject to narrow and exclusive adaptation to his environment than any other animal. In other words, man has retained his versatility whereas other animals have lost theirs. Man is nearer to the original mammalian form, even if the first mammals were no bigger than mice, than any of the other animals. Man can have developed only from an unspecialised origin; in other words, he cannot have developed from anything resembling our present-day anthropoid ape, which can only be a side branch of the main human line of evolution.'

In the meantime the night had grown cold. The midnight constellations were reflected in the dark water. Somewhere zebra hooves clattered over unseen stones. Contentedly we crawled into our sleeping bags.

The events of the following day provided us with new material for our discussion. We made a trip through the net of dry river beds below the great mountain, and at midday we were resting in the shade of a small rock face. Five springbok trotted peacefully past us. The wind was in a favourable corner. I held Otto and we sat perfectly still but without any cover. The animals came nearer until the leading buck was not more than twenty paces away. He stopped, saw us — and then lowered his head to graze.

'Brain unable to interpret what the eye sees,' whispered Hermann. The second animal now came up, and at that moment Otto, who was getting more and more excited, wagged his tail so violently that it hit a stone. The buck threw up his head and whistled shrilly, but was still unable to interpret what he saw. He stood there for about a minute, whistling and moving his forelegs uncertainly, and then his misgivings seemed to get the better of him and he bounded away, followed by all the others.

Half an hour later a black figure appeared over the horizon, sat itself down on a rock ledge and looked into the valley. It was a baboon! It spotted us at once and let out a resounding roar. At the sound other heads appeared, and as the baboons saw us they all gave the same ugly bellow. We stayed where we were and so did the baboons, roaring from time to time to let us know they could still see us. But after about half an hour of this their curiosity got the better of them, and slowly, hesitantly, and with many pauses, they began to make their way down into the valley. They didn't come straight towards us, but from the side, and they didn't all move together. If a group of boulders or rocks barred the leader's view for a moment or two his head would always appear cautiously from behind a rock or a bush, and frequently he would stand up on his hind legs to see over the top of a bush. Finally all nine baboons were about a hundred metres or so away from us on the other side of the valley. To our astonishment they now climbed into two thick bushes, which we knew to be full of sharp curved thorns.

They sat upright in the branches like black devils and watched us. Every time we moved they marked it with an uproar, and the smaller baboons, who couldn't yet bellow like their elders, joined in with loud squeaks. A very small baboon, quite unable to remain still, climbed all over its mother, though usually it remained out of sight behind her back, occasionally looking at us from under her arm, just as a child might look at a stranger from behind its mother's skirts. A half-grown baboon started to creep towards us under cover of rocks and bushes, but it was called back by a loud bellow from the old man of the party, and on returning it received a sound buffet from its mother, which it acknowledged with a loud howl. From time to time the adult baboons chattered to each other excitedly.

I remembered what a Khoi-Khoin had once said to me about baboons: 'Baas, baboons can speak; only they're too clever to let on. They know that if they spoke they'd have to work.' And it had been only too clear that he was sorry that he could speak and so had to mind sheep.

The inquisitiveness of the baboons was even greater than ours and they showed no sign of departing. Finally we got up and went towards them. At that they all piled out of their bushes and fled up the side of the valley whilst their leader covered the retreat by bellowing and baring his teeth.

The subject we had broached gave us no peace.

One evening we were sitting in the twilight together. Bats were darting in geometrical patterns over the bushes and the pool. A silver sickle of moon was in sky.

'I'm still puzzled by this lack of adaptation,' I confessed. 'We've seen that it's made up for by good eyes and a brain capable of interpreting what the eye sees. But the correct interpretation of a constantly changing series of pictures isn't an automatic or instinctive process, but can be learnt only by experience. It follows that the young of such a creature, being without experience, are quite helpless and need the protection of their parents whilst gathering the necessary experience. But how is that possible with roving animals? Perhaps the baboons show us. The mothers carry their babies all the time, and the babies cling on to them. In other words, the hand again! The result is that from the very beginning the little ones take part in and see everything that goes on. They learn from the behaviour of their parents, and they start learning when they're still quite small and therefore highly educable. A jackal on the other hand has to hide its young from the outside world, and they can't leave the protection of their hole until they've achieved a certain degree of independence. When they take part in their first joint chase the greater part of the impressionable highly educable age is gone, so in their case lack of experience is compensated by instinctive reaction. Now supposing that the capacity to learn from experience is the original thing, and that instinct is a substitute for the absence of opportunities to learn, and not the other way round? Could man have retained his original characteristics in this respect too? Perhaps because the development of hands made it unnecessary for him to hide his progeny in caves? Instinct is usually bound

190

up with highly specialised organs to make quite certain they're properly used; at the same time it's invariably based somehow or other on the experience of those animals that went before. But if the experience of previous generations can be gained by the next generation without danger then there's no necessity for hard and fast instinctive reactions. And so we get a permanent capacity to learn from experience, which, in the long run, is superior to any previously determined adaptation. And there's something else: the slower development to maturity may have prevented the awakening of certain instincts, thereby necessarily making man's development even more dependent on learning from experience. And the softness of the skull in infancy enables it to adapt itself readily to the space requirements of a growing brain.'

'All we've got to do now is to trace the development of language in the same way and then we've really and truly progressed from the insect-eater to man.'

'Let's see. When does an animal emit a sound? In pain or in surprise; in anger, or on recognising danger.'

'Take the recognition of danger: the springbok whistles; the baboon roars. Each recognition produces a feeling based on experience. The tone will differ according to whether the object recognised by the baboon is a snake or a leopard. Recognition is based on recollection. Where an animal relies on its eyes recollection consists primarily of pictures. Animals which live together in herds experience the same things together; isn't it therefore possible that the same sound produces the same picture in the recollection of all of them, and oughtn't we to look for the beginning of word formation there?'

'So long as the shock of the experience produced the sound, as in the case of the baboons, we can't talk of word or language. But with growing intelligence and the capacity to learn, children increasingly imitate − in play − the behaviour of the adults and also the sounds they make. In play the sounds are separated from the experience which produced them, and by association they call up the appropriate picture or pictures in the mind. Thus pictures can be conjured up again and again merely by the repetition of the appropriate sounds. In short, children can play with danger − without danger. In this way and because of the long duration of childhood, speech can develop from children's games.'

'Deliberately reproduced pictures in the mind represent the beginning of thought. Thus thought and speaking are twins; they develop hand in hand. As soon as a certain store of words has been collected pictures can be conjured up and linked together at will. What the thinker has not yet experienced in reality he can now experience in thought. And at the same time he can foresee future experiences. Life no longer consists merely of past and present as it does with animals; it has a future too. Thus with speaking and thinking man creates a new dimension for himself. It's astonishing what life can produce with an unburdened childhood at its disposal.

'Yes, it's quite true: without a protected childhood in which there's time for play, mankind would probably never have risen above an animal existence. And perhaps in the future the playing of children will be recognised as more important than technical developments, wars and revolutions. Woe betide the people which forces its children and their games into the strait-jacket of adult politics!'

A Night March and its Consequences

With the arrival of February our easy times came to
an end. The herds had nibbled away all the grass on
the few square kilometres where rain had fallen and
wandered off. The sun greedily swallowed the water
in the water-holes. We had put a water gauge in our
pool and we observed with misgiving that the surface
was lower every day, sometimes by as much as four
centimetres. In the whole area we had found only
one small spring, unfit to drink from, and there was
now nothing left for us but to do as the hunters do
and follow the game.

We realised that we should have to move farther
inland, which would take us closer to the farmed
area, and thus the danger of discovery would be
greater. We therefore had to look for a well-hidden
water source which was difficult to reach and we had
to find it before returning to our cave dwelling,
where there was perhaps no water at all any more. On
a rather too bright morning we packed our things
together, filled our water-cask, checked the tyre
pressure and drove the lorry with whining engine over
the sandy river bed and out of the valley up to the
plains of the Namib, where breadth and glaring light
and the deceptive beauty of dead stone and empty
sky greeted us. The island mountains stood out on
the far horizon like sentries; and as always their
steel-blue shape seemed to hold the promise of hidden treasures and far-off adventure. We felt the temptation though we knew that behind that horizon was
only the continuation of the same old desert.

We drove down the long plains, crossed the old *pad*

193

on the edge of the gramadoelas and then hid the lorry in a gorge. We slept in the sand until the sun had disappeared, and set out again in the ghostly light of a pale moon. We were on foot now, and we trudged for a few miles along the *pad,* a thing we should not have dared in daylight.

The soft light of a high moon lay like a fine mist over the stars, reducing the mountains to small hills and confusing shallowness and depth. The *pad* twisted and turned its way over barren, ribbed watersheds, dipping down between glimmering slate slabs into yawning gorges where there was nothing but barren rock. Here and there the leafless trunk of a sterculia tree protruded from a fissure like a primeval dragon.

Finally the *pad* led upwards again between innumerable rocky mounds rising out of thousands of irregular black shadows. And then to the left ahead of us lay a chain of fissured mountains. We knew that just beyond those mountains began the land of the last farm, which in those days was quite isolated and far away from any other. We knew the farmer, a certain Herr Siedentopf, a German; and more than once we had thought of visiting him. The temptation to look at another human face and to talk to another human creature was very great. We had been unable to resist it altogether and we had more or less decided to visit him; in fact we were wearing our reserve clothing for the purpose. But in the end we didn't dare. The danger of being reported to the police by some farmhand seemed to loom larger the nearer we came to the farm. The future was to show that our fear was well founded. We therefore left the old *pad* and followed a game track southward.

This led us through a pass between hills and on the way we heard stones rolling down the hillside and suddenly a gemsbok appeared ahead of us like a ghost.

Otto raced after it barking, and although we called him back he took no notice and his barking finally died away in the distance. Of course, we had to wait for him, and he kept us waiting a long time. But at last he returned, received his well-deserved cuffing and was put on the lead. And that was that — or so we thought.

But after a while I noticed that he didn't seem to be able to keep up with us and when I stopped he stopped too and stood there with stiff legs, shivering all over. Something was wrong, and Hermann examined him. When he withdrew his hand it was covered in blood. In the flickering light of a match we discovered a stab in his belly, and on his back under the skin was a spongy accumulation of blood. It looked dangerous and we couldn't help remembering Otto's mother, who had been killed by a gemsbok. We felt very sorry now that on top of that we had beaten him. Hermann sniffed at the wound. The intestines seemed not to be punctured, and that was a bit of luck. But we had to go back. Otto couldn't walk any more; his left hind leg seemed quite stiff.

Hermann picked him up but Otto was too heavy to be carried like that for long, so we emptied one of the rucksacks and packed him in so that his head looked out. He was obviously very ill, for he submitted to everything without protest. But what were we to do with him? If we went back to the lorry and drove home we could hardly get to Carp Cliff before sundown. On the other hand we could reach Siedentopf's farm in five or six hours, and he would know how to deal with sick animals. So it had to be Siedentopf after all.

We took it in turns to carry Otto, and we tramped all through the night. And the whole time Otto sat still as a mouse in the rucksack, now and again licking my ear or the back of my neck as a sick child might stroke its mother's hand. As soon as it got light we made a more thorough examination. Fortunately only one horn had caught him, and the wound seemed to run beneath the peritoneum into the thigh muscle. Otto had been very lucky. The wound didn't look so bad to us now and we didn't think that he was in any immediate danger, so we decided not to go straight to the farmhouse but to spy out the lie of the land first for fear we night accidentally run into the arms of a police patrol.

In daylight there was also a danger that someone might see us. Shepherds might be out with their sheep, though the ground around here looked as parched as anywhere else. We made a detour to the north across rolling ground with innumerable shallow valleys. Before we emerged from any of the many pits we had a good look first to make sure there was no one about. We saw no sheep and no sign of human life, and finally we found ourselves in a gorge of the mountain at the foot of which the farmhouse stood.

A small overhanging rock face offered protection from the sun and there we took Otto out of his ruck-sack and gave him a hatful of water to drink. He had fever now and after drinking he lay down and panted while Hermann did his best to keep the flies away from his wound. I clambered up over the hot rock face to the top of the gorge and crawled to the edge from which I could look down over the farm under cover of a balsam bush. The farmhouse with its gleaming corrugated iron roof lay below me like a toy perched on the crest of a hill beside a dried-out river bed. Chickens were clucking, a dog barked, there was the steady sound of axe blows, and I could hear the sing-song voice of a worker. They were the sounds of human civilisation and they warmed my heart. I had never thought it would be so exciting to come across human beings, and my heart was beating hard. The farmyard was empty and there seemed to be no car around. It was therefore unlikely that the farmer had visitors.

Hermann relieved me in the afternoon and he saw a man and a woman sitting on the veranda of the farmhouse drinking coffee, no doubt Herr Siedentopf and his wife. We waited until nine o'clock, by which time we hoped that the house servant would be back in his own quarters. When we finally walked into the yard we were greeted by a dachshund who was almost beside himself at the sight of Otto in his rucksack. At his wild yappings the kitchen door opened and there stood the Ovambo staring at us open-mouthed. We tried to behave as though it were the most normal thing in the world for a couple of men to arrive on foot in the evening at a lonely farm carrying a dog in a rucksack.

'Where's the Baas?' demanded Hermann.

The Ovambo jerked his thumb over his shoulder, and then the door opened again and Herr Siedentopf appeared, looked at us, hesitated for a moment and then said: 'Well, did you ever!' We unpacked Otto in the kitchen and Siedentopf examined him, gave him a sulphate tablet and treated the wound with gun-oil. After that we sat a little awkwardly at a table covered with a white cloth and Frau Siedentopf brought us plates of fried eggs. We finished up with luscious grapes. What wonderful things there are in the world!

After that we sat together chatting over a glass of red wine. In uncertain times the less you know the better, and Siedentopf asked very few questions and we didn't say more than absolutely necessary. A lot more Germans had been interned it appeared. There had been very little rain and the Kuiseb had not

197

flowed again as yet. Siedentopf had been compelled to put his sheep out to graze at a high price up country. The next police patrol would probably arrive at the farm in about a couple of months, by which time the Ovambo would be back with his own people.

We wanted to leave before dawn, but Siedentopf wouldn't hear of it: the dog couldn't be allowed to walk yet, and we should therefore stay on the farm for a few days. The wine and the friendly faces quickly convinced us that this was quite the best thing to do.

That night we slept in real beds, but we didn't sleep well; they were too soft, and the room — despite the fact that the windows and the door were open — was too oppressive and airless. There was a wind outside and it disturbed me that I couldn't feel it. I had a nightmare — the Ovambo came into the house bringing the police with him.

But for all that it was wonderful and we stayed there four days during which time Otto rapidly recovered. Siedentopf then took us in his car to the edge of his land. We got out and shook hands with him. Then the car drove off; Siedentopf looked round once and waved, and we waved back; then we were alone.

We now turned southwards towards the gramadoelas to find ourselves a new place to live. And fortune favoured us. In the big Nausgomab gorge we found a suitable water-hole and near it a good place which could be reached by lorry. It was dark by the time we got back to the lorry and Otto, who still limped, had managed the last part of the way only with difficulty. The next morning we set off early. Beyond the Goagos mountains we drove out into the plains that stretched right to the horizon. There wasn't a blade of grass to be seen, and of course no sign of game. This time I thought of our car-trap in good time. The glaring chalk stretch down to the Carp plateau seemed more barren and bleak than ever. And yet it was a home-coming for us; we belonged to this landscape now by dint of hard work and hunger, sweat and thirst.

In our cave dwelling we found everything covered with a thick layer of white chalk — the work of the winds that had brought no rain. On the game tracks in the canyon there were no fresh spoor anywhere. Only the klipspringer were still there; they found enough moisture for their small bodies in the bushes they fed on. Our water-hole was as dry as a bone. The die was cast; we had to go.

Our packing took a great deal of time and meant a lot of hard work. The wind generator had to be dismantled, the radio wrapped up in blankets. And how many possessions we seemed to have even in the wilderness! The wooden ledge along the wall, the dried hides! We left nothing behind; not a scrap of wood, a stick, or even the smallest piece of wire. There was no cave where we were going to live and we should have to build ourselves a house, and for that we needed everything we had. All that remained behind were the two hollows in which we had slept, the hearth, the stone table, the walls, the remains of bones, a big heap of ashes and a couple of useless tins.

The lorry was loaded high, and we took a last look round from the plateau, waving farewell to all the familiar landmarks; then we started up, driving carefully over the sharp chalky rubble which was so very hard on our tyres. This time as we passed we dismantled our car-trap. It was useless now and we didn't want it to do unnecessary harm.

Housebuilding

As the river had come down in November and again in February there was plenty of water in the Nausgomab water-hole. Above the steep 53-metre-high sides of the gorge we found a small ochreous strip, the remains of an older river bed, surrounded by low rocky mounds all of the same height and obviously representing a still earlier level. It was well-hidden, and although we had no particular view, the reddish stretch of sand rested the eye amidst the general confusion of rocky crests, and at least we could see the Gams mountain from any angle.

Along the northern edge of this flat stretch there was a mound with a steep side which made an ideal backing for our new house and there was plenty of building material around: innumerable schist slabs of all sizes. We carried up all the slabs we needed and then we built four walls at right angles to the rock wall, making three rooms open to the south: a bedroom, a living-room and a garage. It was hard work, and quite astonishing how many slabs you needed for even one of those walls because as they were irregular in shape we had to build the walls very thick if they were to hold. When the job was done the skin of our hands was worn and painfully thin. For the roof we brought up the trunks of young ana trees from the gorge; across them we put all the boards we had; and on top of that our dried hides. We also put our tarpaulin over the living-room, in which we proposed to keep the things most in need of protection, such as our radio, paper, drawing materials and books. Then we piled twigs and shrubs on to the roof as an extra protection against the sun.

We began to explore the neighbourhood. We didn't see much game but we did come across the spoor of wild cattle, and there was a small bitter-water source in the Nausgomab about half an hour away from our house. There was no shortage of kindling wood because more bushes and trees grew around these smaller dry rivers than near the bigger ones further out.

One rather oppressive afternoon — Hermann had gone off on his own — I was assembling our wind-generator. It was already twilight when I heard a shot, and immediately afterwards a second. I was rather disturbed because it was almost dark now and there were no stars in the clouded sky. At last I heard stumbling steps and then Hermann came up to the fire. He was panting and out of breath.

'What's the matter? ' I demanded.

He bent down, took an ember from the fire and lit his pipe before answering. 'My number was nearly up that time,' he said.

'How? A leopard?'

'No, a gemsbok. But I got him.'

Then he made himself comfortable at the fire and explained.

'I was sitting on a mound below the Nonnibusch river and watching a couple of otocyon foxes playing in front of their earth. Then whilst I was taking a look round with my glasses a gemsbok appeared and I realised that it would have to cross a game track a little further on. I went down into the valley and climbed up the other side, and as I got my head over the edge I saw that the gemsbok had just passed, but I was so out of breath that he was about forty metres or so away before I managed to get a shot in. I fired from behind at an angle, aiming for the shoulder. He bellowed, leapt into the air, swung round and then came towards me full pelt. His horns were so close to the ground that I could see small stones flying in all directions. I had no time to aim again; almost before I realised what was happening he was on me. I was just able to vault over the ledge. I thought he'd go over the edge and break his neck, but he pulled up short at the last moment and came down upright with his two front legs stretched out in front of him. He was almost across the valley, limping on three legs, before I got another shot in. I could see I'd hit him and a little later he went down. But it was getting dark and I should have to go right up to him to give him the *coup de grâce* so I didn't care to chance it.'

'Well, what are we going to do about it? If he's badly wounded the hyenas will have polished him off by the morning. How are we going to get there in pitch darkness?'

'With the lorry. The place is readily accessible and only a couple of kilometres away.'

It was fortunate that the battery was still in the lorry. Although the narrow slit in our headlights made an unfamiliar neighbourhood seem even stranger, Hermann managed to find the spot after a wild jolting over bushes and broken ground. In the light of our headlights we gave the wounded buck the *coup de grâce* and then spent the night by the lorry sleeping in a zebra hollow. In the morning the clouds broke and rain fell on our faces. The way back in the first light of dawn was easy. It was the one time we were ever able to retrieve a carcass by lorry.

We had decided to build ourselves proper beds, and Hermann thought his gemsbok hide would come in useful, so as soon as we had attended to the meat we started work in the beds. It wasn't easy to find four more or less straight pieces of wood strong enough for the sides, but in the end we found four suitable tamarisk poles. The shorter pieces for the head and foot were easier. We fitted the frames together by notching, and lashed the whole tight with wet strips of gemsbok hide. We then cut from the fresh hide a long thin strip about two centimetres wide; Hermann salted it lightly and then plaited it across his bed frame. When it had dried it was as firm as a spring mattress. There wasn't enough for my bed as well, so I made a sort of network with the rope I had used in my fruitless attack on the bees' nest. But at least I was able to use my bed at once whereas Hermann had to wait for a few days until his hide strip had dried out thoroughly. We put the bed frames on stone supports in our 'bedroom', the head ends against the rock face, and Hermann enlarged a small niche in the rock near the head of his bed to take his pipe and matches.

The furnishing of our living-room was easier. There was a horizontal ledge along the rock face and on this we made a sort of wall cupboard. It took the box with the radio and other boxes with books, drawing materials and spices. Hermann had his place on the west side; mine was on the east. Between us was the wooden chest which served as a table, and the long driving seat of our lorry made a wonderful couch.

We soon found out that our new home, being on the border between the Namib and the uplands, wasn't anything like so well protected from wind as our old cave home on the Carp plateau, and the east and west winds seemed to chase each other here like wild children playing tag. After the first storm we spent the whole afternoon stopping up holes in the walls with small stones. Clay or something of the sort would have been better, but stones and slabs were all the building material nature provided.

We also found that we had to take the wind into consideration when cooking. In the Namib they say that sand scours the stomach. Maybe it does, but it's disagreeable between the teeth, so in the end we made ourselves two hearths; one for the west wind and the other for the east. This arrangement saved us a lot of wood too. Flour, sugar and other perishable supplies were kept as before in the cabin of the lorry, and its tailboard served us as a kitchen table.

At last we were settled in. Fetching water was not so troublesome here as it had been on Carp plateau. But man is never satisfied: amongst our rocky crags we often longed for the broad vistas over the desert we had enjoyed from our cave dwelling.

Start of a Dry Year

Once again the sun crossed the equator to the north on its annual course, and with that the period of rains was definitely over. Now and again in the evening glowing clouds still hovered over the Gams mountain like fairy castles, but they brought no rain of any consequence, though one night water trickled through our inadequate roofing onto our beds, with the result that Hermann's hide-strip mattress began to stink horribly. He had to sleep on the floor until the strips had dried out again.

The sun no longer reached the zenith, but its rays were still extremely hot, as though it intended covering its retreat with a barrage of burning spears, and in the afternoons the bare stretch of red sand gave off such a heat that our living-room often felt like a bake-house. To improve matters we built a low wall before both living-room and bedroom. In this way a sort of 'front garden' was created, and here we set up a stone table. The slab we used for the top was so heavy that when we were dragging it up we nearly dropped it on our toes.

The landscape became very parched now and already towards the end of March the bushes began to lose their leaves. From day to day the specks of green in our barren stony landscape grew scarcer until finally there was nothing left but a few weather-beaten tufts of grass dotting the slopes — and they were more grey than green.

But both zebra and gemsbok were still in good fettle, impressive evidence of their great capacity for adaptation. One day going round a rock I came across a herd of wild cattle, with black and brown spotted cows and calves. They were not more than fifty paces away and as soon as they saw me they lowered their horns and charged. I quickly retreated to the safety of a rocky mound and as they swept by beneath me I could see their pitiful condition, all empty bellies and loose flapping skin over jutting bones.

A few days later Hermann came across the mangled remains of a cow: the backbone, the torn hide and a much-gnawed head. The sand all around was churned up where the hyenas had fought and scrambled over the stricken beast. It wouldn't rain again now for seven or eight months, and only the toughest, wildest and most cunning of those wild cattle would survive. The struggle was pitiless on the edge of the desert.

On another occasion we saw a herd of zebra grazing down a slope where a few old grass tufts were still showing amidst the stones. They kicked the stones away with their hooves and then with their long teeth they seized the tufts as low as possible and dragged them out, roots and all, vigorously shaking out the sand and earth and then crunching up grass and roots between their powerful molars. It shed some light on how zebra managed to survive and keep fit. But of course this was only the beginning of the dry season.

There was a little steenbok in the neighbourhood and it refused to be frightened away by us. It kept out of sight during the day, but in the mornings we would see the marks of its small hooves in the sand, often quite close to our house. Sometimes Otto chased after it in the darkness, but the little steenbok didn't seem unduly disturbed; he just kept out of Otto's way. There were still enough bushes around containing some moisture to satisfy his modest requirements, and we never saw his spoor at the water-hole.

We fetched water only once a week, but then we made several journeys and filled up our water cask. The last man up carefully effaced all our traces between the water-hole and the rocky slope. In this way we hoped to avoid discovery even if someone should happen to come along the river bed in daylight.

No man can become really familiar with a landscape until he's given names to its landmarks, and in any case, naming is essential for communication and identification. 'Otto pass' was the name we gave to the place where Otto had been tossed by the gemsbok. 'Cattle terrace' was the name of a rock platform where we had often noticed wild cattle. And there was 'Artist's mount', from where Hermann had done a water-colour of the wild gramadoela landscape; and 'Dug' was the name of a certain jutting rock which looked like an upturned teat.

In our labyrinth of hillocks we certainly missed the breadth of Carp plateau, and the grand view we had woken up to every morning. We now had to climb the mountain chain to the north to get a good view, but then the landscape was spread out below us like a relief model. It affected us according to our mood. If we saw it with the eyes of fugitives we liked the sudden drop from the uplands with only one difficult track down, and on both sides a wild maze of ridges and ravines, and a chaos of many thousands of deep shadows, and we knew that we were unlikely to be discovered except by a stroke of very bad luck.

But the eyes of scientists were interested in a different aspect. The micaceous schist ridges were broken repeatedly where the heaving earth crust had split open in the geological past. Between the steep mountain chains lay the nineteen-kilometre-wide Kuiseb valley, a landscape all its own. How had that giant rocky trough come into being in the first place? Had it been gouged out by glaciers in a former ice age? Had it been scoured out by the hot, sand-laden winds of the desert? Had a pause in the rise of the land allowed a river to extend its bed so enormously? Only a great mass of energy and more than one radical climatic change could have fashioned such a trough in that tough crystalline rock. In the original valley lay bastions of chalk, bearing witness to a more humid climate and to a period of geological inactivity in which sand and boulders piled up because the fall of the river wasn't steep enough to carry them away to the sea. And there were the twisting canyons and ravines cut deep in the original broad valley as though with a giant knife, signs of a new rise and of a steeper drop towards the coast. And in the distance, beyond the lighter-coloured Namib plains, rode the blue island mountains, and their uniform level told us that they were no more than the vestiges of a still higher land level in the dim past long since broken up. How many drops of water had to fall, and how many grains of sand had to be carried away by the winds before the firm earth crust of a continent was worn away and the debris carried into the sea, leaving only a few upright rocks behind? And during those aeons vulnerable life had obstinately persisted, renewing its youth from generation to generation and developing into ever new and more beautiful forms.

The eyes of the scientists, accustomed to extracting a few valid laws from a great variety of phenomena, recognised that this whole tremendously varied landscape had developed from a conflict between two opposing groups of forces: the mysterious power lying in the earth's centre which had worked for fifty or perhaps a hundred million years steadily lifting the level of a whole continent; and the destructive forces of the sun, the wind and the rains, working equally steadily to wear away and hollow out every altitude, finally destroying it and casting its debris into the sea. How very different is the order of life which rain and sun must serve for its development and enjoyment.

Spiders, Lizards and Snakes

For the moment life in the desert was good to us and to all other beasts of prey. The game made things easier for us than the previous year when the gemsbok had not visited the water-holes regularly until July, but now the grazing was sapless and this compelled gemsbok and springbok to start coming down as early as April. In addition, the water-holes in the Kuiseb valley were dry and naturally they had to concentrate around the few holes still containing water. In consequence it was an easy matter to sit up for them, and easiest of all at the bitter source. About thirty metres above this source was a small cave in the rock where we could sit hidden in the shade and pick out the best animals. Now and again we lay in wait along the game tracks instead and left them in peace at the water-holes, for we didn't want to frighten them away altogether.

Incidentally, a mystery that had been puzzling us was now solved. When we fired from the shade of our hole in the rock the shots always went true to their mark, but when we fired from anywhere in the sun they tended to stray. Obviously the hot sun beating down on the pistol barrel caused a certain amount of distortion, so we now covered the barrel with sticky tape and had a weapon which was reliable at all times.

As we had no great difficulty in providing ourselves with food we had plenty of time for study and observation. The first time we walked over our stretch of red sand we noticed strange markings in it. The impressions were like a four-leaved clover and about as big as the ring you can make with thumb and forefinger. They lay behind each other like the spoor of an animal, but then suddenly they would disappear altogether. And we knew of no animal which made such marks. We had a good many guesses, and finally Hermann provided us with a working hypothesis: 'It can only be the trail of the excessively rare feathered water waddler. It never shows itself in daylight because it feels ashamed when the other birds laugh at its silly feet. It nests in inaccessible rock crevices and feeds exclusively on fudge and fiddlesticks. On account of its weak understanding it can take only two or three steps at a time.'

'Well, at least that seems to cover all the available facts.' I agreed.

During the day the wind effaced the mysterious traces, but every morning they were there again, and despite Hermann's spoof solution we were still keenly interested in the explanation of the mystery. It came in the end.

Near our house was a nest of black ants, and radiating in all directions from it were well-worn tracks to places where food was to be obtained, including of course our kitchen. From sunup to sundown the ants went busily backwards and forwards along these tracks like human beings along the streets of a busy town. In addition to the worker ants, which were quite small, there were two distinct types of soldier ant, both of them considerably bigger, and one of them about three times the size of the worker ant and having an unusually large head and powerful mandibles.

One morning just as the early rays of the sun lay at an angle over the sand showing up every irregularity, I noticed a fresh spoor of our feathered water waddler. As I was looking at it an ant slid down a declivity in the sand and went half-over the edge of the four-leaved clover-shaped depression in the sand. For some reason the ant seemed unable to recover, and it remained there wriggling. I knelt down to take a closer look and then I noticed that it was held by a very fine almost unnoticeable web which ran round the depression and appeared to be sticky. Suddenly as I watched there was a movement underneath the sand, a funnel-shaped hole appeared, the sticky web bent downwards and, wriggling and struggling vainly, the ant was carried down into the funnel of sand and engulfed.

I called Hermann over and in an experimental mood we pushed another ant into the depression, and exactly the same thing happened. Then we carefully dug up the whole four-leaved clover and found that it consisted of a felt-like web, and as we lifted it up something disappeared like lightning into a slanting hole at the point where would have been the stalk in a real clover, and uncovering this hole we found a small red spider.

It was an astonishing example of ingenuity, combining the normal web of the spider with the behaviour of the lion-ant. The spider, which would not have dared to expose itself openly to the bite of the ant's powerful mandibles, kept safely out of the way in the sand under the web until it had trussed its victim. So much for Hermann's feathered water waddler.

Grass-cutting termites had built themselves a nest amidst the rubble of the hillside. What dry grass they could find they cut into two centimetre-long pieces and carried them into their nest. They too seemed to prefer the neighbourhood of our house; perhaps because we had used tufts of old grass to cover the roof so that a good many dried blades of grass lay around. Unlike other termites, these grass-cutters worked quite openly and didn't bother about the usual earth protection, and on windy days they were hard at work all the time. Like all termites they had soft, white bodies and only their heads were armoured.

One morning coming back to the house from some errand I saw Hermann lying on his belly studying them. He beckoned to me: 'Take a look at that grey ball,' he said, pointing to it with a stem of grass. It looked very much like a grain of sand, and it was much smaller than the termites, which took no notice of it and busily went on cutting grass. One of them happened to come close to the little grey ball, which suddenly was seen to have legs; it darted towards the ant which had ventured too close, swiftly stabbed its proboscis into the soft rear part of the termite and withdrew. The termite went on for a few steps, then stopped and fell trembling onto its side. Nothing happened until the trembling ceased and then the attacker approached again, inserted its proboscis into the termite's body and began to suck.

We watched this several times and discovered that the murderous little ball was actually a small spider whose jaws had developed into a harpoon-like proboscis. It disposed of the termites with such a sudden and deadly attack that they had no time to defend themselves, although with one snap of their powerful jaws they could have killed their assailant easily.

And once again came the question: how could such fantastic adaptations have come about? What force was it which gave living matter such rich variety whereas all chemical and physical phenomena declined from a higher to a progressively lower degree of energy? Did it lie only in the complicated structure of albumen? Was the interlocking operation of mutations and ruthless natural selection enough to account for all the vast and manifold developments of life? We were life and part of life, related to all its various forms around us, and we too were engaged in a fierce and pitiless struggle to survive. What gave us the capacity to wage it? Primarily it was the will to live; a will which refused to surrender to pain, and which forced the flagging body on long after it was exhausted. But was that will perhaps only an illusion of consciousness? Was it perhaps only the expression of the strongest chemical phenomenon in our body? Could you speak of a will to live in animals which lived without that same consciousness? There seemed no solution of the problem from this angle.

Indisputably the struggle to survive played a decisive role in evolution; it ruthlessly extirpated the unfit, and that necessarily guided developments into certain channels. But surely that was too negative a process? Could anything positive come of it? Hadn't we ourselves concluded only a little while ago that man owed a good deal of his development to the fact that much of it took place during childhood, when he was protected and sheltered from the ordinary struggle to survive? On the other hand, we had seen enough to convince us that any development which was not checked and controlled by that struggle must quickly lead to degeneration and extinction. There were contradictions whichever way you turned.

Nevertheless, the more we studied the problem the less likely it seemed that any purely mechanical explanation could be adequate. As it was, everything remained a question of probabilities and we were not satisfied with that; we felt certain that there must be a better solution. It probably stared us in the face — and yet mockingly eluded us.

Our home was now becoming steadily more com-

214

fortable; for example, the bare stone walls were being progressively covered with beautifully marked springbok hides. Now and again the flies became a pest, but that was because there were always bits of meat or bones lying around — Otto had his feeding place next to the garage. We were therefore delighted when a number of lizards took up residence in our thick walls; and the swift and neat way in which such a small dragon made short shrift of a fat blow-fly decided us to encourage the settlement. We caught lizards in the neighbourhood and slipped them into crevices in our walls, where they soon seemed to feel quite at home. Amongst them was a very attractive little fellow in grey with a red tail *(Eremias)* who would rear up and wave his forelegs about in the air. Unfortunately, however, he had cannibalistic leanings and we once saw him swallow a smaller lizard whole. Another type was a fellow with four long brown and grey stripes down his back *(Mabuja)*. The biggest lizard of all, of which we had only one specimen, had beautiful bronze scales all over his body. We soon began to call him 'Phillip' because he was every bit as saucy as an ill-fated mouse we had so named in our previous home.

Under a rock above our house lived a pair of big rock lizards, or *Agamidae,* with blue, red and violet bodies and reddish tails. They were about forty centimetres long and they looked like real fairy-tale dragons. They ran very fast on short legs like a dachshund and they were excellent jumpers. I saw one of the two jump from scratch up onto a rock more than a metre high.

A couple of geckos, a lizard of the *Gekonnidae* family, had also made their home in one of our walls. They had big heads and large prominent eyes like opals, and on their bodies were gleaming blue spots.

215

We were particularly fond of them, but it wasn't often they were to be seen in daylight.

One day we got the idea of feeding our lizards and so we caught flies, pulled out one wing and flung them down for food. It wasn't long before the lizards had grasped the idea and after that they watched our every movement. Next we held out the wriggling flies in our fingers and the lizards would make a few quick steps forward, and with a swish of the tongue the fly was gone. Now we began to whistle every time we gave them flies, and after that we only had to whistle and lizard heads popped out of our wall everywhere. Then we went a step further; we offered them dead flies, which up to then, as far as we could see, they had never touched, but they took them all the same. One day we offered Phillip quite a sizeable piece of gemsbok liver and he took it and swallowed it without hesitation. After that he was missing for three days — sleeping off his gluttony perhaps.

One or two dwarf mice also put in an appearance, and a yellow snake, apparently finding plenty of food in our neighbourhood, settled down in one of the walls. We weren't so pleased about this, having seen a dog bitten by a similar snake die in agony. And we were even less pleased when we came across him on warm days taking a nap on one or other of our beds. We tried to catch him, but we didn't succeed; at the least movement he disappeared into the wall like a flash. Then we tried to drive him out with smoke, but that didn't work either and we came to the conclusion that the hole in the wall went right through into the rock face beyond. We could have shot him of course, but we were loath to waste a bullet; we wanted meat and plenty of it for our bullets, not the wretched carcass of an uninvited snake.

After about three weeks it was again my turn to

216

go down to the bitter-water source and bag a spring-bok and I returned with it about midday — we had since learned the knack of carrying such a beast over our shoulders easily. I was just about to throw it down onto our stone table as usual when Hermann exclaimed: 'Careful! You'll send my most valued patient to kingdom come.' And then I noticed one of our little geckos lying on the table and looking rather dead.

'I was painting,' Hermann explained, 'and there were termites around near the wall. Our friend here came out of the wall to eat them, and I was just marvelling at what a healthy appetite he had when I looked again and there was that wretched snake just about to swallow him. By the time I sprang up the snake had got him and was gone. It made me so wild I got the shot-gun and that old cartridge that would not fit in the chamber, and I scraped it down with my pocket-knife until it did. Then I loaded and put the gun down ready on the table and went on painting. After about an hour that snake stuck its head out of the wall again and that was that. I fired and blew its head off, and its body wriggled out of the hole and fell on the floor. I carefully slit it up with a knife and extracted our gecko. He seemed dead, but I washed him and put him in the sun, and I think he's getting over it. He's able to move a bit, which is more than he could just now.'

Hermann was quite right; the gecko did raise its head a little now and again. That evening he crawled back with some difficulty into his hole in the wall. The following day he appeared again as lively as ever, but he was blind; we could waggle a finger right in front of his nose and he never noticed a thing. The digestive acids of that snake had robbed him of his sight, but three days later he shed his skin and after

217

that he could see again.

'If I'm ever in trouble I'd like to be as lucky as that,' said Hermann.

The Beginning of Winter

Every evening the bright stars of Orion's belt now hung in the west over the Namib. At the beginning of the hot weather they had sparkled over the uplands in the east. The winds blew almost exclusively according to the planetary change from day to night. Soon after sun-up the east wind began to blow from over the uplands. Towards midday it dropped, and then the warm surface of the land drew in cooler air from the west. Once the sun had gone down there was no wind at all and the starry night was quite still.

After a number of warm days the west wind didn't drop towards evening but swung round across the south-west almost due south. When the sun had disappeared beneath the horizon the reddish glow that remained gradually turned into a cold glassy green, and we knew that the first influx of cold air had begun, so we brought our pullovers out from under the beds. The next morning the east wind was blowing strongly, and it boomed and whistled all day long. We made a note of the date in our weather book because we remembered from the previous year that those cold-air influxes would now arrive regularly at monthly intervals.

More and more animals were coming down to water, and even the zebra began to drink during the day, probably because the long journey from their distant grazing spots couldn't be done in a night. It was always fascinating to watch the various animals at close quarters, and again and again we were amazed at their inability to recognise us as a danger at even a few metres distance, provided we sat quite still.

When some slight movement engaged its attention an animal would often raise its head and look straight at us into the pistol barrel without any feeling of impending danger. I always expected it to take fright and gallop off, but no, it would lower its head and continue drinking or just move slowly off. We used to wonder whether an antelope would also fail to recognise a leopard ready to spring as long as it kept still.

The sound of a shot didn't upset them much. They would throw up their heads perhaps and trot off a little way, but if nothing further happened they would soon have forgotten all about it. That wasn't as astonishing as it may seem because very, very few of them had ever had to associate disagreeable happenings with such bursts. Perhaps more extraordinary was the fact that the death of one of their kind didn't seem to disturb them in the least. When one antelope dropped with a bullet in the head the others would just go on drinking as soon as they had recovered from the shock of the sound. They seemed to have no conception or instinctive awareness of death. Of course we didn't show ourselves as long as any of them were in sight, because we didn't want to scare them away from the water source.

But they behaved quite differently as soon as they caught the slightest scent. We had to cross the river bed to get to our ambush on the other side near the bitter source, and we always did so above the source because most of the animals came from below. One day it was my turn to do the shooting and I was taking up my position when three gemsbok came down the river bed from above. The leader stopped and hesitated as soon as he came to my imprint. Then he raised his head and looked around suspiciously and I could see his ears beginning to flick. The others noticed that something was wrong, and they caught his nervousness and misgiving and prepared to flee. With one accord they went back about a couple of hundred metres or so and stood quite still. After about twenty minutes they came forward again. But when they reached my spoor they stopped, hesitated and turned back once more. At the next attempt the leader followed my trail, lowering his muzzle to the ground as though he were a dog, and moving at a tangent across the river bed. When he came to the end of the trail in the sand he even went a few steps beyond it, then stopped and turned back. This happened several times, and the indecision was clearly the result of an inward struggle between fear and thirst. The other two stood and watched, seeming to rely completely on their leader. In the end caution won the day and they all retreated to the shade of an ana tree where they waited for a couple of hours before finally trotting off.

The fact was that this conscious self-control, or whatever you cared to call it, had saved a gembok's life. Later on the leader of a herd of springbok found himself in a somewhat similar situation, but he hadn't so much self-control — or he was thirstier. After long hesitation he came down to the water, and he ended in our pot.

We never had to bother about clearing away the offal of animals we cut up. It was disposed of either by vultures during the day or by hyenas or jackals at night. At home of course the bits and pieces belonged to Otto, and he used to bury the surplus until it was really 'high', always taking the greatest precautions that we didn't see where the precious spot was.

After a while a shrike, with brown and white markings and a cruel head, discovered that the neighbourhood of our house was highly advantageous. He would steal small pieces of meat from Otto's feeding quarters and spike them onto a parkinsonian bush as a reserve store. Otto didn't seem to mind. One day — we had a hide pegged out on the sand to dry — vultures were circling around rather low, and we got the idea of throwing out bits of food in order to accustom them to us so that we could take photographs. We had hardly put out a few pieces and gone back to the house when dark shadows moved swiftly across the sand, and there was a flapping of huge wings as three vultures pounced on the pieces and were away again. Otto observed the process with disapproval.

The next day when we went up on the hill again and scattered pieces for the vultures Otto immediately seized as many as he could and carted them back again, growling at us every few steps. Down below he dropped the meat in his own feeding place, and when we began to laugh he placed himself a-straddle across it. Only when we had stopped laughing and he felt sure we would let him keep the meat would he wag his tail again. Then he followed us into the house without having eaten any of the meat. He was obviously so upset and indignant at what he considered a disregard of his right to all the bits and pieces that we could no longer bring ourselves to lay out any for the vultures.

Otto's behaviour in this matter was strangely 'human', and in fact the longer we lived with animals the clearer it became to us that human and animal behaviour were very closely related. It is quite true that again and again we were faced with that automatic instinctive animal reaction which is so foreign to us, but this was only an adaptation to certain conditions of life, a process which in certain circumstances made the invariably dangerous method of learning by experience unnecessary, or greatly simplified it. As an adaptation to a narrow way of life instinctive reaction could only be something secondary imposed on an originally adaptable and more versatile being. Out of many possibilities one would be chosen in preference to others and then developed to automatic perfection and incorporated in an animal's physical structure. Whatever of it may once have been present was effaced by the long childhood of the human species, and in this way the original human being remained fully capable of development, whereas with animals the common basis became visible only when their instincts were no longer in play.

One day Hermann returned from one of his many trips with his sketch-book: 'I saw the Joseph of springboks today,' he declared with a chuckle. 'His brothers had cast him out. At first there was a whole herd of springbok but when they had gone a single creature came up the river bed. I thought it was a wild dog, but the gait was different, and the nearer the creature came the more puzzled I was. It turned out to be a young springbok, not more than six months old, but a misbegotten one. Its face was almost black, its chest was crooked and it had bandy legs. His companions had obviously ejected him from the herd on account of his strange appearance, and he hobbled up to the water like a crippled child. When he had drunk he began to play around on his own, jumping about in the mud until he was spotted like a leopard. It was really quite touching and I would have loved to stroke him. I've christened him "Joseph". He'd make a nice pet.'

Hierarchy of the Wilderness

It was June now and Orion was no longer to be seen; Scorpio dominated the long cold nights. When the monthly influx of cold air arrived we would sit during the day wrapped up in blankets to keep ourselves warm, and the east wind blew so persistently that our battery was always fully charged. In fact we could even afford to have a light in our living-room and Hermann made us a lampshade. We could now read or write after dark. Two evenings a week we enjoyed excellent symphony concerts from Cape Town, and when accompanied by succulent antelope meat life was quite agreeable.

Then one morning the music was interrupted for an announcement that German troops had invaded Russia. 'He seems to have forgotten Napoleon,' said Hermann slowly. After that we listened religiously to the news broadcasts twice a day. We followed the swift advance of the German armies, the development of great battles, and the whole fascinating operation of that vast war machine as it rolled deeper and deeper into Russia. We found it difficult not to let ourselves be swept away in the general frenzy, although we knew very well the mass misery and suffering behind the news.

In the meantime our own particular trouble was lack of water. The levels of our water-hole sank slowly but inexorably, and the antelope, which usually put a bit of fat on in winter, remained thin. Only the zebra still looked fit and well and as though they lacked nothing. We tried to shoot one but the bullet glanced off the hard slanting horselike skull. The animal fell and seemed dazed for a moment or two, then scrambled to its feet and clattered off in a cloud of dust. The next time we picked out a young one, and we got him, but there was no fat on the carcass. The wild cattle looked so pitiful that we didn't bother about them at all.

We had our hunting expeditions well organised now. From the hill behind our house we could see over the rocks to our ambush. If one of us was sitting up there and had shot a gemsbok he would spread out a white cloth, which was clearly visible from the house, and the other would then go down to help in the job of skinning, cutting up and transporting the meat back to the house.

One morning before sunrise I was sitting up as usual when I heard the crunching of gravel followed by a loud smacking of wet chops. A horribly ugly hyena was at the pool. After drinking it licked its forepaws and then trotted off along the game track which led down the river bed. I was following it with my eyes when I noticed a leopard coming along the same track but from the other direction. The two animals came closer and neither gave any indication that it had spotted the other. The leopard's fur was ruffled and it slunk forward like a big cat towards the hyena, whose high shoulders and great head with its enormous jaws made it the taller. The two animals were quite close to each other but still neither of them made any attempt to give way.

When they were not more than five paces apart they both stopped and looked at each other for the first time, standing motionless for several seconds, apparently weighing each other up. Then the leopard gave a low growl, and at that the hyena turned sideways, backed off the game path and sat down on its haunches like a dog. The leopard then stalked past

225

silently like a great lady after a short and triumphant exchange with a rival, going not towards the water, but up the northern side of the slope. The hyena sat there and watched its rival depart, and when the leopard was about two hundred metres away the hyena gave vent to its wounded feelings in a long drawn-out cackle. The leopard didn't even bother to look round. The incident was grotesque, a caricature of human behaviour, and it struck me that the 'all too human' behaviour of men was in reality 'all too animal'.

Coming back with a springbok one day Hermann left his field-glasses behind in our ambush. There seemed no great harm in that; no one but ourselves was likely to go there. It was three days before he went to fetch them. He was gone a long time and when he returned he laid the component parts on the table silently.

'When I got down to the river bed,' Hermann said, 'I saw the solitary tracks of a big baboon, and I felt a certain misgiving. How right I was! He had poked around in our ambush and my glasses were gone. I began to search and about two hundred yards down the bed I found a lens on a rock slab, and as I went further I discovered the other pieces one by one. Everything you could unscrew was unscrewed. The fellow must have been at it for hours. He just chewed off the leather covering. Unfortunately there's one eye-piece missing. Maybe that baboon's wearing it as a monocle.'

Hermann reassembled his field-glasses, but owing to the missing eye-piece he could use it only as a monocular now, which was a great nuisance, because the vastness of the area made it necessary to use our glasses constantly. However, about two weeks later he was lucky enough to come across the missing eye-piece.

'I was going down to the water, and nothing was further from my mind, particularly as all the other bits and pieces had been much lower down. But once I had got beyond the ana tree I had an odd sort of feeling that I ought to go over to the other side of the river-bed. I hadn't quite got there when I saw something glint in the sand. I bent down to see what it was — and it was the missing eye-piece. It's a bit scratched, because the wind's had ten days to scour it with sand, but it's much better than nothing all the same.'

What had drawn Hermann over to that spot where the missing eye-piece lay? Was there some secret telepathic force at work? We remembered the frogs and we thought of the almost incredible feats of messenger pigeons. How did they find their way back to their lofts, often hundreds of kilometres away? It isn't satisfactorily explained by assuming the possession of some mysterious sense of direction, because what's the good of knowing where north is when you don't know where you are? And how does a seal find its way through changing wind and tides to an isolated island in the sea?

All these and similar questions to which we could find no satisfactory answers confirmed our feeling that no purely mechanistic interpretation, and in general no interpretation which assumed that a living being was only a complicated physio-chemical machine, was adequate — and that applied not only to human beings, but to life as a whole. So far so good, but where was the proof that there was a power superior to chemical and physical phenomena? We tackled the problem first from one angle and then from the other, but we made no progress. It was quite true that many of the almost incredible perfor-

227

mances of animals and plants could be adequately explained by highly developed and perfected chemical and physical reactions operating entirely within material limits, but the fact remained that day after day our life on the edge of the desert demonstrated the fundamental difference between living and non-living matter.

One evening Hermann raised the subject once more: 'Why does evolution only suggest that the problem of life can't be satisfactorily solved on a purely materialistic basis? Why doesn't it provide us with some proof? Perhaps there is no absolute proof,' he continued, 'because the accident of arbitrary mutation is embodied in evolution. Where chance is a condition of the experiment you can't demand a definite result. Chance is innate in the generational change. To avoid chance and thus the calculus of probability there would have to be evolution without either birth or death.'

Suddenly the solution dawned on me.

'You said that if there were evolution without generational changes,' I began. 'But there is such a development where the individual man or animal is concerned. Every human being and every animal develops during the course of its life.'

'True enough,' admitted Hermann, 'but can you prove that that evolution isn't purely mechanically determined by the interplay of heredity and environment?'

'Yes, I think so. Take our lizards, for example. In just three days they learnt that a whistle meant food. The utmost their predecessors can have learned is that a buzzing noise indicated the approach of a fly. But the introduction of a connection between a whistle and the feeding reaction of the lizard required a readjustment and an extension of inherited charac-

228

teristics. And such a readjustment and extension is what we call development, and in this case it was certainly no question of a mutation.

'And such readjustments happen constantly. In the Stone Age there was a man who was the first ever to trace the outline of an antelope in the sand. In doing so he was not only using one part of his body in a way it had never been used before, but he was deliberately creating something entirely new, to wit, a picture. Before that no such thing as a picture had ever existed — not even as an idea. Thus life was not merely able to adapt itself to its surroundings, but it could create new things and give old things a new significance. And for this neither a generational change with accompanying mutations nor any natural selection in the struggle to survive was required.

'Now that certainly fits in with the conclusions we have already drawn regarding human evolution. We decided that it was precisely the protection of children from the struggle to survive which favoured learning and new developments. But where any form of animal life is subjected too intensely to the struggle to survive we find narrow physical adaptations and rigid instinctive reactions which make further development impossible. Darwin was quite right when he said that the struggle for existence with the consequent survival of the fittest was responsible for adaptation in the animal kingdom. But as most adaptations hamper the capacity for further development their influence on life in general is negative, which is, after all, precisely what you would expect from a force operating primarily through destruction. Everything which is narrowly adapted to certain conditions are constantly changing. But where does that lead us? Above all it explodes all those wretched arguments which try to justify war and brutality on the ground that a ruthless struggle for survival furthers development. It furthers certain developments, but it drives them into a blind alley and leads ultimately to extinction.

'In other words, the feeling which revolted against such an idea was right, which isn't so very surprising because feeling is a judgement based on life as a whole whereas consciousness and understanding are newly acquired and not as yet highly developed faculties.'

The next morning I was up early and from a hill top I watched the sun rise over the mountains. Turning my eyes from the bright horizon I spotted a group of gemsbok on a bare patch of ground below me. They were certainly wonderfully vital animals, and the early morning light clearly modelled the rippling muscles under their shining skin and their long horns glistened like burnished swords.

When I got back Hermann had cooked a sort of sweet omelette with currants, but without eggs, for breakfast, and hot coffee sent little clouds of exhilirating aroma into the cool air. From the radio came the powerful chords of a Beethoven symphony, but you might have thought it emanated from the wild and broken landscape all around.

Later on we reverted to the subject which had occupied us the previous evening. We had seen that individual animals could develop during their lives without the benefit of mutation or natural selection. What was the basis of this marvellous capacity? What was learning? What was experience? A simple example occurred to me: I am thirsty and therefore I go to drink; but then I discover that the water is salty. This is an experience not easily forgotten, and with it goes naturally a picture of a water-hole with salt-encrusted edges. If that experience is repeated a few times I soon draw the conclusion that a salt-encrusted edge means that the water in the pool is salty, so the next time I see it I pass the pool even if I am thirsty. In other words, I have learned from experience. Some kind of memory seems to be one of the basic attributes of life — even unicellular beings possess a certain capacity to learn from experience. How is a conclusion drawn?

Is it true that every conclusion is based on some requirement, thirst for example? It would seem so, since it can change as the requirement changes. Water is something good when I am thirsty and can drink it, but something bad when I fall into it and am in danger of drowning. Doesn't this classification of experiences into 'good' or 'bad' determine the conclusion we draw? Thus learning is something more than a process of association, that is to say the interlinking of successive happenings in our memory; it is closely connected with relative values and our judgement of values.

This seemed to be an important realisation which raised learning above all purely physical phenomena, for good and bad are not physical qualities even when they apply to physical things. And we could now link up this conclusion with some earlier ideas of ours when we decided that every feeling, even the simplest such as the perception of pain, involved a passing of judgement. Doesn't every feeling judge an experience in relation to a need? For example, the disappointment of a thirsty man when he finds that the water he wants to drink is salty. Or the feeling of relief a man experiences in the cool shade of a hillside out of the burning sun. Could one in fact go further and say that need was first made conscious by feeling?

More and more ideas developed. Was the capacity to pass judgement a spiritual attribute? If it were then

231

a spiritual force was at work in all feelings, even the simplest. But was the expression 'force' an appropriate one in this connection? Probably it was, because a feeling sent electrical impulses through the nervous system to set muscles into movement; in other words, it produced effects which could be produced only by forces in the strictly physical sense of the word. But the decisive thing was nevertheless that these forces were guided by judgements based on feeling. But feeling considered as a judgement does not necessarily run parallel with physical phenomena; it can run counter to them; it can approve or disapprove — in other words, it is superior to physical phenomena.

I had often asked myself whether life in all its multifarious forms was merely a strange accident in world evolution, and now I felt that I had obtained proof that it was nothing of the sort: life was raised above the phenomena of the inanimate world precisely by feeling. Here then was something truly remarkable: a force which determined values, something non-material, and guided physical phenomena through them. It was thus a force of a higher order, and by establishing values it broke through the rigid framework of purely physical phenomena.

Each value would have to be measured in terms of the force which passed judgement and created all values. Forms of life which were seen to allow this force the greatest latitude and afford it the greatest possibilities of development would necessarily be the most vital and the most valuable. And conversely, those forms of life which were seen to be bogged down in mechanistic adaptations would be the inferior, the less valuable. It was immediately obvious of course that those forms most successful in the struggle for survival need not necessarily be the most valuable. There were many examples in the history of life to show that precisely the most perfectly adapted, the physically biggest and strongest, the most numerous creatures, the lords of whole periods of life, died out in the end with monotonous regularity leaving the torch of life to be carried forward by smaller, more modest and often previously almost unnoticed forms of life, until they too fell into the trap of all too perfect adaptation. The museum show-cases were full of the fossilised remains of once powerful and highly adapted forms of life which had nevertheless died out.

These considerations gave rise to one burning question which was now given point by the radio reports of the fierce fighting in Russia: was the human being the next candidate for the museum show-case? But our happy recognition that the development of life was being guided not by sheer chance, but by a non-material force, inspired us with hope that in the end humanity would be able to escape from the compulsion of suicidal wars. Could there have seemed a more forlorn but gallant hope in the year 1941?

Our bare feet had traced two parallel paths in the red sand, and we were exhausted; our stomachs were rumbling and our midday meal was only a memory. We ate a large piece of gemsbok meat, caught flies for our lizards and browsed in the already ten-times-read books of our small library.

Fats Grow Scarce

The water level in our drinking hole continued to sink, thus widening the stretch of sand we had to cross when fetching water. It was therefore no longer easy to efface our tracks so that the result looked natural. In view of the proximity of the farm this was unfortunate, because at any time someone could come down the river-bed in daylight in search of honey. Somehow or other we should have to disguise our traces if we were to feel safe.

We cut old tyre rubber into shapes of gemsbok and zebra hoofs and nailed them onto a pair of discarded shoes. The resulting spoors were not quite true to nature, but amidst the many spoors at a water-hole they were good enough to escape detection, so from now on we always wore these shoes when we went to fetch water.

But as soon as one problem was solved another arose. Our fat supplies were running short. For weeks, apart from a very little marrow fat, none of the animals we had shot had provided us with any. And what would happen in the next few months when they would become even leaner? Our observations and experience seemed to indicate that gemsbok in calf were a bit plumper than the others, probably because nature stored up a little fat to serve them during the lactation period.

For three days I sat up with our shot-gun and one of our home-made bullets at a water-hole visited by gemsbok. Group after group of gemsbok and zebra filed past me at a distance of ten or twenty paces, but not a single cow seemed to be near calving time.

Finally however, three female gemsbok approached and one of them was obviously in calf and she was picking her way along the twisting and turning game track rather awkwardly. For some time they stood at the foot of the slope and looked around cautiously. Did they notice anything strange about the ana tree in whose roots I was hiding? Flies were crawling over my nose, eyes and ears and for about a quarter of an hour I heroically resisted the temptation to brush them away. Then the three cows came forward and I slowly raised my shot-gun. The sound of the shot reverberated like thunder and the three animals reared, swung around and galloped off.

But the one I had aimed at didn't get far; the shot had penetrated the shoulder blade and she could not clamber up the rocky slope. She tried once or twice and then stood helplessly looking round. The other two stopped a little higher up the slope and waited for her, and then went on.

I was wondering why the stricken cow hadn't collapsed long ago, because those home-made bullets of ours made dreadful wounds. She now turned back towards the river bed, going slowly forward on trembling legs. As she came closer I could see that my aim had been bad. The shot was too low; it had missed the heart and probably entered the lower part of the lung. The cow went slowly up river and stopped between two ana trees.

I dared not show myself for fear the poor brute still had strength enough to escape, and it was a disagreeable wait. After about an hour she lay down. It was pitiful to watch her, and I would willingly have given her the *coup de grâce* although we now had to think twice before we used a bullet, but I couldn't get near her unobserved because she was lying with her back into the wind, so if I made a detour to get behind her she would scent me, whilst if I went into the wind towards her she would see me. Was it instinct that made her take up that position? Or had she learned by experience that she should always look in the direction from which no scent could come?

Another wretched eternity passed with slowly moving shadows and the buzz of irritating flies, and then her horns gradually sank down into the sand. I made my way towards her cautiously now and as I advanced her rump twitched for the last time and she lay still.

The first cut into her paunch revealed wonderful white layers of fat. And then came the little calf ready to be born — and that was a sad sight. There was already milk in the udder and the intestines were quite empty. She had probably gone down to drink for the last time before calving.

I drank the milk from the udder and then I carefully removed every scrap of fat. When I got back to the house with my first load I found a gemsbok haunch on the lorry tailboard and on the table a message from Hermann; he had shot a fat cow at the bitter source and asked me to come and help him. This was too much of a good thing, and each of us now had to haul his own gemsbok home. It was long past nightfall when we finally got our loads back and we were dead tired.

We were as delighted with our new riches of fat as children with an unexpected present, and to celebrate our success we decided to bake an apple-turnover with dried fruit, cinnamon and cloves.

After that we shot two more gemsbok cows in calf and obtained more fat, but then the calving period passed and the cows which were suckling were even leaner than the other animals. Once when returning from a reconnaissance through the more desolate part of the gramadoelas I was striding along lost in thought and paying no attention to Otto who was with me, when suddenly I heard a pitiful sound overlaid by Otto's growling. Looking up I saw that Otto had seized a new-born calf and was shaking it excitedly. I shouted and rushed up to save the poor little beast, which Otto had found under a bush, but I was too late. The mother had probably gone down to the pool to drink. I remembered the needle-sharp horns of the gemsbok, and as I was unarmed I put Otto on the lead and dragged him off hurriedly. Otto couldn't understand why he wasn't allowed to eat his prey, but I had no wish to be anywhere near the spot when the mother returned.

Steadily our world grew more parched and desolate. Sometimes we asked ourselves whether cruelty was an essential ingredient of life. Wherever you looked life seemed the enemy of life. In our own case the growing dryness intensified the struggle for survival and made it more ruthless; and we ourselves had to be more ruthless if we did not want to perish.

Again and again we were confronted with the ridiculous inadequacy of any attempt to explain the whole of development merely through natural selection in the struggle for survival. In a hostile environment development was impossible without a struggle, but if natural selection in that struggle were the only active force how could there ever have been any striving towards beauty, friendship and peace. And yet this striving, which cannot be reconciled with the laws governing the struggle for survival, exists even in the animal world.

For example, in New Guinea there is a bird which builds a real little house of twigs when it goes courting. And in front of this little house it makes a sort of garden which it decorates with bright flowers, pretty feathers and beautiful shells. When everything is ready it performs its courtship dance in this little garden, picking up with its beak, as though in pride and satisfaction, the little treasures it has collected there. It is not a particularly beautiful or striking bird but it happens to be a distant relation of the bird of paradise, whose courtship display is so superb. Thus it would seem that the urge towards beauty is very highly developed in this particular bird family. And what I always find a most remarkable thing is that the sense of beauty in birds is so closely related to the sense of beauty in human beings.

Friendship also exists in the animal world, and no one who has had anything to do with animals for any length of time can have failed to witness examples of it. But how would such things be possible if life were controlled only by the harsh struggle for survival?

And I mentioned peace — how could even the conception develop in a world of struggle? We could just as well ask ourselves how a permanently hungry man could conceive of the idea of satiety? How could the conception of timelessness develop out of time? In other words, how could it come about that life had an urge towards something non-existent?

This miracle is implicit in the capacity of living things to feel and judge. All pairs of opposites developed from the original pair: pain and pleasure. Pain, the basic experience of the capacity to judge, impelled a search for something non-existent. The opposite fundamental experiences of life, pain and pleasure, gave life the possibility of seeking an opposite to every state and every conception. And this realisation now shone like a bright jewel over our harsh and barren world. Suddenly we were able to understand how life could strive for the impossible, how human beings could toil persistently towards the impossible, and how we ourselves, although engaged in a ruthless struggle to survive, could still love our fellow creatures. And how often life has persisted obstinately until the seemingly impossible has been made possible! Blessed be the ridiculed who strive with determination to achieve the impossible. They are the ones who carry forward the banner of life, theirs is the privilege to reach for the skies.

And we realised another thing too: when life becomes rigidly instinctive, when it is compelled to make narrow physical adaptations, the creative capacity to judge and operate with opposites becomes lost, and that particular form of life inevitably becomes ripe for extinction.

And what about man? In a laborious and dangerous life not guided exclusively by instinct he has preserved and developed his capacity to judge and to learn from experience, and he had therefore succeeded in emerging from the merely animal world. The power to judge has achieved its highest expression in him. Could this truth provide us with a yard-stick for judging human institutions and human behaviour?

Undoubtedly it could! Everything is evil which tends to rob man of his capacity to judge and to compel him to any kind of uniform instinctive behaviour, and such a tendency must inevitably lead to his extinction as shown by all the other extinct forms of life. And isn't it crystal clear that mass propaganda, cunning advertisement, mass parades and mass meetings are specifically the influences which tend to push man in that direction?

We went up to the hill behind our house as the twilight rose out of the gorges behind us and a purple glow enveloped the summit of the Gams mountain. The green and gold window of evening closed in the west and we knew that there would be frost on the

239

uplands during the night, and that tomorrow the
east wind would be roaring among the rocks.

Man's Peril

During all the months Hermann and I had lived together, sharing hard work and short commons, joy
and thought, there had never been any serious quarrel
between us or any really harsh words. But now we
began to get on each other's nerves. At first it was no
more than pin-pricks, but it grew worse. 'We'll have
to build a roof over the veranda before the sun gets
too hot,' Hermann said one morning.

'There's plenty of time,' I replied. 'And then, it's
not at all certain we'll be able to stay here anyway.
The water isn't going to last much longer.'

My objections irritated Hermann and he lost his
temper, and before we knew we were at it hammer
and tongs, calling each other disagreeable names.
When it was all over we grinned sheepishly, but the
atmosphere remained strained.

We had both known this was bound to happen one
day, and we had long ago decided that when it did
we would separate for a while. I therefore determined
to go off on my own at once and see if I could get
some good photographs of animals at what we called
Crow's water source. I packed up my bread ration, a
leg of springbok, a little dried fruit and my sleeping-
bag, and off I went with my rucksack on my back. It
was about eleven o'clock at night when I left and the
moon had just risen. In its light I made my way along
age-old game tracks, through gorges and over hills
and ridges.

The night was as still as a church, a web of feathery
clouds moved across the face of the moon, and the
dust of the storm still lay over the jagged mountain

tops like thin silver smoke.

The Crow's source lay in a barren gorge between almost vertical canyon walls and when after a few hours tramping I made my way cautiously down the natural rock steps into the valley I suddenly heard a low growling. I stopped and held my breath. No doubt a leopard! Very slowly and with infinite caution I retreated and made my way into a side gorge where I found a small stretch of sand on which I lay down and went to sleep. I woke up at daybreak and after a frugal breakfast I hid my rucksack behind a rock, went to the source and made myself comfortable on a ridge above it. When I turned my glasses onto the spot where the leopard had warned me off I could see a black-and-white pattern beside a craggy rock which I made out to be a mangled zebra foal. Obviously I had disturbed the leopard at its feeding, a very dangerous thing to do. Through my glasses I saw something move amongst the grey rocks. Two jackals were prowling around the scene of the night's tragedy. With pointed muzzles and tail between their legs they were sniffing the scent of what the leopard had left, keenly alert and prepared to take flight at a moment's notice.

And suddenly as I watched, the leopard stood there on the rock, spitting like a great cat. The two jackals disappeared like magic, and with a single graceful spring the leopard landed beside his prey. He sniffed the remains of the dead foal for a moment or two and then took it in his mouth and carried it up the track between the rocks. I was sorry that he was too far off for a photograph.

For some time everything was quiet, and only a couple of rock pigeons went to the source. Then a herd of zebra came trotting up gaily, filling the grey gorge with cheerful life. Perhaps they had walked all night to get here and drink in the morning, and when they had drunk their fill they stood around quietly in the burning sun with lowered heads. Just one foal rolled over and over gleefully in the sand. Suddenly a stallion threw his head into the air and whinnied shrilly, and as though they had waited for the signal, another herd came out of a side gully. The stallion advanced a few steps and the other herd trotted past to the water without taking any notice of him.

But then the leading stallion of the new herd stalked up to him. For a little while the two circled round each other with heads held high and tails arched. Suddenly they rose on their hind legs and with their forefeet hailed blows at each other's chests and shoulders. Clouds of dust and sand half concealed the striped flanks and haunches of the two contestants. Then, as though at a word of command, they both turned their rumps on each other and kicked away mightily, sending bunches of tail hair flying into the air. The battle ended as quickly as it had begun. Honour seemed to have been satisfied and the second stallion went peaceably down to the water, whilst his rival moved off leading his own herd away down the gorge. Later on gemsbok and a pair of klipspringer arrived to drink and I got some good photographs.

Towards evening I went down to the source and had a drink myself. The water had a sweetish taste, something like Glauber salts. Then I gathered kindling and made a fire. I cut a spit from a tamarisk tree, put my leg of springbok on one end and stuck the other into the sand so that the meat was just out of reach of the flames. Before long the wonderful smell of roasting meat was all around me, and as I sat, turning the spit from time to time, I dreamily watched the glowing embers and the dancing golden flames.

243

The following morning I took up my position at a game track which ran along a ribbed watershed in the hope of getting a few pictures with a different background. Nothing exciting came my way and I finally decided to try my luck along another game track which led through a metre-wide gully. Fifty paces from the entrance I came upon a dead gemsbok lying between the stones with twisted neck and torn throat. The blood had been sucked and great gobbets had been torn out of the haunches. It was clearly the work of a leopard. The gemsbok was a first-year bull and not full grown, but all the same I was amazed that the leopard should have dared to go within range of those horns. Then from its traces I realised that it had lain in ambush right by the game track behind a rock and had torn open the gemsbok's throat at the first onslaught. This was the only time I ever came across a gemsbok which had been killed by a leopard. Thinking that the gemsbok's liver would make a tasty supper I pulled the carcass into the shadow of the rock.

What the leopard had managed to do ought not to be impossible for me. A strong east wind was blowing steadily and I crouched in a niche right close to the entrance to the gorge. I had been waiting there over an hour when a herd of twenty-seven zebra came by. I pressed myself back against the rock and didn't move a muscle as they filed passed me unsuspectingly. I could have touched them with my outstretched hand as their acrid horselike smell hit me in the face. It was difficult to understand why their clear, bright eyes didn't spot me. When gemsbok appeared a little later I crouched back even further into the rock, for at such close range their sharp horns were very intimidating; but they didn't see me either.

That evening, sitting by the camp fire, I thought

the matter over. The explanation certainly couldn't lie in the eye itself, because it could spot a moving man at a thousand metres and see clearly that he was neither gemsbok nor springbok. The explanation must therefore lie in an inability to interpret what the eye saw. But wasn't interpretation the essential prerequisite of recognition? And wasn't interpretation also a form of judgement? Suddenly I realised that the sense organs were at the same time organs of judgement, and that with the development of the senses from mere feeling to tasting, smelling, hearing and seeing, the capacity to judge developed, becoming capable of increasing differentiation. Sense organs were obviously useless unless supported by the capacity to judge. And through the development of his senses man's capacity for judgement had been sharpened on his environment as a knife is whetted on a stone. Thus development of life and of capacity to judge went hand in hand, and thanks to man's faculty of conscious thought his capacity for judgement had risen to a completely new dimension. Could there be even higher stages ahead? There was no obvious reason why not. It was an exhilirating thought.

On the fourth day I went back to our house and we had a grand reunion. Hermann and I were delighted, and so was Otto who wildly wagged his tail.

The idea of adaptation to an out-and-out struggle for survival leading to ultimate extinction was still in Hermann's mind. He had drawn an imaginary graph of man's ability to kill. First sticks and stones were the only weapons and with them prehistoric man could kill one of his kind at a time. Then bow and arrow arrived, and man could now kill his fellow man at a considerably greater distance, but still only one at a time. Then came the Romans with the mechanical catapult. With this weapon man could

245

kill perhaps five or six simultaneously. Next there was gunpowder, but this discovery led to no striking 'progress' in man's art of killing. Only in the past fifty years or so had man's capacity for multi-slaughter made great strides with the use of machine-guns, gas grenades and so on. And now we have large bombs and the promise of still larger ones — not to mention more and more devastating explosives — and there is no limit to the number of simultaneous victims.

And what about the future? Already the lives of multitudes could be destroyed by one bomb. The ultimate logical development would be the destruction of all life by the action of one man.

Although at that time we knew nothing about the atomic bomb and its many variations, we felt that once such a devastating weapon became feasible someone would manufacture it and someone else use it. How right we were! Our graph seemed another confirmation of the ultimate evil of any extreme struggle for survival. How infinite is the wisdom of the Bible: 'Blessed are the meek, for they shall inherit the earth.'

Was there no possibility of saving mankind from self-destruction? The extinct animal species had been forced unwittingly towards elimination, but in man, life, for the first time, had mustered sufficient consciousness to recognise dangerous trends in his development.

What were these dangers? Progress of science, man's increasing technical mastery? No, the real danger threatening man lay in those gigantic social and political organisations, being ends in themselves instead of means, using the instruments of education and propaganda to suppress individual judgement by creating instinctive mass reaction. These organisations hinder man's spiritual development, reduce the

246

capacity for moral judgement to a low level, and hand over society to the insensate lust for power of a few individuals.

Those primitive hunters who lived together in small kin groups did not show reckless courage for its own sake. They had to be reckless in order to survive. But the hypnotising power display of vast organisations which exhibited and glorified power, trained man — without necessity — to recklessness and the unquestioning acceptance of death and annihilation. There lies man's road to extinction.

The Water-tank

The southern half of the earth faced the sun once again, and the dry year took its terrible, scorching course. We had built a roof for our veranda, hauling up large quantities of boughs and twigs and using a smooth silver moringa trunk as a support.

For over a month now not one of the animals we had shot had yielded us a scrap of fat, and even the flesh had begun to take on a bluish and unappetising appearance. One evening we were carrying water to the house from the water-hole when we heard Otto barking excitedly, and full of foreboding we began to run. Had someone discovered our house perhaps? Or had . . .? When we came in sight of the house everything seemed as usual. Otto was still barking somewhere a little further off. Then immediately before our door we saw fresh gemsbok spoor. We threw down our loads, and Hermann, anxious for Otto's safety, pushed a bullet into the chamber of the pistol, and off we ran.

We found a shaggy gemsbok, little more than a bag of bones, lying in a small gully, with Otto dancing around it, barking wildly and easily avoiding the feeble lunges of the poor beast's horns. When he spotted us he rushed up, wagging his tail delightedly and then ran back to the wretched gemsbok, barking louder than ever. We ended the business with a quick shot in the head.

Our delight at obtaining a gemsbok so easily didn't last long. The meat of the shrivelled muscles was a dirty yellow in colour and it smelt musty. Even Otto sniffed at it and turned up his nose in disdain. We had wasted a bullet and we now had the trouble of getting rid of the wretched cascass.

The only animals which still looked in good condition were the zebra. Hermann shot a particularly plump beast, but he had to use three bullets for the job and we really couldn't afford that. Whilst cutting it up we studied its anatomy carefully in order to discover a vital spot: the shoulder blade was narrow, the ribs broad and widely spaced, and the heart was very big. We paid particular attention to the position of the heart in relation to the pattern of the stripes, and after that we could drop a zebra at sixty paces with one shot in the heart.

The zebra had no fat left either, but at least their flesh was as juicy as ever, and it made a particularly good goulash, which we christened zebrash for short.

Every day hot winds swept over the parched land. The water level in our hole had now sunk below the gravel and we had to dig deeper and deeper to get at it. In the end the hole became so large that after use we put a slab of rock over it, which we covered with sand. This had a double purpose: first of all it acted as camouflage from prying eyes, and secondly it retarded the process of evaporation. But the level of the water fell constantly. About a metre down we found a small spotted frog in its dry-period hibernation. It woke up but it had the good sense to stay where it was.

We were really worried now; after all, it could be months before the river flowed again, though with a bit of luck next month — which was October — could bring a shower and perhaps fill a few puddles. Hermann suggested that we ought to make ourselves some sort of container to store enough water to last us a month or two. But we hadn't that number of petrol tins and if we dug a hole in the ground how could we make it watertight?

Could we perhaps build a tank of rock slabs? Five slabs the size of a table-top ought to hold enough water for a couple of months. But, once again, how could we make the joints water-tight? What about strips of wet gemsbok skin? At least there was no harm in trying, and our table-top could serve as a ready-made bottom for the tank. We spent a whole day searching for four suitable slabs, and then came the fiddling job of fitting them together and fastening them in place.

It wasn't particularly difficult to trim them to the right shape, and we found that we could easily break them off clean along a straight edge with sharp blows of our hammer. But after that the edges had to be smoothed and slots cut into the two long slabs and into the base slab. We took turns at this long and laborious task. We had only a small cold chisel, which had to be whetted a dozen times a day; and the cutting took us over a week, but in the end the sides and ends of the tank fitted fairly well into the bottom.

We now cut strips of rubber from an old tube and fitted them into the joints, winding strong wet strips of gemsbok hide round the sides of the tank. This attempt at waterproofing proved a failure and the tank leaked in many places, so we had to try something else. Clay would have done the trick easily enough, of course, but desert climates don't encourage its formation. We now tried stuffing up the joints with wood shavings and cloth fibres. Then we mixed melted rubber and motor oil until we had a highly viscous substance, and with that, the wood shavings and cloth fibres we managed to make the joints really watertight.

The next problem was to prevent the water tasting

of oil and rubber, and this we did by sprinkling fine clayey sand on the mixture until no more oil seeped through. The tank took us two whole weeks to build, and it took us another three days to get it half-full. To slow down evaporation we closed the top with another stone slab, leaving a three-cornered hole through which we could scoop out water, and this hole we kept covered with a cloth. We were ready for the rain now and very proud of our achievement!

Flight

The rain didn't come, but a different kind of surprise was in store for us. About a week after we had finished the tank Hermann came striding back from a hunting trip with bad news.

'Police!' he exclaimed with a twisted sort of grin. 'Two carloads of them on the old bay *pad*. They must be looking for us.'

The police, it appeared, had been searching the area through their glasses from the top of a hill. There wasn't much danger that they'd spot us that way, but obviously for some reason they suspected that we were in this part of the world. Very much later we learned that when he returned to his own people the Ovambo at Siedentopf's farm had talked about the white men he had seen there — two white men with a dog who had come in out of the Namib. The talk had finally reached the local commissioner and he had reported it to Windhoek.

The whole afternoon we lay concealed on the hill behind our house, but we saw nothing suspicious, and the following morning we approached the old *pad* cautiously and we saw from the tracks there that the police cars had turned and gone back. The danger had passed for the moment, but there was always a possibility that they would send out a real search expedition, and then just one piece of bad luck could be our downfall, and unwillingly we decided to move again.

We had become very much attached to our little stretch of red sand between the hills, so when we started our packing we were both feeling depressed.

Sadly we filled up our water containers and then cut the gemsbok straps of our laboriously constructed water tank. The *pad* itself was the shortest way to the edge of the plains, but we didn't dare to use it; unless there was rain our tracks would remain visible too long. We therefore crossed the *pad* taking good care to efface the tyre marks, and then we worked our way around the foot of the mountain towards the north. The route went across boulder- and debris-strewn wastes, through hot sandy river-beds and across a labyrinth of rock-ribbed slopes. We crossed the mountain chain diagonally through a wild pass, shifting a lot of slabs and boulders on our way, and finally came to a maze of gorges to the south of the river-bed camp which we had used the previous February. The dried-out courses were deeper here and it cost us a good deal of sweat and much grunting to get the lorry up the second gorge to a half-way suitable camping place under a stunted aru tree. By this time it was evening.

How were we to find a water-hole in this maze? Only along a game path of course, but how could you tell which of the innumerable paths actually led to water? Many of them just went from one grazing ground to the next. Twelve months ago we had been ignorant of such things, but in the meantime the desert had become familiar to us, and we had learnt that 'water paths' show the spoor of all kinds of animals, including, in particular, beasts of prey; whereas 'grazing paths' rarely show more than two kinds of spoor. Thus after examining a path for a few hundred metres you could usually tell whether it was leading to water or not.

The following day we got up early and separated to go about our search. The first day all I found was a small and quite useless salty source, and Hermann found nothing at all. On the second day Hermann found a source, and brought back a sample of the water which seemed only slightly bitter. Hermann thought it tasted much better cold out of the water-bag than at the spring, but in any case it would have to do. This source lay in a small enclosed valley surrounded by tamarisk trees and evergreen salvadora bushes. The salt, which split up the rock, had undermined and worn away the sides of the valley into a semi-circle, leaving a few sharp ribs and columns standing like scenery in an amphitheatre. Water trickled into four pools and each of them had a different taste.

We found a reasonably suitable living site in a small side gorge about a kilometre away. It took us another half-day to get our lorry there, but then we could breathe more easily; the place was out of the way and we felt safe again. But the next time we went to fetch water we found that baboons had fouled the pools, so we called it 'Baboon's Hole'.

The sun was beating down so fiercely now that we had to get a roof over our heads as quickly as possible. Fortunately there were a good many dead bushes in the gorge so we built ourselves a hut using some branches and taking advantage of a clump of thorn bushes that stood like a small hedgehog at a point where the gorge widened. We tore our hands on the thorns as we lugged up loads of wood, and the sweat ran down our foreheads and necks and dried in salty crusts whilst the sun burned in the sky and rock and sand threw up a scorching heat.

It was incredibly hot, and we were so exhausted that we could carry only small burdens and were unable to work for more than an hour at a time. The strong laxative quality of the water weakened us even more and it was weeks before our insides got used to it. However, our new house gradually took shape and it was finished at last, its walls partly covered with hides. On Hermann's birthday we had got as far as setting up the wind-generator, and we had a combined birthday-housewarming celebration, but you couldn't have described it as a recklessly joyous affair. We used our last flour to make an apple turnover, and there was no more coffee. I had carved two new pipe stems as a birthday present, but the trouble was that his tobacco supplies were almost exhausted. No, the outlook wasn't encouraging.

Hunger Again

The first longingly awaited clouds raised their white heads timidly over the mountains, and twice towards evening there was sheet lightning in the east and the north, but after that the skies were as clear as burnished steel again. And nowhere was there the slightest trace of game. Perhaps eighty or ninety kilometres away rain had fallen, and now the hungry herds were eagerly making their way into the wind that had brought them the smell of wet earth.

Our food supplies were nearing exhaustion; all we had left was a little maize flour, some beans and a bag of dried meat. We had plenty of seasoning, but little to use it with. Our daily rations had become wretchedly small; the outlook for the immediate future was not very hopeful. Once again we crouched down at the water and waited for steppe quail, but there were so few of them now that one shot might with luck bag four birds, just enough for one meal. We couldn't afford to use cartridges at that rate, so we made small traps out of oblong tobacco tins and rubber bands, but they were no more successful than our gemsbok-hair snares had been. If we covered the traps with wet sand they didn't snap to properly, and if we used dry sand the birds noticed and avoided them. We tried catapults, but we very rarely scored a hit, because the birds heard the slap of the rubber and were in the air before the stone arrived.

The small black berries of the salvadora bushes were ripening, but there was only a thin layer of flesh over the hard stone, and it had a rather tart, sweetish taste. We knew the fruit wasn't poisonous because we had found its stones in the excrement of birds and baboons, and though we couldn't eat much of it raw, we discovered by dint of experiment that if we stewed the berries long enough we got a syrup which didn't taste too bad. We stripped all the bushes around the source and our harvest gave us about two and a half pots of jam. It wasn't much of a food on its own, but this time we hadn't the Bushmen's source to refresh ourselves at. We were so weak that we were unable to go far on our hunting trips, and sometimes if we got up too suddenly everything would go black before our eyes.

We were so hungry that we even began to think about another visit to Siedentopf, but we realised that if the police had been looking for us they would pretty certainly have promised the Ovambo a reward for information concerning us. No, it was too dangerous. But supposing we just drove straight into Windhoek or Swakopmund, bought what we wanted and cleared off again before the police had a chance of spotting us? We were engaged in discussing this tempting possibility when we heard the drone of an engine in the distance. We went out to have a look; no doubt it was an aeroplane and we spotted it circling nearer over mountain and gorge.

'If they are looking for us they're not likely to have much luck like that,' said Hermann. 'A needle in a haystack would be easier to locate than us in this maze of ridges, gorges and shadows.'

The plane circled round once or twice and then flew off in the direction of Windhoek. After that neither of us referred again to the suggestion of going into town.

One day Hermann caught a porcupine and that lasted us for three days, but afterwards we were hungrier than ever. Clouds appeared in the sky, but no rain fell, and then it was December. All we could think of or talk about now was food. Hunger often kept us awake at night and so we would discuss all the meals we would cook — if only we had the proper ingredients! It was a simply inexhaustible subject.

And then after a seemingly endless period we began to find fresh spoor on the game paths. But even when we spotted an animal we weren't lucky. Hermann got in the first shot, but the gemsbok galloped away so spiritedly that he felt sure he had missed it and didn't bother to go in pursuit. But the next day we saw the vultures circling and we dashed off towards the spot — just in time to snatch a haunch before they finished the lot. The meat was slightly high, but otherwise quite good. We took all the bones we could find back for Otto, and in consequence he ate only part of his ration of beans, and greedily we immediately shared what he had left.

Then I fired at a gemsbok from an ambush at the water-hole. I was using one of our home-made bullets and he bled pretty freely. He made off but I felt fairly certain he would lie down before long and I went in pursuit. I followed for a kilometre or so, but the blood trail grew fainter and fainter and became very difficult to follow, so I went back for Hermann and Otto. Otto joined in the hunt enthusiastically and took us for another kilometre or so, but by that time his nose was so dry he couldn't smell a thing. Hermann went back and fetched water, and then we went on again, but in the end we lost all trace in a hot, barren area, and a day, hopefully begun, ended somewhat discouragingly.

On one of our prowls we spotted part of a beehive below an overhanging rock and we knocked it down with stones. Five cells were still full of crystallised honey. We shared it between us and were quite certain that we had never tasted anything so wonderful in our lives. There seemed to be no inhabited bees' nests anywhere; the drought had lasted too long. We searched hopefully for a nice puff-adder which we could fry in its own fat, but we were unlucky. Later on when the need was past I did kill and fry one, but there was very little meat on it.

Often, whilst sitting up at the water-hole or near one of the game paths, I was sure I heard the clatter of zebra hooves in the distance and my mind would fill with glorious expectations of zebrash, but as the minutes passed I would realise I had only heard the rumbling of my own belly. And so the days crawled by; a merciless white light beat down on us and we were weak and hungry.

Once a big warran lizard about a metre long scuttled away from under my feet. I rushed after it and managed to catch it by the tail just when it was about to disappear in a crevice. I gripped the wedge-shaped scaly tail with both hands and pulled with all my might, but the lizard had puffed itself up inside the crevice and it hung on like grim death. I got a firm foothold, leaned back and waited for about five minutes, then I gave a sudden mighty tug. I think I gained about a centimetre or so that way, but when I relaxed the lizard got even with a sudden jerk forward. My next jerk had no effect whatever and I realised that with brute force even allied to persistence I was unlikely to achieve anything against the antediluvian nerve and muscular system of this huge lizard.

By my side lay my knobkerrie, a thick stick with a heavy rounded head, but I couldn't do anything with it, because the lizard was protected by the rock. And my gun was thirty metres away where I had left it when I first began to chase the brute. I could probably reach into the crevice with my knife, but then I should have only one hand to hold on with and if the brute jerked forward again I shouldn't have the strength to hold it, particularly as the arm I was holding it with would have to be bent. Then I got a better idea.

With my right hand I took the leather lace out of one boot and fastened it round the base of the lizard's tail, where it narrows a little, and the other end of the lace I tied round my knobkerrie so that it lay across the crevice. Now the lizard couldn't get into the hole and I had both hands free. I put one foot on its tail to stop it from swishing then I drove my knife through the hard scales into its body. It was ten minutes before the dying reptile's muscles relaxed sufficiently to let me pull it out of the crevice.

That lizard provided us with two good meals. The flesh was firm and white and tasted like a cross between chicken and salmon. Strengthened by this good food we decided to try our luck at a small bitter source about two hours journey away. We set out in the middle of the night and made our way there by the light of a half moon, walking slowly and resting a good deal. Shortly before daybreak we got there and ate a double portion of maize porridge — if we bagged nothing then that one meal would have to serve for the journey back too.

When the early morning light began to turn the black gorge into grey and we could make out its gloomy sides, we spotted the black stripes and white bellies of gemsbok in our glasses. There wasn't much water in the pool and they would drink a little and then wait patiently until the hollow filled up again. Hermann tried to get closer but before he was near enough for a shot the early morning breeze, which was blowing first in one direction and then the other, betrayed his presence, and the gemsbok fled.

We found ourselves places to sit up now: Hermann above the water-hole and I near a much-frequented game path, and there we waited all day long. The scorching sun rose steadily to the zenith, seemed to stay there for ages, and then finally sank into a sea of red fire over the Namib. The day had seemed like an eternity, but apart from a few birds and a lizard or two we had seen no sign of life throughout the parched landscape.

We met and discussed our next move, and then Hermann took Otto home. The pistol was useless in the half-light and I remained behind with the shot-gun with a good view over the sandy stretch by the water where the steppe quail would land. As I had not altogether given up hope of a gemsbok or a zebra I loaded one barrel with shot and the other with one of our home-made bullets. As the outlines of the rocks grew fainter in the twilight I heard the call of the quail and then they began to drop out of the sky onto the sandy stretch ahead. More and more landed as I watched, and my heart began to beat harder; a shot would certainly not be wasted. As soon as I heard them moving towards the water I took careful aim in the general direction and fired. When I ran to the water I couldn't believe my eyes: I hadn't bagged a single bird. Then I realised that I had fired the bullet instead of the shot.

Words cannot describe my disappointment, and I completely lost heart. I almost gave up and went to sleep, but I knew that if I did I should sleep right through the night and in that case it would be very doubtful whether I should have strength enough to get back next day under the broiling sun. I therefore started back at once. The journey through the dark night — the moon didn't rise until much later — was a nightmare. Our shot-gun wasn't really heavy, but it cut into my shoulder as though it was made of lead, and my feet dragged over the hard stones as though I was hobbled. Sometimes I seemed to be gliding along without feeling on dark clouds, but then the scratch of sharp thorns would bring me back to earth again. I had to sit down frequently, but the rest did me no good and getting up was torture. The stars above me blinked like evil eyes in the warm air rising from the hot desert. Finally a distorted sickle of yellow moon appeared over the mountains and threw confusing shadows before my stumbling feet.

When I staggered into our wretched hut Hermann told me it was two o'clock. He could see that I had brought nothing and he asked no questions; instead he took off my shoes and gave me a drink of our salvadora-berry syrup with hot water and brandy. When I woke up the next day the sun had already gone down.

The Second Christmas

Fortunately that trip from which I returned empty-handed marked the end of our run of bad luck for a while. Two days later Hermann came back to the hut joyfully carrying meat on his shoulder. He had shot a zebra stallion through the heart with the pistol at eighty paces.

We fell on the meat like starving wolves, and devoured a good portion of it raw. Then we grilled juicy steaks over the fire — we had no more fat for frying. It took us a good many journeys to bring in the dismembered carcass because by this time we were so weak that we could no longer carry much, but we got it all in and for four days after that we worked hard making biltong, smoked meat and meat extract. For the time being we ate nothing but meat in order to save what little maize and beans we still had.

In the meantime less and less water trickled into our pool, and one morning we found that baboons had fouled the place again. They probably did it deliberately in order to keep the pool for themselves, because their stink is so horrible that other animals don't care to use a pool after them. We did our best to clean it up, scooped the water out and cleaned the basin with sand and soap, but when the water ran in again it still stank. We had to scour the hollow out three times before the water was fit to use again, but then we fetched and carried until our water container was full. But the next day the water stank of baboons. We were nonplussed. In the desert you don't pour away something like 160 litres of water with a light heart. In the end we decided to use it to wash our clothes, which hadn't been washed for six months. When the washing was over they didn't look clean, but at least we knew they were cleaner, though when we turned in with our freshly washed bed-linen the smell of it left us in no doubt that we were living at Baboon's Hole. We were so annoyed that we decided to take counter-action at the first opportunity, but before we had a chance to do anything Christmas was upon us.

There was no question of any feast such as we had prepared the previous year, but we did our best. We allowed ourselves a double portion of maize and we made it more tasty with a teaspoonful of sugar that we managed to shake out of the fabric of our long-empty sugar sack. And then we heated up all our empty dripping tins and collected about two teaspoonfuls of fat. It was rancid, but to us, who had eaten nothing but fatless zebra meat for a couple of weeks, it tasted wonderful.

Hermann was suffering from lack of tobacco now and the deprivation made him moody and occasionally disagreeable. Shortly after Christmas he announced bluntly: 'I'm going in to get some tobacco.' I could see many objections to that suggestion, particularly after the advent of the aeroplane, but from his tone I knew that he was determined so I said nothing. And I must confess that I was greatly attracted by the thought of bread and sugar again, so when he put the rhetorical question about what was to happen if there was no rain again this year, I gave in and we began to discuss the proposal. I wanted to go too, but Hermann pointed out that if we both went we would have to take Otto, which would attract too much attention — they were already looking for two men with a dog.

Then we discussed where. Swakopmund was nearest, but as it was on the coast we thought that the police might be more alert there, so we decided on Windhoek.

'There might be check-points on the roads into Windhoek,' I pointed out.

Hermann shook his head. 'Not on New Year's Day; they'll all be sleeping off their hangovers. But we'll have to alter our number plates. Every policeman in the country probably knows ours by heart.'

Then there was the question of which storekeeper to go to, an important one, for we had no money.

'Grossarth,' Hermann proposed. 'I'll take the Leica and he'll give me credit on it. With my beard no one will recognise me. There are enough bearded Boers around anyway.'

Hermann had obviously been thinking the matter over and he had an answer for everything.

We altered our number plates so that they read W810 instead of W1018. Then there was the problem of our tax disc. We hadn't paid tax of course, and every year the disc to be stuck on the windscreen had a different colour. All we could do was to make it unrecognisable as naturally as possible. It had been cloudy over the uplands for the past few days and rain had almost certainly fallen somewhere so that the sight of a mud-splashed lorry ought not to arouse much attention. I therefore made some mud and soon our lorry was thoroughly splashed, particularly that disc. Hermann trimmed his beard, put on his long khaki trousers and his one clean shirt (they were the only decent clothes he possessed) and was ready.

We didn't say much to each other when he drove off; each of us knew that we were taking a risk and that the future was insecure enough anyway. It was New Year's Eve. The sound of the engine sounded very loud at first, but then it died away and Otto and I were left alone to await the result of a very dubious undertaking. It was just as well that I had learnt patience from the wild animals of the desert, for Hermann could hardly be back for a few days. But when he did come would it be with a police escort?

In the night of the third day a bank of cloud sailed forward over the mountains and in the morning it began to rain. I took off my clothes to enjoy it the more and climbed up to the highest point over the gorge to assess the prospects. I was studying the all-important cloud movements when my ear caught the distant sound of an engine. Was it Hermann returning before I expected him? Had he been caught? But I could hear only one engine and it sounded rather familiar. Then our lorry came in sight, jolting and swaying over the rough ground. Otto and I rushed to meet it and I sprang up onto the footboard. Otto was barking wildly and jumping around madly in his excitement. Hermann pulled up, took the pipe out of his mouth and grinned:

'Excuse me, Mr Adam,' he said, 'but am I right for the Garden of Eden? I haven't any fig-leaves: would a few figs do?'

So all was well! Otto had already leapt into the back of the lorry and he was sniffing around at the sacks and cases there.

'He can smell the bacon.' Hermann said.

I sighed. Words failed me. Bacon!

When we were in our hut Hermann produced a package of coffee as though he were a magician turning dross into gold. The aroma was indescribable. 'A mocha, laddie. I think I've earned it. I drove down from the mountains without lights.'

In the meantime I was unpacking unimaginable luxuries: figs and peaches! I went weak at the knees before I had seen half of it and I had to sit down. When the coffee was on the table Hermann told his story.

'The first incident was just behind the Langenberg. I came across five hyenas tearing a zebra to pieces, whilst at a respectful distance a dozen jackals sat round in a circle. When the lorry hove in sight the lot fled. You should have seen 'em. The next occurred at the old *pad* where I noticed fresh car tracks. I had a closer look at them and they were Firestone cords, the sort the police use on their Fords. At a sandy river bed they turned back. After the first shock I realised that if they'd been looking for us they would not have gone back so soon, so I drove on quite happily in their tracks, but I took good care to see they didn't turn off anywhere to some outlying farm, and I kept my eyes skinned to make sure I didn't overtake 'em. On New Year's Eve I slept in the hills outside Windhoek.

'The next morning — it was New Year's Day — I met a solitary car. But hold your hat on! — it had the same numbers as ours! I was so rattled I nearly drove into a tree. By the time I got to Windhoek I was so upset I was praying. But there was no car-check and not another car in sight. I went straight to Grossarth, got down, put my pipe between my teeth to steady my nerves, and knocked. Old Grossarth himself opened up, looked at me without recognising me, and obviously thinking I was a Boer, said: *'Kom binne, Meneer!'* ('Come in, sir.')

'I followed him into the shop and as I still hadn't said anything he said: *'Wat kan ek vir u doen?'* ('What can I do for you?')

'And then he recognised me. As it was a holiday I couldn't get anything and it seemed too risky to stay in his house all the time, so I drove the lorry under a

267

camel-thorn bush to conceal the tax-disc and I spent the day there with a box of figs and some peaches from Grossarth's garden. The next morning he got me what I wanted and I drove back here. Once I was outside Windhoek I didn't see a single car and I drove past the last farm and down the hills without lights. As I could hardly keep my eyes open I stopped for a few hours and had a sleep. When I woke up I drove on, and here I am.'

He was very modest about it, but I realised clearly what a performance that drive had been, one which required unremitting alertness and lightning decisions. That mountain *pad* twisted and turned and skirted sheer drops, and now and again it was so narrow that a lorry had no margin to spare at all. I asked him whether he had thought to efface his trail when he left the *pad*.

'I think I did something even better,' he replied. 'I didn't efface the tracks but I drove round the Langenberg massif on the south side in a wide circle and rejoined the *pad*. Whoever wants to can follow my tracks, and if they try they'll find themselves back where they started and they won't know whether I branched off somewhere along that thirty kilometre circle or earlier still along the *pad*. I don't think they'd have patience enough to search the whole route on foot.'

We grinned like naughty schoolboys and decided to celebrate Christmas Day again now that we could do it properly.

It appeared that it had hardly rained in the uplands at all, and sheep and cattle were dying of thirst in large numbers.

That evening the west wind rose again and the prospect of rain became even more uncertain.

Desert Rain

January passed into February, and the sun still dominated the sky unchallenged. Day after day death poured down on the earth, its scythe a sheaf of burning rays, and its harvest as generous as in war. The air trembled over the plains as it does over a hot oven, and the gramadoela gorges yawned like the portals of hell. Hyenas and leopards had easy game with their exhausted prey, and in the shade of the few bushes and trees myriads of sand ticks waited for the wretched animals.

At last, on February 14th, great white clouds billowed up over the mountains. In the evening they retreated once more before the west wind, but the next day they sailed overhead like fully rigged ships, and by evening thunder was rolling heavily over the Namib. Humid masses of air from the Indian Ocean had swept across the African continent and reached the edge of the desert.

The next day we began to prepare ourselves a shelter from the expected rain, because the wattled roof of our hut was not water-tight. About forty metres up we found a long narrow space between fallen rock and the mountain side. We built a stone wall on the eastern side and made a roof with our tarpaulin, weighting it down with stones. In this way we had a narrow shelter which would keep out the rain. All our perishable goods were in the driving cabin of the lorry as usual and the lorry itself was safely parked under an overhanging rock face.

From our point of vantage we marvelled at billowing clouds bigger than we had ever seen before. Here and there deep blue shadows were already creeping over the rock ridges and the gorges. At twelve o'clock a dark-grey mass moved slowly forward over the Quabis range, gathering momentum as it advanced; then it tipped over into the plains, rolling forward like lava from a volcano. Where it touched the plains great veils of sand rose up at once and were swept off into the Namib like reddish ghosts. We were still staring after those whirls of sand when amidst a ceaseless rolling of thunder the great cloud collapsed in a grey swirl and disappeared so completely that not even a wisp of mist was left. The whole thing had lasted perhaps a quarter of an hour, and an hour later we heard the roaring of water rushing down the main gorge. We ran quickly to see it as it swirled along, a tumultuous frothing bore of brown water over two metres high, flattening the tough bushes in its path, uprooting trees and tossing them into the air like matchsticks. It seemed almost incredible that a short downpour could produce such a volume of water.

Clouds were rolling up higher into the sky now and obscuring the sun. By three o'clock it was dark and eerily quiet. Suddenly there was a rumbling of thunder and it did not stop.

'Quick!' I shouted. 'We're going to get it.'

And I ran back to get the radio into safety. After that everything went very quickly. A powerful gust of wind bent the bushes flat, uprooted a small tree and flung it at our feet, and almost blew us over. The first drops fell when we were making the second journey with our bedding. On the way back the rain was pelting down so violently that we could hardly breathe; flashes of lightning lit up the grey curtain of water, and the thunder rolled and reverberated incessantly. Within minutes the water was rolling down the sides of the valley into the river, raising the level of the rushing torrent so that it now overflowed its banks and swirled into our hut. In the nick of time I rescued our small battery from knee-deep water, and as we worked and slaved to save our things before the hut fell in, as it threatened to do at any moment, the water came up to our thighs. At the gorge bend there was a roaring waterfall now and debris had piled up at every bush. The swirling water was slashing our legs with briars and I trod on a thorn and drove it into my foot. Hermann brought up the last of our belongings and we crouched at the entrance of our shelter and stared at each other in alarm: 'Where was Otto?'

We called to him as loudly as we could, but there was no reply. We looked in all directions, but we could see nothing but water. Finally we discovered him sitting at the back of our shelter behind the radio, trembling and looking very frightened. In our great relief we laughed heartily at the pitiful sight of him. Gradually the clouds broke up, became ragged and swept by; the thunder died away in the west over the Namib, and the flow of the gurgling water began to ebb. The cloud-burst had lasted half an hour, and we measured ten centimetres of rain, more than the yearly average of a good many towns in Europe.

Night fell and sheet lightning could be seen stabbing the clouds on the horizon like searchlights; and then, somewhere away to the south, the incessant roll of thunder continued. Otto got as close to Hermann as possible. I could quite understand him, I had never before in my life heard such thunder or experienced such a cloud-burst.

The drought was over and every day great towering clouds rose over the uplands, bellying up into the sky to a height of 10 000 metres and more. On one occasion we counted from ten to fifteen of them

271

along a front of about 200 kilometres. They would stand there for a while like giants in shining armour on guard over the blue mountains which mark the barrier of Africa against the desert. Then forked lightning would play around their dark base and they would begin to roll forward majestically over the mountains and down into the plains.

It was as though a good fairy had broken a spell that had rested heavily on the land, and now the scorched and battered life began to raise its head again with all the vigour and confidence of youth. Within four hours, bushes that had looked dead began to show tiny shoots of green, and in the shade of the rocks ferns began to unroll delicate light-green leaves. In twenty-four hours the evening sun breaking through a bank of clouds turned the fine new blades of springbok grass into a mist of gold-green bloom. The desert was alive everywhere: seeds that had lain dormant for years came to life and pierced the crust of earth; almost overnight the balsam bushes covered themselves with green leaves like young birches; a delicate tracery of green creepers began to wind over the red sand; and the first yellow flowers opened their petals to the sun.

Once again we laid out a small garden, fetching the water from the over-brimming holes. Rock doves were billing and cooing from morning to night; a pair of garden-warblers nested under a piece of bark near our lorry; before long we found the speckled eggs of the quail amidst the grass and stones; and the lukewarm water of the pools swarmed with little crab-like insects whose eggs had survived the years of dryness and scorching sunshine.

Dream, Fantasy and Imagination

The game now spread out over the wide plains and it became more difficult to hunt. The antelopes no longer came down to the pools, for they found sufficient moisture in the green, succulent grass, whilst the zebra had a choice of innumerable water-holes. If we had only possessed a rifle, even a poor rifle! But with our pistol it was very difficult, despite our increasing skill and our endless patience, to get near enough for a shot.

One day Hermann came back after dark. 'We can fetch a gemsbok early in the morning,' he said. 'I thought at first I could get him this evening, but another gentleman was keeping watch.' And he hung the pistol up on its nail.

'All the morning I was on a rocky mound watching the neighbourhood,' he went on. 'Finally a single gemsbok came into the valley to graze. I couldn't get nearer than about eighty paces, but I tried a shot. He galloped off up the side of the valley into the wind and then stopped. I managed to creep up unobserved behind a rib of rock and when I bobbed up I came practically face to face with him. He looked at me aggressively and came forward a step or two so I shot him straight in the forehead. He stumbled for a moment but then came at me again. I dodged down behind the rock and there he was above me, his horns rattling against the rock as he tried to get at me. I don't think I ever made myself so small in my life. The drop was too much for the wounded beast, otherwise things might have gone badly with me, but after what seemed an eternity he turned and went away. When he had disappeared over the brow of the hill I followed. The opposite slope caused him difficulty and finally he lay down, with the wind behind him. There was no way of getting up to him unobserved. I looked at him carefully through my glasses and I could see where the bullet had entered his forehead; it was a bit low.

'It obviously wasn't easy for him to keep his head up but he didn't relax his vigilance. After about half an hour he suddenly leapt to his feet and trotted off with his tail switching and disappeared into the next valley. I jumped up and followed, taking cover behind a bush. I saw a second gemsbok bull grazing there. The wounded gemsbok went up to him and they sniffed at each other; then my gemsbok clambered up the other side with some difficulty and squatted down in the shadow of a rock, taking no further interest in anything. I could have got up to him easily enough now, but for the next three hours the other gemsbok stayed there grazing and never moved more than fifty metres away.

'Once the wounded gemsbok raised his head, bellowed and then collapsed, whereupon the other gemsbok trotted up and nudged him with his muzzle a few times until he raised his head again. Quite obviously the second gemsbok knew the other needed help. Perhaps that isn't so surprising, for he must certainly have smelt blood. But how did the wounded one know that the other would keep watch for him? Because he certainly did know it; the difference between his keen vigilance at first and his complete lack of caution afterwards was too great to be accidental. And you must remember that they were both bulls, and therefore not necessarily well disposed towards each other. I was so moved by it all that I wasn't even sorry I couldn't get up for a shot before it grew dark.

I dare say he'll die in the night.'

Early the following morning, before the sun was up, we started off to where the wounded bull was lying, but when we got there both animals had gone. There was a small pool of blood where the wounded beast's head had lain, and the spoor of the two bulls led westward. We followed the trail for about an hour and then as we saw no further traces of blood we gave up. Apparently the wounded bull had recovered its strength in the coolness of the night.

Incidentally, we weren't the only ones who were finding it difficult to come by our meals; the beasts of prey were in trouble too. Every night the hyenas besieged us; no doubt they were after Otto, and sometimes their blood-curdling howling went on uninterruptedly for two hours and more at a time. In the mornings we could see that five or six of them had been prowling around hoping for the best. Every evening we tied Otto up and just let them howl – we couldn't afford to waste ammunition on them.

But the brutes did find the place where he had hidden some of his bones. This must have been a real shock for Otto because when he found out his behaviour changed. Previously he had always taken the greatest care not to let us see where he buried his bones, but the next morning he dug up a bone and brought it in with the sand still on it and buried it in front of our eyes near the water cask. Then he went off and came back with another one, which he buried, again in full view, near the smoke oven. In other words, on the basis of a disagreeable experience Otto had changed an instinctive action in one important particular.

We had learnt something else: that even instinctive actions could be adapted on the basis of experience to changed conditions, and not merely by mutation and selection. But how had Otto come to his decision? On the basis of conscious thought? Or by an unconscious intuitive process?

It was about this time that we noticed a change in the subjects of our dreams. Animals began to play an increasing part in them and the distinction between human beings and animals became blurred. There seemed no particular mystery about this; after all, for a couple of years now our whole life had revolved around them; they were our only fellow beings and our existence depended largely on them. Supposing we had led such a life not merely for a couple of years, but from childhood onwards! How natural such deams would be! Perhaps this was the origin of mythology — to be found in the heritage of all peoples — in which human beings and animals mingle and merge into each other. Was it too much to suppose that it developed quite naturally from the chase?

Round the fire in the evenings, whilst the owls were hooting and the hyenas howling, we told each other all the fairy tales we knew. And there were very many of them in which human beings changed into animals, and vice versa. There were wolves and werewolves, princes who were turned into savage bears, the stag of St. Hubert, Reineke the cunning fox, and so on. Domestic animals never played the same role, and such stories as 'Puss in Boots' were much later inventions. Practical experience was making it easier for us to understand an age-old feature of human development.

How did dreams come about anyway? Were they pictures of experiences strung together, sometimes arbitrarily, sometimes with a meaning, but always expressing some desire or fear? After all, wasn't man's thought a similar series of pictures and imaginings, if a little more controlled by consciousness? What was imagination if not a more or less purposeful game with pictures and memories? And imagination was the basis for dreams and thought, the unconscious and the conscious activity of the soul of man. Dreams proved that even unconcious fantasy and imaginings could have a very real significance. For example, problems often found a solution in dreams when the conscious mind had failed. And that was almost to be expected, because imagination was essentially connected with feelings and the capacity for judgement which characterised human life.

And of course, pictures and feelings of the unconscious exercised an influence over the body. After all, hypnosis could produce blisters, and unconscious anxiety could produce illness. Primitive negroes died when they heard that a sorcerer had cast a spell upon them, or when they had inadvertently broken some often quite ridiculous taboo. And on the other hand, belief and confidence could help to overcome serious illnesses. Yes, there was no doubt about it: unconscious pictures and imaginings could exercise a decisive effect on the body.

And this unconscious working of the mind certainly wasn't limited to human beings. We had seen Otto obviously dreaming in his sleep: whining, scraping with his paws, clearly trying to run.

But one question with regard to the evolution of life was still proving difficult. We had decided that chance mutation could not adequately explain everything. And on the other hand, acquired characteristics and experience were not necessarily inherited. But how could controlled mutations, without which so many rapidly concluded developments were hardly understandable, actually come about? Was there perhaps some power in the imagination of the unconscious, reflecting itself in dreams, which could produce controlled mutations?

The more we thought about it the more likely it seemed. Here was a force which could intelligently link up experiences and at the same time exert its influence on the physical state of the body. No doubt imagination and fantasy existed wherever life could produce memories, which were after all a sort of hopes and fears. Given a species living for generations under similar conditions and experiencing the same hopes and fears, wasn't it conceivable that the unconscious imagination could recognise new possibilities in those experiences and produce controlled mutations to achieve them?

If a human being could develop blisters as a result of suggestion, was it too much to suppose, putting it crudely, that the wish to fly could start a development towards the growth of wings? And almost every dream showed that such impossible wishes could arise in the unconscious.

Imagination has always been regarded as a heaven-sent and creative force, but perhaps it is even greater than man has ever dreamt. Perhaps it impelled the birds of paradise to the development of their fantastic display feathers, and the weaver-birds to their technique of building such ingenious and complicated nests; after all, there are thousands of bird species which get along perfectly well without building elaborate nests. Wouldn't that fit the facts far better than the theory of chance mutations and destructive natural selection?

We looked around and life was lovely and worth living, and every small flower seemed to confirm it. But imagination didn't necessarily produce beauty. It probably played its part in all the phenomena of life. Why did a spitting snake invariably aim at the eyes of its enemy, the one place where its poison could be effective? Selection? But many snakes, including its close relative the cobra, lived perfectly satisfactorily without doing anything of the kind.

And how did all this apply to human beings? We had already agreed that by the development of his consciousness and by his unlimited ability to learn from experience, man had obtained greater freedom from the force of circumstances than any other living being. This process of emancipation also applied to his imagination, which could therefore turn to good and evil.

But what was good and what was evil?

An answer even to this question must be possible because to live means to judge. We had already drawn one important conclusion from the story of evolution: good was something which encouraged the capacity to develop; bad something which forced it into a blind alley leading to certain extinction. This was an answer, but was it the whole answer?

Visit to Paradise

For two weeks it rained almost every day. Then the storms became less frequent, and after three weeks the rainy period was over. About twice the average amount of rain had fallen and the wide plains of the Namib were green and flowery as far as the eye could see.

During the rains we lived cooped up in the small, narrow space we called our *'wagon-lit'*, but soon we were longing to get out again into the open and much more friendly world. The Karikas mountain had always attracted us, and there was sure to be clean rain water in its granite hollows. It looked almost near enough to touch, but it took us a good six hours over the burning plain to get to the foot of it. This time the trip was very different: there was grass with silver feathery heads everywhere, and flowers, masses of them in patches of yellow, blue and violet. Round a pool of water grew a light green belt of dwarf fern and many gaba bushes whose white flowers attracted the sun-birds. At the bottom of each long calix were drops of pure nectar, and we gathered quantities of them and sucked them as we went along.

In the distance we could see herds of game grazing, and springbok leaping and cavorting, and we knew that before long the zebra would be plump again. We came to a small round valley which looked like a spring meadow strewn with flowers and there was luscious green grass growing in the shade of a clump of trees. Birds were flitting here and there and rock doves were cooing. We stood and marvelled; it was a little paradise but it would last only for as long as the moisture lasted. A little higher up in the rocks we found a hollow with water and we settled down under a rock roof for our short stay in paradise.

Not far away we found a place full of *uintjies*. These were bulbs of a certain kind of grass and for an hour we gathered as many as we could; in the evening we ate them roasted, enjoying their rather nutty taste.

To the left of our overhanging roof the rain had worn a furrow into the soil and below the upper sand layer we came across the remains of old ashes and skilfully fashioned stone tools and spear heads which were probably more than twenty thousand years old. We explored the neighbourhood and soon we had a fine collection laid out in the sand. As we could not carry much with us we made sketches of the better pieces. The calcareous nature of the sand indicated that at one time the climate had been more humid than it was now, and perhaps in those far-off days this valley had seemed an ever-lasting paradise.

We wondered how those early hunters had lived; perhaps not very differently from the Bushmen of our own day. They had probably lived and hunted in small kin groups, following the game as it moved here and there, no doubt defending their hunting grounds against intruders, but apart from this there seemed no reason why they should have developed any pronounced warlike qualities. The indefinite extension of hunting grounds is not an advantage, for as the area increases so the intensity with which it can be exploited diminishes. There can have been very little temptation to attack and kill a hunter for his possessions, because it was easy enough for any-one to fashion his own spear, stone knife or bow and flint-tipped arrows. Similarly, an animal, once killed, would remain edible for only a few days. And certainly no hunter, finding it difficult enough to feed himself and his family, would get the idea of keeping slaves; they would merely be more mouths to feed.

And his children, in whose hands lay the future of the group, would probably have grown up very much like Bushman children. Before the war we had come across Bushman families in the Kalahari. Very small children were carried on their mother's backs in a skin whilst bigger children trotted at her side. Children were always with the adults, taking part in everything, so they never felt out of it. When we saw adults dancing together in the moonlight the children were happily beating the rhythm with their feet.

Bushmen had no possessions that a child could break, and all educational rules arose out of danger or necessity, apart of course from those which had a magic or mythical background, perhaps based on dreams; and these too were accepted naturally because the group lived them and explained them with understandable legends. As a result children never felt themselves at odds with their environment, which naturally included the world of the adults. In consequence they developed no vices or destructive urges. You never heard a child being scolded and you never saw a child spanked.

Perhaps the serene childhood of such people was the basis for the belief that the world is ruled in an orderly fashion by a spirit, perhaps even a good spirit; a belief which is found amongst most primitive peoples, and which represents the root of later religious developments. We found nothing surprising in the fact that this simple but logical form of living had survived for hundreds of thousands of years down to our own day. But what had forced development to go on beyond this hard but blissful life?

We sat by the fire and discussed the problem whilst

the flames cast fitful shadows up the granite sides of the valley.

The far horizons attracted us as they always did, and we decided that as soon as possible we would make a tour of exploration as far westward as water conditions would permit. But for the moment we were still keenly interested in the immediate neighbourhood. We measured and sketched the shoulders and the irregularities of the mountains, the remaining evidence of age-old landscapes over which the dinosaurus probably once wandered.

We also looked for more patches of *uintjies,* but we didn't find any, though we did come across a kind of wild lily which didn't look too poisonous. We roasted one of the bulbs and we each ate a small piece of it as an experiment. It tasted excellent, but we waited for a few hours to see what happened, and then, as nothing did happen, we ate the rest of it. After that we collected a rucksack full of bulbs and had a real meal of 'onions'.

The next day Hermann complained of weakness and griping, and my own stomach felt a bit upset, so we decided to go home straight away. But after about an hour we were doubled up with pain and we felt so exhausted that we had to sit down and rest every twenty minutes or so. Those 'onions' obviously contained too much oxalic acid for our stomachs, and we had only one thought now: to get back to our hut and take a strong dose of castor oil.

We got back at last and immediately we both had our 'medicine'; to our amazement it didn't taste a bit like castor oil, more like salad oil. We had a look at the bottle; it was castor oil all right. We took another couple of spoonfuls each, and it still tasted quite good. In spite of colic we had to laugh when we thought of the tastes we had got used to since living in the desert.

'If anyone had told me that when I was a child!' Hermann exclaimed. 'And to think I used to fancy myself as a gourmet!'

The castor oil had no great effect, but we recovered completely after a day or so. And then we pulled our first radishes.

Hyenas, Footprints and Magic

The hyenas were still besieging us, and they gnawed at or carted away anything we happened to leave more than ten paces or so from our hut. Even a tin with nails disappeared, and one night they carried off our pump which we had left lying around. We found it again, but they had gnawed bits out of the handle and eaten part of the rubber; fortunately we had some spare tubing.

One morning when we were sitting down to breakfast, Otto sprang up and rushed out barking wildly. About eighty paces away sat a hyena and watched with interest as the dog came closer, but Otto was wise enough not to get too close. The hyena got up and trotted off only when I approached with a club.

We could never quite rid ourselves of the fear that the hyenas might get Otto, and therefore we always scolded him when he went off on his own, but it didn't stop him. One day we spotted him through a gap in the wall of our hut as he returned from one of these forbidden outings. He didn't come straight back to us but first went round to the back to his heap of bones, and there he deliberately made a great deal of noise, throwing his bones around and putting them back again — obviously to give us the impression that he had been there all the time. When he finally came into the hut, it was clear that he had a conscience. He was looking at us sideways, wrinkling his nose and wagging his tail wildly. We couldn't help laughing, and that seemed to make him more conscience-stricken than ever.

A few days later he repeated the manœuvre on returning from a similar trip, but after that he gave it up, having apparently realised that we weren't taken in.

'Now that was a deliberate attempt to deceive,' I pointed out to Hermann, 'and you can't do that without some sort of logical thought.'

Hermann agreed, but commented: 'It's a good example of how education develops the intellect and depraves morals.'

One night I managed to get a bit of our own back on the hyenas, or at least on one of them. We had discovered that zebra occasionally drank at the saltiest of our four little sources, so one moonlit night I sat up for them on a ledge of rock about sixteen feet or so above the bed, armed with shot-gun and one of our home-made bullets.

Now and again shreds of cloud swept across the face of the moon. There were no signs of zebra, but after a while I heard a noise in the sand. I could tell it was not the sound of zebra, and then I saw a very big hyena coming up the river bed. It kept to the rock face and when it sidled round the corner it was directly below me. Silently I picked up a large piece of rock and dropped it on the brute, scoring a direct hit in the middle of its back. It let out a startled growl and fell flat on its belly with its legs out-spread like a frog. It was my turn to laugh, and it sprang to its feet and raced off madly, the sand spurting up behind it in the moonlight.

We didn't go to the source very often because quite close to our hut was a good water-hole, but one morning when there were light clouds in the sky we did stroll over. With a shock we spotted the imprint of a human foot in the sand. Had the police sent out trackers? And, if they had, had they found us? We hadn't been at the source for some time and the mark

286

wasn't fresh. Did it mean the arrival of a police patrol at any moment? Or was it the imprint of a Klipkaffir — a tribe of primitive negroes formerly kept by Khoi-Khoin and Herero as slaves — or a Khoi-Khoin who perhaps had as much reason to keep out of the way of the police as we had?

Making sure to tread only on stones in order to leave no trace we followed the trail. After a while a second trail linked up with it. Then the two parted and joined again, and a little later we spotted dog imprints and saw black spots of blood on the stones. Finally we came to the hide, skeleton and head of a zebra foal. We examined these remains carefully and we could find no trace of a bullet wound anywhere. It looked as though dogs had brought the zebra to bay and that the men had cut its throat. The method didn't suggest police.

In a small hollow in the rock face beyond the source we found the ashes of a fire, half-burnt and much-gnawed bones, and signs that two men had slept there. We decided that the intruders were Klip-kaffirs, and that they had stayed there for not more than twenty-four hours, otherwise we would have found more foot-prints. We felt relieved. It looked as though the two lived in the western gorges of the Khoma uplands and that the big rains had brought them out this far. However, they would certainly have relations and friends on some farm or other, or in the Otjimbingue reserve; which meant that if they had found our spoor they would probably betray us with their chatter. But nowhere did their tracks lead anywhere near our hut and we were very glad that we had left no traces anywhere near the source.

'Pity we didn't notice them,' said Hermann. 'We could have given 'em a spooking to set 'em running till they dropped. They would never have come back.'

That gave us an idea, and we decided to make things hot for them if they ever did return. We still had a few cartridges belonging to a small pistol we had surrendered to the authorities on the outbreak of war. I opened them up, removed the powder and rammed it tight into the hollow of a dried-out bone, stopping up the hole with a piece of wood. I then hid this miniature bomb under the ashes of the fire. Anyone who tried to cook on that again would find himself crowned with his own cooking pot. In the meantime Hermann had artistically made the imprints of a couple of giant feet in the sand. If trackers came across that they would fly for their lives.

With this we considered that we had effectively protected the source. As long as we lived in the hut no one visited the spot again, but perhaps the magic worked later on when we were no longer there.

Tour in the Namib

The delicate birchlike green of the balsam bushes had darkened; the foliage was denser, and the leaves were much bigger than we had ever seen them before. Innumerable black-and-yellow-ringed caterpillars were crawling on them, steadily eating away the leaves. All three kinds of balsam bush were attacked by this pest and some of the bushes were already stripped. Thousands of caterpillars swarmed around searching for new sustenance and before long there wouldn't be a leaf left anywhere.

And the caterpillars weren't the only pest. Small green *dikpens*, at first hardly visible, quickly developed into black insects several centimetres long which ate everything that came their way, even their own body when it was injured. When they were disturbed they stretched out their long feelers and chirped angrily, and if they were touched they emitted a revolting yellow fluid. They swarmed everywhere, and at night we would wake up at the feel of their long, brittle legs crawling over our faces.

They were an example of extreme adaptation and they had become mere machines for destruction — and we destroyed them too whenever we had a chance. When the struggle to survive demands the utmost efficiency then such murderous automatons inevitably develop. Extreme efficiency in adaptation was obviously a dangerous ideal. On the other hand, it seemed little short of miraculous that life was also capable of goodness, justice and love; that it was capable of ideals far beyond self-interest and far above the promptings of its belly.

Efficiency could be really fruitful only when it was guided by these unifying principles. Efficiency alone and for its own sake was a blind alley inevitably leading to destruction. Mankind could develop further only if it succeeded in raising the rich diversity of life into a higher unity through goodness, justice and love.

In the meantime the hyenas were becoming such a nuisance that we decided to set a trap for them, but before we could do so they were gone, and a couple of days later the wind brought us a distant sweetish smell of decomposition. It came from the carcasses of dead zebra which lay around everywhere with swollen bellies. Apparently some epidemic had broken out amongst them, perhaps from eating stale grass. Every puff of wind carried the smell to us and great numbers of vultures wheeled around in the sky under the clouds that had once again rolled over from the uplands. Even marabou came in to get their share of the offal.

We decided to go out into the wide plains of the Namib where the game had gone, exploring the neighbourhood for perhaps a couple of weeks. As the nights were cold now we had to take extra things for warmth, and we needed sketch-books, compasses, a barometer, field-glasses, our pistol, water-bags, a water canteen and supplies of food, so when we set out our rucksacks were heavy.

The light-coloured plains extended endlessly before our eyes, and compared to the speedy animals of the plains our progress seemed wretchedly slow. On the second day there were vultures circling above us in the sky; obviously they reckoned that we could hardly last much longer. When we lay down under a thin bush for our midday rest they dropped down in lazy spirals, turning their repulsive heads as they sailed past to see how much life was left in us. We cocked a snook at them, but they didn't understand that, and Otto barked furiously. When we got up they flapped away in disgust.

What a delight it was to find a granite hollow full of cool water in the evening! The first light of the morning lent delicate colouring to a fairy landscape, stretching away in a golden glimmer to the horizon. But even in that beauty there was danger and the fear of death. Otto trotted with me to one of the humped granite rocks that lay in the plain like tortoises. I was looking around for stone implements when suddenly I saw Otto standing over a horned adder. Before I could drag him away the snake had reared and buried its fangs in his nose. When I got Otto back to our camp Hermann wasn't within call and it seemed ages before he reacted to my frantic signalling. I couldn't hold Otto and cut open the bite as well. When Hermann came we did it together and put permanganate of potash crystals in the incision; as some consolation we gave Otto a big piece of biltong and a lump of chocolate.

We watched him and waited in fear and anxiety to see what would happen. In fact nothing at all happened and Otto wasn't even out of sorts. Perhaps the bite had been confined to the cartilage of the nose where the poison would only gradually enter the bloodstream, or perhaps Otto had been bitten by an adder before and had developed immunity.

The magic of the desert is hard to define. Why does the sight of a landscape of empty sand, rocks, slab and rubble stir the spirits more than a view of lush green fields and woods? Why does the lifeless play of light, colour and distance have such an invigorating, fascinating and elating effect? Perhaps because no limitations are imposed by other forms of life; perhaps because the mind of the beholder is presented with a *Fata Morgana* of unlimited freedom. And on such far horizons the outline of a mountain draws the eye like an island in the endless ocean.

The last landmark to the south-west was Barrow mountain. It stood close to Kuiseb canyon, but much further west than we had ever ventured. There was certainly water in the canyon now, so why not chance it and make the trip? We tramped for kilometres over the same endless stretches of sand and rubble through a landscape which changed imperceptibly — if at all; yellow grass, at first still in large tufts, and later in small, sparse tufts here and there amongst the harsh white rubble. And nowhere a sign of game! An aard-wolf sprang up and raced away before us, vigorously chased by Otto. The aard-wolf is an insect-eating, useful relative of the hyena, provided with a powerful stink gland, and for a long time Otto reeked constant witness to his victory. That night Hermann refused to allow him to come anywhere near his sleeping-bag but when you're tired out you sleep like a log, so that when Hermann woke up in the morning there was Otto lying snuggled up to him as usual. The sleeping-bag stank for a week after and Hermann was pestered with evil smells even in his dreams.

We spent a second day tramping monotonously through a lifeless landscape, but towards midday we came in sight of a stretch of small ugly dunes and before long there was fresh grass at our feet. Then came one of the fascinating sights we had always expected from those blue horizons. Suddenly we stood on the lip of a wide pit and looked down at a *vlei*, several hundred metres long, its broad surface rippling in the breeze. And all around herds of grazing zebra as far as the eye could see! We sat down trying to count the animals in one sector of the great hollow; there must have been about three thousand in all!

As soon as they scented us one herd after the other made off, stamping and whinnying. But from the other side, down wind, more and more herds would advance at a tangent. It was just like a circus performance. When they spotted us they would halt like squadrons of cavalry at a command, standing close together and looking towards us with pointed ears and twitching nostrils. Then they too would turn and gallop away, and almost immediately another herd would wheel in to take their place. What a contrast to the loneliness of the previous few days! Before our eyes was a living kaleidoscope of rippling stripes, waving tails, flowing manes and prancing hooves.

Otto was dragging desperately at the leash, but we wouldn't let him loose. We would gladly have shot a zebra, but none of them came nearer to us than about a hundred paces, and in this featureless hollow it was absolutely impossible to steal up any closer unobserved.

The reddish water of the *vlei* was inviting, but we feared that our feet might get too soft and tender, for we wore no socks in our heavy and much-repaired boots. We drank some of it but took none with us, since our water-bottle was still half-full and the mountain seemed very near now; there were bound to be good water-holes in its gorges, so why load ourselves up unnecessarily?

As it turned out we had grossly underestimated the distance, because the flat, unbroken plain gave the eye nothing to measure with. We tramped on for another three hours until the edge of the plain suddenly ended in the wild lateral gorges of the Kuiseb canyon. By this time we had left the area of the recent rains behind and all the water-holes were dry. The terrain was so savage, rocky and deeply fissured that we had difficulty in finding a place to stretch ourselves out on, but in the end, when the sun had already disappeared behind the jagged blue mountain top, we found a small patch of sand in a narrow cleft of rock. At one end of it there were many little round holes in the sand, and we saw a small brown bee crawl out of one of them and fly away. They proved to be lined with little wax cells containing a mixture of pollen and honey, obviously the breeding cells of a kind of bumble bee. We cleaned out the lot.

The next morning we clambered to the top of the mountain which offered a fantastic panoramic view. To the north lay the light, featureless plains over which we had come, running right up to the mountain and then breaking off suddenly into dark gorges. To the south stretched a gramadoela world, a rocky maze of black canyons, jagged ridges and gleaming ribs of slate. And beyond that were the rolling red dunes, wave after wave, poised like a petrified sea of blood.

The rock was already hot and we were both thirsty, for we had drunk only very little water for breakfast. We had to find a way down into the canyon to get water, and it wasn't easy. We knew we could not follow a side gorge, for after running a short distance between vertical walls it disappeared into incalculable depths. The only other possibility seemed to be a watershed, but after hours of tramping that might also end in a steep drop impossible for us to negotiate. However, we had already lived long enough in the desert to know what we were about. Zebra had lived in this savage gramadoela world of barren rock for tens of thousands of years, and so we studied the area through our glasses until we spotted a big zebra track that obviously went towards the canyon. We followed this and when it branched we continued along the bigger of the two tracks. For hours we trudged over rocky mounds and along narrow ridges, deeper and deeper into a hot chaos of rocks, getting thirstier and thirstier all the time. There wasn't a great deal left of the original big path, but it was still visible and we hoped desperately that in the end it would lead us down into the canyon. Despite our anxiety to get to a water-hole and quench our thirst, we allowed ourselves sufficient time to measure the age-old river terraces which were still visible here and there.

The sun was low on the horizon when the ridge ended in a steep rock face; opposite us towered a dark vertical wall; and in between lay the Kuiseb canyon. Anxiously we stared into the gorge; it looked impossible to find a way down through the intricate chaos. But the remains of our zebra path clearly led out over a rib of rock and we continued to follow its zigzag descent between rock faces. Now and then it ran within a hair's breadth of the abyss, switching round sharp corners and dropping down in great steps to a lower shelf. We descended over two hundred metres into the rocky depths of the wilderness and there we were greeted by the cool sound of splashing water, and soon we stood beside a wonderful, crystal-clear stream which flowed over sand and stones as though in some fairy grotto.

We threw off our rucksacks, dropped to our knees and drank and drank until we could drink no more. The air was mild and humid. How much it must have rained on the uplands for this wonderful stream to be running a month later!

The next morning, after a night's sound sleep, we decided to explore up-canyon as far as the entrance to the Gaub gorge, and with our boots strapped to our rucksacks we paddled up the clear stream, the wet sand squelching between our toes, a delightful feeling after the long march over the rocky surface of the plains. Already the rays of the morning sun squeezed through jutting rock towers, the glittering water sent reflected light dancing in rococo patterns up and down the dark walls of the canyon, and on the southern walls red sand like molten lava glowed in all the fissures.

But our path soon became more difficult. The canyon narrowed and the water became deeper. The sand slid away under our feet and we were often up to our knees in water. Finally we gave it up. To the north were the gramadoelas; to the south the dunes, and we chose the latter.

We now entered into a strange and eerie world. There were sharply defined mountains of red sand with knife-edged ridges and deep, soft hollows. The sand ran away in streams under our feet, vibrating like the low note of a bass-viol until finally the whole dune would be humming and singing. Laboriously we made our way through the loose sand, welcoming the tightly packed windward sides of the mounds and sinking knee-deep into the hot sand on the lee sides. Our boots became as heavy as lead but we couldn't take them off and go barefooted, the sand was too hot.

Even the dunes were not entirely without life; small lizards darted here and there, but as soon as we came near there was a whirl of red dust and they were gone, boring their way out of sight like lightning. On one occasion we slid down into a funnel-shaped declivity that might have been the trap of a giant lion-ant and by the time we managed to climb up the loose sand on the other side we were panting and exhausted.

The west wind rose in the afternoon and the first puffs blew thin veils of sand over the rolling dunes, and before long the veils had become red flags which swirled into the air from every ridge. All contours were blurred by an endless stream of hissing sand swept over the slopes and down the lee side until the sand there came into movement too, and in quick succession all the dunes began to drone. It was as though we were making our way through a spell-bound world: the dunes resembled great red waves, stationary, yet in motion. Red curtains fluttered against a deep-blue sky, our feet trudged through a red flood tide, and as the wind swept over the dunes the sand all around hummed and droned — a ghostly and most uncanny sound. We pressed on until after sundown, when the wind slackened; and falling asleep we could still hear the whispering of the sand as it trickled over us.

The following morning there was no wind, and as the sun rose the thousandfold new patterns the wind had etched into the dunes stood out in clear-cut golden relief. Beyond the next ridge the dunes gave way to rolling stretches of chalk. We walked faster now towards the distant Gaub canyon, and the next water-holes.

'There must be game ahead,' said Hermann, though there was no sign of any for the moment, and as the area seemed easy to watch over we didn't put Otto on the lead. But quite suddenly we came to the edge of a large shallow valley which was dotted with gemsbok, springbok and zebra in large and small herds. Before we had even taken in the vast picture properly — the valley was several kilometres across — Otto was off like the wind, ignoring our shouts. He had his eye on a couple of springbok and the chase went in a wide sweep round the edge of the valley and between other groups of game until finally he was so far away that we could see him only through our field-glasses.

'I wish there weren't so many gemsbok,' said Hermann anxiously. And at that very moment we saw Otto abandon the springbok and turn his attention to a couple of nearby gemsbok. There was absolutely nothing we could do.

As we watched we saw one of the gemsbok turn towards him with lowered horns, but then it seemed to change its mind and it turned away with Otto still at its heels, disappearing from view beyond a rise in the ground. Hermann began to run now. How slow we were by comparison with those swiftly moving animals! And how helpless in those broad plains! And once down in the dip we no longer had a view over it all. We had left our rucksacks on a little hill, and as we ran inquisitive animals on all sides raised their heads and stared at us. Hermann believed the chase had gone to the left and he went off in that direction whilst I went straight on towards the spot where we had last actually seen Otto.

Otto had been our faithful companion for two lonely years now and he meant a lot to us. We were intensely worried about him. If a gemsbok had speared him and he was lying wounded somewhere he would be very difficult to find. I zigzagged forward in the hope of coming across him and I constantly looked around with my glasses. After an hour's search I decided to try in a new direction, but first I went on to the next ridge of ground. Through my glasses I saw a dark point on a small chalk plateau in the distance. No antelope was as dark as that, and I began to hurry. As I came closer the dark-brown thing moved and then it began to bark. It was Otto.

'Otto! Otto!' I shouted and I ran as fast as I could.

He continued to bark but he made no attempt to run towards me. I ran up the slope towards him and there he stood with his legs straddled and there was foam at his chops. When I got to him he rolled over on his back and I could see that he was bleeding from a wound behind the left shoulder-blade. I picked him up and carried him back to where we had left our rucksacks. He looked as though his strength had lasted just long enough to keep him on his feet until I came. I put him down on my sleeping-bag and I was a little relieved that the bleeding seemed to have stopped, but I didn't dare to give him any water until we had examined him more thoroughly.

Hermann came in sight and I tried to make signs to him, but he was obviously down-hearted at not having found Otto; he was trudging back with lowered head. When he had reached the foot of the hill I shouted: 'Otto's here! I've got him.' He looked up, spotted Otto beside me on the ground, and a great smile lit up his face. When he came up we carefully examined Otto's injuries. The stab behind the shoulder-blade wasn't dangerous; it just went under the skin along the ribs. The left back leg was speared too, but that could hardly be fatal either. And as soon as we had given him some water Otto got up and limped around quite happily on three legs. It occurred to me then that he had probably turned over on his back when I arrived because he had a bad conscience and could remember the cuffing he had received after his first gemsbok adventure.

In the meantime all the animals had galloped away and we had lost our dinner. We were hungry, tired and empty handed, and we hadn't much water either. We went on now, with Otto limping along on his three sound legs behind us. That evening Hermann bagged a young zebra and we were able to eat our fill again, but we were so far away from water that we couldn't stay, so we walked through the night, taking a supply of freshly grilled steaks with us. A hopeful hyena followed the rich odour for a long time, and now and again we could hear sand crunching unpleasantly close behind and then we would turn and hurl stones at the brute to keep him at a respectful distance.

We found the water-holes in the Gaub canyon full to overflowing and some of the pools were so big and deep that we had to climb up around them. With only three legs Otto couldn't clamber up so well and twice he fell off a ledge. We tried to persuade him to swim and in the end he got the idea and paddled along cheerfully through the deep water.

We went on for another four days and one evening in a sandy river bed we found only a hole with salty water. As water evaporates so its salt content increases, but we dug a hole in the sand quite close and soon struck almost fresh water.

For a fortnight in all we had tramped across glimmering plains, over blue hills and through deep canyons, and when we returned to our permanent quarters we were glad to be home again. Eager for news we switched on the radio and learned of Rommel's brilliant operations in the desert, and because it was the desert the reports interested us keenly.

End of a Baboon

It was a big day for us when we bagged the first fat
zebra, for we had an indescribable longing for fat,
and now the grazing was becoming more lush the
game was getting plump. During our own shortage of
fat we were reminded of the Klipkaffirs' idea of
heaven. When a Klipkaffir dies he wanders over a
stony waste until he comes to the heavenly kraal,
which is fenced in by thorn bushes. At the entrance
hangs a gourd full of warm fat, and next to it a
scoop. Before he enters heaven the Klipkaffir may
drink as much fat as he likes. Such is heaven to the
Klipkaffir, for he lives on the edge of the wilderness
and usually in great hardship. When we first heard
this legend it struck us as a mere curiosity; now that
we had some personal experience of life in the desert
we could see the point. For two days our big iron pot
was on the embers full of juicy rib pieces, and whenever we felt like it we fished out generous titbits
and drank spoonfuls of the warm, fatty liquid.

The water in the holes was rapidly disappearing
now, or becoming so salty by evaporation as to be
undrinkable. We pulled a few more radishes and
mangelwurzel and then we had to give up the garden.
Once again the fresh-water supply had not lasted
long enough to let tomatoes and carrots ripen — not
to mention Hermann's tobacco plants.

The rich green of the balsam bushes had vanished
from the landscape, and the hundreds of thousands of
black-and-yellow caterpillars which had eaten all the
leaves were dying miserably in the hot sand and on
the granite rocks. They even came into our hut and

we found them in our beds.

Fat zebra were scarce now; in fact it was becoming difficult to bag anything, because the game had gone out into the endless, rolling waterless plains where we couldn't live, and we were again prowling around hopefully day and night, but in vain. Once I was sitting up at our small source looking out for zebra, but instead of zebra a horde of baboons arrived. I could hear them calling and chattering long before they came in sight. I pressed myself back in my rock crevice to remain unobserved and I took an old shot cartridge we had saved up for just such an eventuality — we had not forgotten that the baboons had fouled our water source once before.

Then the leader of the baboons appeared, a big fellow with grey hair on his back. He sat down and scratched himself, looking around and grunting and mumbling. The rest of them appeared only after he had started to climb down, and squatting on their haunches they watched his progress. When he got to the water he bent over and stuck his calloused behind in my direction and I let him have the charge of shot. He fell face forward into the pool and when he picked himself up and got out he was limping. It looked as though a pellet had penetrated his spine. I hadn't wanted to kill him, but now I felt I had to, and I did so with a heavy blow from my club across the back of the neck. His band had watched the whole proceedings from above, shrieking with excitement and alarm. Now they fled, and they never came near our water source again.

The dead baboon was about the size of a Bushman and I carted his carcass away from the spring into the rocks. I severed the head and took it back with me, together with a lump of the flesh for Otto, but he sniffed at it, his hairs bristling, and then rejected it

302

in disgust. We boiled all the flesh off the head and used the skull as a table decoration. One of the canines was broken off and the stump had been worn level. The other was at least as powerful as the canine of a leopard. It had a sharp cutting edge, and working with a similarly sharp edge on the tooth below it provided the baboon with a perfect pair of scissors — weapon and tool in one.

Hermann fingered the powerful ridge bone which served as a fulcrum for the great muscles of the baboon's jaw. 'With this sort of thing a skull just can't spread to allow the brain to develop,' he observed. 'But what power! Small wonder that even a leopard doesn't care to mix with baboons!'

Power was the right word. The white polished skull with the great jaw clearly showed wherein this power lay; it lay in an ingenious arrangement of bones and dentine, inanimate matter built into a living organism. What constituted power? The teeth of the baboon, the leopard and the lion, but they consisted of bone substance and dead dentine as hard and without feeling as the solid rock. Powerful claws were so much dead horny substance. The horn of the rhinoceros, the scales of the crocodile, the great curved talons of the eagle — just so much horny substance. And it was the same with insects: a hard armour and strong mandibles of chitin, a somewhat similar substance, and perhaps glands filled with poison.

In short, the strength and power of all animals was based on the use of inanimate matter, matter without feeling. All successful adaptations in the struggle for survival consisted in the accumulation of inanimate matter. And it was precisely these adaptations which led again and again to the extinction of forms of life which had once been the most successful. Was there any lesson in this?

It seemed to us there was. Inanimate matter, incapable of forming judgements, was also incapable of development. In fact it opposed any change by its very nature, being solid and inert. Obviously, therefore, the more inanimate matter a particular form of life carried in its structure the less readily it adapted itself to changed circumstances. Now as the world steadily changed with the increasing age of the universe every loss of adaptability spelt death.

Suddenly we saw the physical reason why again and again the seemingly most successful forms of animal life, those with the strongest bodies and the most powerful jaws and claws, died out, whilst precisely those forms of life which appeared more delicate and vulnerable survived; it was because they remained capable of development and therefore adaptation.

'Continued adaptation means continued pain,' Hermann pointed out. 'And it could hardly be otherwise, because pain is one half of the power to form judgements. Any form of life which insulates itself too successfully against pain fails to notice any change in its environment until it's too late.'

But what about man? Hadn't he developed beyond all other forms of life precisely because he was not specifically adapted, because he had no long, powerful teeth, and because instead of dangerous claws he had soft, delicate hands much better suited for recognising the nature of things by touch rather than subjecting them by force?

And what about the power of man? His natural strength was also based on an accumulation of inanimate matter, but with fists and muscle alone no man could ever subject a large number of his fellow men to his will. To do that he needed steel, aeroplanes, bombs, newsprint and printer's ink, i.e. inanimate matter in a thousand different forms. And now-adays he has them, and there is a danger that his spirit will lose control over all this accumulated matter; that great machines will become crueller masters than the worst of slave-drivers; and that this mass of accumulated matter will force mankind into more and more destructive wars. Was the time already at hand when the use of ultimate means of power, the absolute weapon, would lead to universal destruction? Was it really the fate of mankind to go the same way to extinction as so many other powerful forms of life had gone before?

The future looked black, but man's fate was not so inevitable as that of the animals. A door of escape was still open. The power wielded by man was not incorporated in his body, he could abandon it and thus win back his powers of adaptation. Above all he had the ability to know himself and thus recognise the dangers of his own development. And understanding — in theory at least — implies the possibility of redemption.

But would mankind use this escape? Wasn't there a danger that the struggle for survival had made power seem desirable for its own sake?

All power operates on a narrow basis; it rests on a few chosen faculties, and always ruthlessly exploits the weak. But history has shown again and again that the weak of the present have become the strong of the future, whereas power of today has provided the ruins of tomorrow. Who can know today what attributes and capacities will be vital in a thousand years' time? Only the preservation of all our attributes, including our weaknesses, can carry us safely through into the uncertain future.

But how can it be done? Certainly not by force which does not preserve but destroys. There is only one thing which preserves all things, including the weak, and that is love.

The truth which we had felt vaguely all along had become a reasoned certainty: man could command the future only by love. It was the message which had been given to men almost two thousand years ago. 'Though I have the gift of prophecy, and understand all mysteries, and all knowledge; and though I have all faith, so that I could move mountains, and have not charity, I am nothing.'

Quail-trapping and Bird-catching

Once again we had been out and about for a week looking for game without spotting a single animal. But at least the steppe quail came daily to the pool, and returning tired and hungry to our hut one evening I said impatiently to Hermann that it was quite ridiculous that we couldn't think of any method of catching those quail. He looked at me thoughtfully and then he said: 'The Italians catch them with nets; we haven't tried that.'

We made ourselves a net of well-waxed thread and when we had finished it was rather less than a metre by fifty centimetres wide and just about enough to cover the small patch of sand at the little source. It would have to be set up so that it snapped to instantly, for those quail flew off with incredible speed.

It took us a day and a half to manufacture this net and try it out, but at last we had it ready, and the burning question was whether the quail would consent to walk into the trap. The next morning we set it up at the pool, and waited patiently. Hermann sat with the line in his hand ready to jerk it as soon as the birds were beneath the net whilst I looked on anxiously from a little distance. Before long we heard the first calls in the sky; then there was the sound of wings and seven quail dropped out of the sky and landed about twenty paces from the water. After a moment or two they hurried down to the water with quick little steps. In my excitement I almost forgot to breathe.

The first quail walked underneath the net without the slightest hesitation, followed by another and then another until five birds were there. Hermann jerked the line, the supports were released and the net snapped down. There was a wild flapping of wings and a couple of birds shot into the sky, but when we rushed up we had three of them safely in the net.

We had only just time to put the net up again when the next batch arrived. This time we got two of them. After that we left them in peace for a while; we didn't want to frighten them away altogether. We were tremendously elated at our success. There were quail in thousands, and they all came down to drink. From now on there would be no need to go hungry even if all the bigger game disappeared beyond reach.

A little later I was sitting under a bush near our hut plucking the quail, and a gentle breeze swept the feathers around my feet. Suddenly from behind the bush appeared a red hairy body, moving with ugly, angular movements on long hairy legs. It was a bird-eating spider as big as the palm of your hand. With its front claws it seized a ball of feathers and thrust its poison fangs into it, stabbing again and again when it found no resistance. I called Hermann, and as we watched a second spider arrived and also seized a ball of feathers. The warm smell of the newly killed birds had obviously drawn them out of their holes. We didn't much care for such ugly and poisonous brutes in our immediate neighbourhood so we killed them both.

The next time we went to fetch water we found a sun-bird in the pool. Its head was still above water but it was already very weak. We took it out, and although it was soaked it weighed practically nothing; it was much lighter and smaller than the bird-eating spider and would never stand a chance against those insects. We didn't know where the bird roosted but we put it into a bush to dry. It seemed a shame that such a beautiful little creature should have such ugly and merciless enemies.

The rain had produced a great variety of insects, and a stick locust about twenty centimetres long flew into our hut on spotted gossamer wings and landed on a doorpost, folding its wings below two grey wing-covers, and what had previously been recognisably an insect became a small, narrow twig. The protective mimicry was so ingenious that there were even the indications of small thorns on its back.

The development of such camouflage seemed adequately explained by natural selection, but it was not long before we noticed that in insects it was not always confined to physical structure. I was leaning against a rock watching a herd of zebra when a steel-blue ichneumon fly landed in front of me on the sand. For a while it crawled around and then, apparently satisfied that it had found the right spot, it began to dig. With its angular forelegs it picked up the sand, ran backwards with it, dropped it, went forward again, picked up a new load, went backwards with that, and so on. The whole procedure went like clockwork.

Before long the ichneumon fly was out of sight in the hole it had dug, whilst the pile of scooped-out sand grew like a tip heap before a mine. This went on for about a quarter of an hour and then the fly flew away. But before long it was back, this time holding a locust between its forelegs. The locust was bigger and heavier than the ichneumon fly but it had obviously been paralysed and it offered no resistance, and when the ichneumon fly laid it to one side for a moment or two it made no attempt to escape. The fly was now crawling around looking for the hole it had dug and it was a good minute or so before it found it. Then it went back to the locust, but it had lost that too, though it found it fairly quickly. Then it mounted on its back holding the locust with its forefeet, and I realised why the hind legs of an ichneumon fly are so long: they reached down to the ground on either side of the locust. Walking forward the ichneumon fly now dragged its victim towards the hole. At the entrance it put it down again and disappeared inside. Apparently it had discovered that the hole wasn't big enough, for it now began to enlarge it, using the same technique as before.

This renewed digging went on for a few minutes, then the ichneumon fly seized the locust and dragged it into the hole. I don't know whether the eggs were already in the locust's body, or whether they were inserted afterwards in the sand hole. After a while the ichneumon fly reappeared and began to fill up the hole carefully, and as I watched I was amazed at the ingenuity with which it camouflaged the place. When the hole had been filled in and levelled there was a small heap of sand over, and the ichneumon fly carefully smoothed this out too. It carried up several stones and placed them irregularly over the hole, which was now really unrecognisable. But even that was apparently not enough and the fly dug five spoof holes and then made them look as though they had been carelessly filled in. After which, satisfied that everything possible had been done to nourish and protect its eggs, it flew away. The whole business had lasted about an hour.

Could natural selection be said to explain all this adequately? On the assumption that the ichneumon fly had enemies which looked for its breeding holes to destroy its eggs it was clear that natural selection would cut off the progeny of all ichneumon flies which took insufficient trouble to bury their prey. But how to account for the instinct which impelled the ichneumon fly to disguise the location of an already invisible hole with stones and then to dig misleading holes in the neighbourhood? Could that little bit more or less play any important role in natural selection? Was it possible that the unconscious imagination of life was responsible for this ingenious bit of camouflage, and not natural selection at all? We knew already that this imagination always strives to carry development to its furthest possibility.

Discussion at a Sick-bed

It was winter again. The nights were cold, and in the mornings it was often only a few degrees above freezing. Apart from our source we knew of only one other water-hole in the neighbourhood. There was still rainwater in this hole which lay in the big river bed about half an hour's walk from our hut. We could see from the traces around it that zebra sometimes went there to drink and so now and again we took it in turns to sit up close by. As there was no moon at this period of the month we used to set off early in the morning, because on a dark night zebra are absolutely invisible, but before long it became clear that they came there only at night. Incidentally, we weren't the only ones who, due to the excessive rains, suffered from short rations; there was 'Old Scarfoot' for example.

He was a big leopard. We had never seen him in the flesh, but we had often come across his spoor, and the scar was clearly visible in the imprint of one paw — hence his name. No doubt a Bushman could have told us which paw was scarred — our wisdom didn't reach that far. After a cold morning (6° centigrade, we noted in our weather book), Hermann returned about midday with the information that he had run into Old Scarfoot.

'Was I pleased that Otto wasn't with me!' he exclaimed, filling his pipe. 'The sun wasn't up and I was just turning all unsuspecting round the last sharp bend — in fact I was filling my pipe, the pistol squeezed under my arm — when I suddenly came face to face with a leopard, a big brute. He was coming down river and the bend had kept him out of sight. We weren't more than four or five paces apart. We both stopped and looked at each other. I was thinking fast. If I seized my pistol it meant letting my tobacco tin drop, which would have been a pity, and the brute would have been on me before I could fire. So I just stood quietly and looked at him. I noticed that he was soaked. The water was dripping off his belly. I don't know how long we stood there looking at each other, but then he growled softly, went over to the other side of the bed and slowly continued his way. It was as though he were saying: 'I don't really want any trouble with you, you long, forked creature, but I'm not afraid of you either, so don't think I am.'

'Was I relieved! But I was also very curious to know how that leopard had got so wet on a cold morning. His spoor led back to the water-hole — it was old Scarfoot all right. He had obviously been in the water, and after a while I realised why: the four small water turtles were missing. He must have been damned hungry to bother to scoop those stinking things out of the water and eat them. When I thought about that half-starving leopard I went weak at the knees. Perhaps if he hadn't been so wet and uncomfortable he wouldn't have let me get away so easily.'

It wouldn't be long now before game put in an appearance again, and in the meantime we could scrape by trapping quail. There had been a good deal of rain, so this year the animals would be plump and there would be ostrich eggs and wild honey. From our original 300 rounds of ammunition we still had 120 left, and with that we could probably last out for another eighteen months. After which we could always fall back on bows and arrows, and we had also worked out plans for trapping bigger game than quail. In short, we felt that we had mastered life in the desert and we were happy and contented.

But then Hermann fell ill.

He had been complaining for some time about pains in the back, and we thought he had strained a muscle, or had a twinge of rheumatism perhaps. But the pain got worse. He tried sun baths and putting hot sandsacks on his back, but nothing did him any good. Finally we came to the conclusion that it was probably nerves and that the real cause was a lack of vitamins; since the rains we hadn't had much fresh meat. Perhaps we ought to have eaten our quail raw, but we had been unable to bring ourselves to do so – even Otto turned up his nose at raw bird flesh.

One cold morning Hermann stayed in bed. I had put a can of glowing embers in the hut. Some quail were grilling on it and blue smoke was rising into the many bars of light which fell through the chinks in the brushwood roofing. The whole room was warm and comfortable and we chatted about the history of development. Was it possible that agriculture had developed out of man's cult for the dead? If seed were buried with the dead, then if it sprouted the result would be a particularly luxuriant growth, and it was interesting to note that the fertility rites of agricultural peoples were originally all associated with human or animal sacrifices.

However that may be, agriculture and cattle-breeding had given man's life added security. But at the same time it made the keeping of slaves economically worth while, so that war and discipline became as important as husbandry. Rivalry now began between the peoples and their civilisations, and this increased the savagery which had first developed in man's soul in prehistoric times when he had changed from a near vegetarian diet to animal food. Today this development had reached a point where it threatened the whole existence of mankind; not only were those savage instincts deliberately fostered but man had ever-increasing technical powers of destruction at his disposal.

It was as logical as the development which had led to the extinction of once powerful prehistoric saurians; power inevitably led downward into the abyss at an increasing speed.

'In that case,' objected Hermann, 'how was it possible that even before the danger became imminent and easily recognisable, the message 'Love one another' could be proclaimed?'

'Through suffering,' I replied. 'Pain and suffering provoke reaction, induce change, encourage learning; pain necessarily mobilises all the defensive forces of body and soul, and it could hardly be otherwise. Men naturally try to change any situation which involves pain and discomfort. Is it therefore so astonishing that they should sometimes long for love and justice in place of hatred and cruelty? Life after all is accustomed to moving in contradictory feelings and ideas.'

'That's true. And then in addition to individual pain there's also sympathy with others who are suffering, which in turn produces a desire to help.'

Hermann puffed at his pipe and continued: 'It's quite true: sympathy and a desire to help go together. Where natural sympathy is not suppressed or distorted the community will soon find ways and means of correcting errors and abuses even if only a minority suffers from them. Sympathy is an important feature of human society and there's no doubt it's played a big part in social development. Any attitude which fails to appreciate this and condemns sympathy as sentimentality will hinder the timely correction of evils, and injustice and suffering will lead to the accumulation of explosive and destructive forces.'

After a minute or two Hermann said: 'I think I can answer my own question of a moment or two ago: sympathy and pity attach the individual to his kind; through them he can share in their sufferings. And as a result of this relation saints and martyrs can take the sufferings of a generation, of many generations, on themselves, and open up new paths through their teachings born of suffering. On this plane the individual can be far more closely bound up with the community, in fact with humanity as a whole, than through any biological tie, because tradition keeps that past suffering alive in human memory and therefore operative throughout the generations. In this way the death of Christ on the cross is still a force today. Without his agony his teachings would have been forgotten amongst many others. Christian teaching gives complete expression to the great truth that in man's soul the forces of redemption are closely linked with the capacity for suffering. Suffering, death and resurrection, Good Friday and Easter Sunday are closely related.'

There was a long silence in our hut flooded by the midday sun, and in my mind I wondered whether, living in a period of great suffering, we might not one day ourselves experience the Easter Sunday of ressurection and redemption.

Hunting Trip

Hermann's pains now extended to his legs and he began to find it difficult to walk. Fresh liver full of vitamins might help, I thought, so I decided to try my luck at the Goagos source.

The way there went through small ugly gorges at first. Slabs of rock lay down the slopes, and there was a good deal of coarse grass whose prickly seed got into my boots as I tramped along. Coming across an aru tree with ripe fruit I picked a handful of the pea-sized berries and chewed the thin layer of tart fruit off the hard kernels. I knew they contained a high proportion of tannic acid so I didn't eat many.

At last I left the barren gorges behind and found myself on the edge of the Namib. The scene had changed again: the dry grass was waving in the wind like ripe corn, covering up the rubble of the desert with a golden carpet, and to the north the granite domes were like familiar islands in the sea. And there was game. Zebra were grazing peacefully, and springbok were dancing and leaping about. And the most beautiful sight of all was the many kids and foals that played around; there were little gemsbok playing within reach of their mothers' long, slender horns, and zebra foals that looked like painted toys. Once again vigorous, joyful life had been triumphant over the cruel, ancient desert.

In the zebra hollows which two months ago had been full of rain water were groups of round tsammas pumpkins. They were like green Easter eggs now, but soon they would be ripe and golden and then the animals would eat them. Unfortunately they were too

317

bitter for us.

The lovely day made me happy, and as I walked I tried to avoid crushing any of the desert flowers. But for all that I had to remember why I had come, and I noted with satisfaction that the herds were grazing against the east wind, a common habit of animals of the plains, instinctive behaviour which greatly reduced the danger of ambushes. If the east wind held for a day or two longer they would move forward into the neighbourhood of our hut.

It is almost impossible to get within pistol shot of a large herd of grazing animals, because they never graze simultaneously; some of them are always looking round ready to spot any suspicious movement. But before long there were fewer of them, and I saw one gemsbok bull on his own. He hadn't noticed me and I managed to get nearer to him under cover of a small hollow, where I took off my boots to avoid their crunching on the stones, and left my rucksack and field-glasses. Then I crawled forward cautiously, keeping my eyes glued on him and moving only when he was actually grazing. Whenever he raised his head I kept motionless. I got to within sixty paces of him when he looked up and seemed to feel that something was amiss. He was staring straight at me now and my heart was beating hard, but I didn't move a muscle. After a while he seemed satisfied and he lowered his head again. I got to within fifty paces of him. Should I shoot? If I missed, or merely wounded him, and he came at me I wouldn't have much chance in this open country. I therefore decided to get even closer and I edged forward until I got to within forty paces of him. About five paces ahead of me was a slab of rock and I decided to crawl that far before chancing a shot. Then suddenly and right in front of me a bustard rose into the air with a loud squall. It shook

318

me to the core and startled the gemsbok too and he sprinted off thunderously, his hooves hurling stones in all directions. He stopped after a while, but he was too far away for a shot and he was now thoroughly alert. I gave up.

After that my way led through an area without game of any kind and as the hot sun almost touched the horizon the Goagos mountains seemed only at arm's length, their foothills stretching out into the plains like the paws of a beast of prey. When the sun had gone down I had a drink and filled my bottle at the spring. The valley was deserted and the sand showed few signs of game — the grazing grounds were still lush enough so the antelope had no need to come down to the water.

I went to the small cave-like hollow where we had previously slept and gathering an armful of kindling I soon had a small fire burning in the fast-falling darkness. I put on extra things for warmth, cooked myself a double portion of maize, enough for both supper and breakfast, and when it was ready I beat out a piece of biltong and ate the meat flakes with the porridge. As a special treat I had a small piece of smoked zebra fat. Then I made myself tea in a canister adding two precious teaspoonfuls of sugar.

After supper I leisurely tended the fire thinking of Hermann and Otto. What was to happen if Hermann didn't recover? Obviously we'd have to go back to civilisation to get him proper medical attention, and the harsh years of freedom would be followed by the harsher years of internment. Would the time we had spent in the desert have been wasted?

My thoughts were rather sad but the silence of the all-embracing night comforted me. The Southern Cross sparkled in the almost gothic arch of my cave above the two Centaurus stars, and somehow I knew

319 .

that the hard times we had been through had not been wasted. We had taken a wild, desolate and magnificent tract of land, and made it our home. We had lived with the lovely beasts of the wilderness as few civilised men had ever done before us. We had lived savagely, as beasts of prey live. We had often eaten with blood still on our hands. Nevertheless, we had lived as thinking, sensitive men; and the ruthless struggle for existence had not made us callous or brutal, but given us an understanding far beyond the narrow limits of our life in the desert. We had learned that life could transmute bad into good, and extract both beauty and significance from ordinary things. We had learned that there is a force capable of judgement in all life; in other words, a spiritual force, a force which expresses itself in feeling, which judges all things through feeling, approving and denying, and thus transcends the rigid course of the inanimate world.

Whilst stars radiate their energy indifferently and atoms disintegrate with age, life uses those energies to build up a new and different world, a freer and higher world, a world of values. Its own evolution was proof of this; in the course of time it had developed from the unicellular creature to the thinking human being deliberately seeking and creating values. Was that not supra-material and thus a spiritual, a divine phenomenon?

It grew colder and I held my hands to the fire. The peace of the vast desert night encompassed me and I felt that with my new-found understanding I would never despair again.

I scooped myself a hollow, took my rucksack as a pillow and went to sleep. I slept lightly and during the night I heard the crunch of paws in the sand of the river-bed as some beast of prey prowled past. I turned over and felt glad that life was so near.

When I made my way in the cold, grey light of dawn to where I proposed to sit up there was a wild bitch near the source and she barked at me hoarsely. It was probably her prowling I had heard in the night. No doubt her young were somewhere near. At first only birds showed themselves, then a single springbok came to the water and I bagged him with a lucky shot. I ate some raw flesh on the spot and, carrying the heavy beast over my shoulders, I made my way back to Hermann and Otto, who, I knew, would be anxiously awaiting me. Unfortunately not even fresh liver made any difference to Hermann's condition.

As I had foreseen, there was soon an increasing number of animals in the neighbourhood, and one morning I was woken up by the sound of a shot. Soon afterwards Hermann came limping in, still in his night clothes. 'He's lying on the other side of the course,' he said, as he crawled back into bed.

He had heard a zebra quite close to our hut and he had dropped it with a shot in the heart. I stalked and bagged a gemsbok, and one night when the moon was full I got a zebra at the water. Our supplies of fat were filling up satisfactorily, and we had plenty of smoked meat and biltong. But I had a good deal more work to do, because Hermann could only just crawl around and he was unable to lift or carry anything heavy.

We hoped that complete rest and plenty of good food, particularly raw meat, would restore him to health, and for almost a month he spent most of his time in bed, sketching prehistoric stone implements and doing a bit of water-colour painting, for which he had a real talent. But it was no use, and there were days when the pain extended from his back to his neck and his head. In the end we decided that the time had come to call it a day.

I got the lorry ready, and I worked for a couple of hours preparing the way out of the gorge, for the heavy rain had gouged impassable channels in it. The next day I drove out with Hermann. Before we entered Windhoek we stopped at a farm to find out from the farmer, whom we knew, what the general situation was. As it happened the farmer's wife was ill and he was just preparing to take her into Windhoek to hospital. We agreed that he should take Hermann too and then report the matter to the police.

I hadn't yet decided what I should do; I found it difficult to give up my liberty in the desert in exchange for internment so I drove back, made the usual loop to deceive any pursuers, effaced all traces of where I finally left the track, and then waited with Otto to see what would happen. Towards evening on the second day the police arrived: seven of them in two cars, armed to the teeth. It appeared that friends had persuaded Hermann that I could not possibly survive alone in the desert, so he had told the police our hiding-place.

Epilogue

We were in prison for two days, and after that we were transferred to a room in the isolation ward of the hospital. Hermann was treated with injections of vitamin B extract and he soon began to recover.

When the police arrived to fetch me they had no more water so they had to replenish their supplies from our source. I said nothing but I secretly looked forward to the effects, which lost no time in making themselves felt. A fortnight later one of the policemen said to me: 'Man alive, I've only got to think of that water and I feel like running!'

It took us a long time to get used to wearing proper clothes and two weeks later, when we had to stand trial, the shoes we were wearing were so uncomfortable that once in court we surreptitiously slipped them off.

We were charged with a whole battery of offences: failure to notify our change of address, failure to pay our dog licence, failure to pay motor-car tax, failure to hand in our radios according to the war-time regulations, the illegal possession of arms, the shooting of game without permission, and so on. We might have got it hot and strong, but the magistrate who tried us showed understanding for our adventure and sympathy for our position, and merely imposed a series of small fines. A friend of ours lent us the money to pay, and that was that.

The higher authorities were lenient with us too and we were not interned; in fact, shortly before the end of the war we were taken into government service as geologists, and we went out surveying for suitable

323

well-drilling sites in areas which had previously been uninhabitable. The knowledge and experience we had gained in the desert helped us to provide many a farm with a better water supply and to turn barren spaces into arable land.

Hermann was killed in a motor accident in 1946 and his grave is in Windhoek cemetery.

Otto lived on for a few years after our return to civilisation, but as he got older he became increasingly deaf — particularly when he didn't want to hear. One day he disappeared altogether and I never found out what happened to him.

South West Africa is developing rapidly now. A new generation has grown up for whom the available farm lands were insufficient. There were good years in the Namib with plenty of rain, and its eastern edge, a parched wilderness in the dry years, became grass steppe. It was inevitable therefore that farmers with sheep should take over some of the desert land in which we had lived. In fact the authorities built a road through the Kuiseb canyon not far from Carp Cliff, and it runs through the desert to Walvis Bay. Gemsbok, whose flesh is the tastiest, have become rare. Whenever zebra showed themselves they were shot and if they were only wounded the hyenas finished them off. And no man will ever again see a herd of four thousand springbok in this neighbourhood as we once did.

Martin Orkin

SHAKESPEARE AGAINST APARTHEID

Reading, teaching and performing Shakespeare depend upon interpretation of the text. The cultural background of the interpreter will determine the meaning and conclusions drawn from the plays. South African students, scholars, critics and teachers have consistently been influenced by simplifications of Anglo-American versions, as well as by the dominant socio-political milieu of the country itself. Accordingly, discussions of Shakespeare's plays – and in particular the tragedies – have too often reflected the distorted racial/ethnic and political stereotyping prevalent in South African thinking. Apartheid is legitimised in the classroom, lecture hall and theatre. All other approaches to the plays are belittled or ignored. Martin Orkin demonstrates how Shakespearean texts are open to multiple readings. By drawing on a number of different scholarly sources – traditional and modern – he suggests that the study of Shakespeare can be the foundation of a new, positive vision, rather than providing the intellectual underpinning for oppressive regimes.

200 pages, a paperbook

Bloke Modisane

BLAME ME ON HISTORY

Blame me on History, first published in 1963 and recently unbanned in this country, is the autobiography of William 'Bloke' Modisane. He was one of the team of black writers of the 1950s who created *Drum* magazine and was a reporter, short story writer and boxing correspondent. He lived in Sophiatown until 1958 when it was bulldozed flat by government order for being too close to white suburbs. When this happened Modisane left too and spent time in Britain, where he acted in Athol Fugard's plays *No Good Friday* and *The Blood Knot,* before settling in West Germany where he turned playwright. But he always felt very much an exile, and as he said in the opening paragraph of his book, 'something in me died, a piece of me died, with the dying of Sophiatown.'

As one of the first black urban intellectuals Modisane became host, in his single room in Sophiatown, to many searchers for the real Africa, introducing such people as Dame Sybil Thorndike, Adlai Stevenson and many South African whites to shantytown life and shebeens. *Blame me on History* gives an insight into the vitality and essence that was Sophiatown, which unfortunately now only lives on in writing.

Modisane died in March 1986 in Dortmund, West Germany.

320 pages, a paperbook

John Conyngham

THE ARROWING OF THE CANE

Written by John Conyngham, a major new literary talent, this novel was joint winner of the 1985 AA Mutual Life/Ad. Donker Literary Award.

Set on a cane farm in Natal, *The Arrowing of the Cane* chronicles a stage in the life of James Colville, sugar planter and pragmatic liberal. The novel is the story of one man's conflict not only within himself, but also with the society that surrounds him. Haunted by historical associations and faced with the dissolution of his world, James Colville is determined to record the present as truthfully as possible for posterity.

'One of the most significant works to emerge from South Africa . . . Extremely well-written, highly evocative, this novel captures the essence of our pathetic predicament' — Beryl Roberts, *Sunday Times.*

This book defies description — it demands to be read.

160 pages, a paperbook

Ridley Beeton

FACETS OF OLIVE SCHREINER

A Manuscript Source-book

Olive Schreiner always had an effect on people – no-one who encountered her was afterwards neutral about her. She was adored or thoroughly loathed. In this collection of letters, diaries and other manuscript sources, Ridley Beeton integrates her warmth and arrogance, her anger and love, her brilliance and contrariness into a comprehensive portrait of Olive Schreiner the woman and writer. The emotional/intellectual entanglements with Karl Pearson, Edward Carpenter and Havelock Ellis are extensively covered. The facets presented are based on primary sources held at research centres, and are linked by notes which give further information about the people who influenced her, or under whose guidance she worked.

275 pages, a paperbook